Measuring the Mind

Is it possible to measure psychological attributes like intelligence, personality, and attitudes and if so, how does that work? What does the term 'measurement' mean in a psychological context? This fascinating and timely book discusses these questions and investigates the possible answers that can be given in response. Denny Borsboom provides an in-depth treatment of the philosophical foundations of widely used measurement models in psychology. The theoretical status of classical test theory, latent variable theory, and representational measurement theory are critically evaluated, and positioned in terms of the underlying philosophy of science. Special attention is devoted to the central concept of test validity, and future directions to improve the theory and practice of psychological measurement are outlined.

DENNY BORSBOOM is Assistant Professor of Psychological Methods at the University of Amsterdam. He has published in *Synthese*, *Applied Psychological Measurement*, *Psychological Review*, and *Intelligence*.

Measuring the Mind

Conceptual Issues in Contemporary Psychometrics

Denny Borsboom
University of Amsterdam

CAMBRIDGE UNIVERSITY PRESS
Cambridge, New York, Melbourne, Madrid, Cape Town, Singapore, São Paulo, Delhi

Cambridge University Press
The Edinburgh Building, Cambridge CB2 8RU, UK

Published in the United States of America by Cambridge University Press, New York

www.cambridge.org
Information on this title: www.cambridge.org/9780521102841

© Denny Borsboom 2005

This publication is in copyright. Subject to statutory exception
and to the provisions of relevant collective licensing agreements,
no reproduction of any part may take place without the written
permission of Cambridge University Press.

First published 2005
This digitally printed version 2009

A catalogue record for this publication is available from the British Library

ISBN 978-0-521-84463-5 hardback
ISBN 978-0-521-10284-1 paperback

Cambridge University Press has no responsibility for the persistence or
accuracy of URLs for external or third-party Internet websites referred to in
this publication, and does not guarantee that any content on such websites is,
or will remain, accurate or appropriate.

Contents

Preface	*page* vii
1 Introduction	**1**
1.1 The measured mind	1
1.2 Measurement models	3
1.3 Philosophy of science	5
1.4 Scope and outline of this book	9
2 True scores	**11**
2.1 Introduction	11
2.2 Three perspectives on true scores	13
2.2.1 The formal stance	14
2.2.2 The empirical stance	21
2.2.3 The ontological stance	30
2.3 Discussion	44
3 Latent variables	**49**
3.1 Introduction	49
3.2 Three perspectives on latent variables	51
3.2.1 The formal stance	52
3.2.2 The empirical stance	56
3.2.3 The ontological stance	57
3.3 Implications for psychology	77
3.4 Discussion	81
4 Scales	**85**
4.1 Introduction	85
4.2 Three perspectives on measurement scales	88
4.2.1 The formal stance	89
4.2.2 The empirical stance	95
4.2.3 The ontological stance	100
4.3 Discussion	118
5 Relations between the models	**121**
5.1 Introduction	121
5.2 Levels of connection	122
5.2.1 Syntax	123
5.2.2 Semantics and ontology	128

	5.3 Discussion	133
	5.3.1 Theoretical status	133
	5.3.2 The interpretation of probability	138
	5.3.3 Validity and the relation of measurement	140
	5.3.4 Theoretical consequences	145
6	**The concept of validity**	**149**
	6.1 Introduction	149
	6.2 Ontology versus epistemology	151
	6.3 Reference versus meaning	154
	6.4 Causality versus correlation	159
	6.5 Where to look for validity	162
	6.6 Discussion	167
References		173
Index		183

Preface

About five decades ago, the visionary Dutch psychologist A. D. De Groot started building an extraordinary academic group at the University of Amsterdam. It consisted of psychometricians, statisticians, philosophers of science, and psychologists with a general methodological orientation. The idea was to approach methodological problems in psychology from the various angles these different specialists brought to the subject matter. By triangulating their viewpoints, methodological problems were to be clarified, pinpointed, and solved. This idea is in several respects the basis for this book. At an intellectual level, the research reported here is carried out exactly along the lines De Groot envisaged, because it applies insights from psychology, philosophy of science, and psychometrics to the problem of psychological measurement. At a more practical level, I think that, if De Groot had not founded this group, the book now before you would not have existed. For the people in the psychological methods department both sparked my interests in psychometrics and philosophy of science, and provided me with the opportunity to start out on the research that is the basis for this book. Hence, I thank De Groot for his vision, and the people in the psychological methods group for creating such a great intellectual atmosphere.

I unfortunately never had the chance to collaborate directly with De Groot; but he did, in the years he spent at the University of Amsterdam, appoint two people who had a direct and substantial influence on all of the work reported here: Don Mellenbergh and Jaap van Heerden, the supervisors of my PhD research. This book is single-authored because I conceived of it and wrote it. But in terms of the genealogy of the ideas that led to this work, and the general spirit in which the research is carried out, I am greatly indebted to these two remarkable men, both for their contributions to my research and for the atmosphere of intellectual freedom they created. Several chapters in this book are partly based on, or use material from, papers we have published jointly. Specifically, the paragraphs on the platonic true score interpretation in chapter 2 are taken from Borsboom and Mellenbergh (2002), chapter 3 is a slightly adapted version of Borsboom, Mellenbergh, and Van Heerden (2003), and chapter 6 is adapted from Borsboom, Mellenbergh, and Van Heerden (2004). Another person who deserves special mention is Peter Molenaar, who was never directly involved with my research but played a highly stimulating role in the background. With his uncanny ability to connect theoretical insights from distinct areas of mathematics, philosophy, and science, he repeatedly probed me to broaden my intellectual horizon; and his insights on the relation between inter-individual and intra-individual variability were among the primary factors that stimulated the theoretical developments in this book. Also, I would like to thank several people who have, in one way or another, significantly influenced the development of my research: Conor Dolan, Harrie Vorst, Ellen Hamaker, Sanneke Schouwstra, Gitta Lubke, Han van der Maas, Maarten Speekenbrink, Joel Michell, Keith Markus, Dan Cervone, Günter Trendler, Ton Smolenaars, Brian Haig, and Ingmar Visser.

My deepest gratitude extends to those closest to me. I thank my parents for their faith in me; Maaike for being such a wonderful sister; and, above all, Helma for her support and love. This book is dedicated to my son, Kick. I hope that, whatever you will do in this beautiful life, you will do it with passion.

1 Introduction

1.1 The measured mind

Psychological measurement plays an important role in modern society. Teachers have schoolchildren tested for dyslexia or hyperactivity, parents have their children's interests and capacities assessed by commercial research bureaus, countries test entire populations of pupils to decide who goes to which school or university, and corporate firms hire other corporate firms to test the right person for the job. The diversity of psychological characteristics measured in such situations is impressive. There exist tests for measuring an enormous range of capacities, abilities, attitudes, and personality factors; these tests are said to measure concepts as diverse as intelligence, extraversion, quality of life, client satisfaction, neuroticism, schizophrenia, and amnesia. The ever increasing popularity of books of the test-your-emotional-intelligence variety has added to the acceptance of psychological testing as an integral element of society.

When we shift our attention from the larger arena of society to the specialized disciplines within scientific psychology, the list of measurable psychological attributes does not become shorter but longer. Within the larger domain of intelligence measurement, we then encounter various subdomains of research where subjects are being probed for their levels of spatial, verbal, numerical, emotional, and perceptual intelligence; from the literature on personality research, we learn that personality is carved up into the five factors of extraversion, neuroticism, conscientiousness, openness to experience, and agreeableness, each of these factors themselves being made up of more specific subfactors; and in clinical psychology we discover various subtypes of schizophrenia, dyslexia, and depression, each of which can be assessed with a numerous variety of psychological tests. In short, scientific psychologists have conjured an overwhelming number of psychological characteristics, that can each be measured with an equally overwhelming number of testing procedures. How do these procedures work?

Consider, as a prototypical example, the measurement of intelligence. Intelligence tests consist of a set of problems that are verbal, numerical, or figural in character. As can be expected, some people solve more problems than other people. We can count the number of problems that people can solve and look at the individual differences in the computed scores. It so happens that the discovered individual differences are relatively stable across adulthood. Also, different tests for intelligence tend to be positively correlated, which means that people who solve more verbal problems, on average, also solve more numerical and figural problems. There is thus a certain amount of consistency of the observed differences between people, both across time periods and across testing procedures.

As soon as a way is found to establish individual differences between people, all sorts of correlations between the test scores and other variables can be computed. So, we can investigate whether people with higher intelligence test scores, when compared with people who obtain lower test scores, are more successful on a job; whether they make more money, vote differently, or have a higher life-expectancy. We can look into differences in intelligence test scores as a function of background variables like sex, race, or socio-economic status. We can do research into the association between intelligence test scores and neural speed, reaction time, or the amount of grey matter inside the skull. We find a diverse array of associations and mean differences. Some are large and stable, others small and difficult to replicate. And so the mechanism of science has been set in motion. Under which conditions, precisely, do certain effects occur? Which variables mediate or moderate relations between intelligence test scores and other variables? Are these relations the same in different groups of people? Once the scientific engine is running, more research is always needed.

However, a nagging question remains. Do such tests really measure something and, if so, what is it?

This book originates from my attempts to make sense of this question, which is encountered in virtually every field where psychological tests are used. In the past century, it has become known as the problem of test validity. Test validity has proven to be an elusive concept, which is illustrated by the fact that empirical validation research tends to be highly inconclusive. The issue remains problematic, in spite of the fact that psychological tests have come to belong to the standard equipment of social science research, and in spite of the enormous amounts of empirical data that have been gathered in psychological measurement. In fact, after a century of theory and research on psychological test scores, for most test scores we still have no idea whether they really measure something, or are no more than relatively arbitrary summations of item responses.

Introduction

One of the ideas behind the present book is that part of the reason for this is that too little attention has been given to a conceptual question about measurement in psychology: what does it *mean* for a psychological test to measure a psychological attribute? The main goal of this book is to investigate the possible answers that can be given in response to this question, to analyse the consequences of the positions they entail, and to make an informed choice between them.

1.2 Measurement models

To the psychologist, to question what it means to measure a psychological attribute may seem somewhat odd. Many are under the impression that there exists considerable consensus among methodologists on how psychological measurement should be conceptualized, or even that there *is* only one theory of psychological measurement. One reason for this is that textbooks on research methods tend to propagate such a harmonious picture. However, this picture is inaccurate. Several distinct theories have been proposed for psychological measurement, and these sometimes differ radically in the way they conceptualize the measurement process. In order to make an informed judgment on the merits of psychological testing, it is critical to understand and evaluate these models.

There are three important types of measurement models, each of which is discussed in a separate chapter in this book. These are the classical test model, the latent variable model, and the representational measurement model. Each of these models proposes a way of conceptualizing theoretical attributes, and specifies how they relate to observed scores. They provide blueprints for ways of thinking about psychological measurement.

The *classical test theory model* is the theory of psychological testing that is most often used in empirical applications. The central concept in classical test theory is the true score. True scores are related to the observations through the use of the expectation operator: the true score is the expected value of the observed score. Thus, a researcher who sees intelligence as a true score on an intelligence test supposes that somebody's level of intelligence is his expected score on an IQ-test. Theories of psychological testing are usually related to a more or less coherent set of suggestions or prescriptions that the working researcher should follow, and classical test theory is no exception. For instance, a typical idea of classical test theory is that the main task of the researcher is to minimize random error. One way of doing this is by aggregating scores on different tests; the longer the test, the more reliable and valid it will be.

The *latent variable model* has been proposed as an alternative to classical test theory, and is especially popular in psychometric circles. The central idea of latent variable theory is to conceptualize theoretical attributes as latent variables. Latent variables are viewed as the unobserved determinants of a set of observed scores; specifically, latent variables are considered to be the common cause of the observed variables. Thus, a researcher who views intelligence as a latent variable supposes that intelligence is the common cause of the responses to a set of distinct IQ-items or tests. A typical idea associated with latent variable theory is that the researcher should set up a statistical model based on a substantive theory, and that the fit of the model should be tested against observed data. Only if this fit is acceptable is the researcher allowed to interpret observations as measurements of the latent variables that were hypothesized.

Finally, the *representational measurement model* – also known as 'abstract', 'axiomatic', or 'fundamental' measurement theory – offers a third line of thinking about psychological measurement. The central concept in representationalism is the scale. A scale is a mathematical representation of empirically observable relations between the people measured. Such an empirical relation could be that John successfully solved items 1, 2, and 3 in an IQ-test, while Jane solved items 1 and 2, but failed on item 3. A mathematical representation of these relations could be constructed by assigning John a higher number than Jane, which indicates that he solved more items, and by assigning item 3 a higher number than items 1 and 2, which indicates that it was less often solved. In doing so, the researcher is constructing a scale on which persons and items can be located. Because this scale is a man-made representation, much like a map of an area, the researcher who views intelligence as a scale supposes that intelligence is a representation of observable relations between people and IQ-items. A typical suggestion associated with this theory, is that the task of the researcher is to establish these relations empirically, to prove that they can be represented in a formal structure with a certain level of uniqueness, and to find a function that gives a mathematical representation which is isomorphic to the empirically established relations.

As may be suspected from this discussion of measurement models, and as will certainly become clear in this book, classical test theory, latent variable theory, and fundamental measurement theory present radically different ideas on what measurement is and how it should be done. One of the aims of this book is to show how these theories differ, what these differences mean in the context of psychological measurement, and to evaluate their potential for furthering progress in psychological measurement.

What are the proper grounds for the evaluation of measurement models? At first glance, it may seem that the objective is to choose the 'correct'

Introduction

or 'true' model. However, this is not the case. Measurement theories involve a normative component, in the sense that they suggest evaluative dimensions to assess the quality of testing procedures, but they cannot themselves be candidates for truth or falsity. The reason for this is that measurement models are not scientific theories. The relation that measurement models bear to scientific theories is very much like the relation a blueprint bears to a building. A blueprint may be invaluable in constructing a bar, but one cannot have a beer inside one. Analogously, a generic measurement model can be invaluable in setting up a testable substantive theory about how intelligence relates to IQ-scores, but it is not itself testable. For instance, a latent variable model for general intelligence could be tested by fitting a common factor model to IQ-scores, because this model yields testable consequences; however, if the model is rejected, this has consequences for the theory that intelligence is a latent variable underlying the IQ-scores, but not for the common factor model as a measurement theory. The common factor model would, at most, be useless as a measurement model for IQ-scores. It could never be true or false in itself.

Measurement models are blueprints for (parts of) scientific theories, they can suggest ways of thinking about scientific theories, but they are not themselves scientific theories. They have no empirical content of themselves. Therefore, the type of evidence that works in evaluating scientific theories, which is empirical, does not apply to conceptual frameworks for thinking about such theories; and the benchmarks of truth and falsity, which are invaluable in empirical research, are useless in evaluating measurement models. The proper ground for the evaluation of conceptual frameworks like measurement models lies not in their empirical implications, but in their philosophical consequences. We may find such consequences plausible, or they may strike us as absurd. In conceptual investigations like the one we are about to begin here, plausibility and absurdity play roles analogous to the roles of truth and falsity in empirical research; they show us which way to go.

1.3   Philosophy of science

The evaluation of measurement models in terms of their philosophical consequences implies that such models are at least in part based on philosophical theories. This is, indeed, one of the main assumptions behind this book. The central idea is that measurement models can be considered to be *local* philosophies of science. They are local in the sense that they are concerned with one specific part of the scientific process, namely measurement, rather than with general questions on the aims and function of scientific theories. The latter type of philosophical theories could be called *global*.

Examples of global theories in the philosophy of science are theories like the logical positivism of the Vienna Circle or Popper's falsificationism. Such theories are based on general ideas on what scientific theories are, on how scientific research should proceed, and on what the best possible result of scientific research is. Global theories on philosophy of science and local theories on measurement models have something in common. Namely, in both cases a central question is how abstract scientific concepts, like intelligence, are connected to concrete observations, like IQ-scores. The difference is that in global theories, the connection between theory and observation is always related to more general ideas on the scientific enterprise, but hardly ever formalized, while in theories of measurement, the connection between theory and observation is always formalized, but hardly ever related to more general theoretical ideas. However, it would be surprising if such similar enterprises – formally specifying the relation between theoretical attributes and observations in a measurement model, and general theorizing on the relation between theoretical attributes and observations from a philosophical viewpoint – touched no common ground. And indeed they do. In fact, in this book I will consider measurement models to be local implementations of global philosophies of science within the context of measurement. The question then becomes: what philosophical viewpoint does a given measurement model implement?

To answer this question, global philosophies of science will be evaluated according to the status they assign to theoretical terms like 'intelligence', 'electron', or 'space-time'. I will divide these theories into two camps, corresponding to the answer they give to a simple question: does the value of scientific theories depend on the existence of the theoretical entities they mention? For instance: does it matter, for the theory of general intelligence, whether or not general intelligence exists?

Theories that answer this question positively are called *realist* theories. Realism gives the simplest interpretation of scientific theories, and it has therefore been described as science's philosophy of science (Devitt, 1991). For the realist, theoretical concepts refer directly to reality, so that intelligence and extraversion are conceptualized as having an existential status quite independent of the observations. The meaning of theoretical concepts derives largely from this reference to reality; general intelligence, for example, would be conceptualized by a realist as an unobservable, but causally relevant concept. We learn about intelligence through its causal impact on our observations, and when we use the term 'intelligence', it is this causally efficient entity we indicate. Such views are embodied in the writings of many theorists in psychology (Jensen, 1998; Loevinger, 1957; McCrae and John, 1992; McCrae and Costa, 1997). In this book, I will argue that latent variable models are an implementation of this line of thinking.

Theories that answer the question whether theoretical attributes and entities exist negatively are sometimes called anti-realist theories (Van Fraassen, 1980; Devitt, 1991). There are many different theories that sail under this flag, like empiricism (Van Fraassen, 1980), instrumentalism (Toulmin, 1953), social constructivism (Gergen, 1985), and several variants of logical positivism (Suppe, 1977). Of course, when a realist scheme of thinking is denied, an alternative account for the meaning of theoretical terms, and for the successful role they play in the scientific enterprise, must be given; on this account such theories differ. For the reader to get some idea of the lines of reasoning that are commonly employed in anti-realist theories, it is useful to give a brief overview of some of them.

The logical positivists held that scientific theories could be partitioned into an observational and a theoretical part. In their view, a scientific theory could be represented as a set of sentences. Some of these sentences contained theoretical terms, like 'intelligence'. Such sentences were considered to be part of the 'theoretical vocabulary' (Suppe, 1997). The sentences that did not contain such terms, but only referred to observational terms, like 'John has given the response "13" when asked to complete the series 1, 1, 2, 3, 5, 8, . .', were thought to be directly verifiable; they formed the so-called 'observational vocabulary'. A set of 'correspondence rules' was considered to coordinate the theoretical and observational vocabularies (Carnap, 1956). These correspondence rules were supposed to play the role of a dictionary, which for every theoretical sentence returned a set of observation sentences that could be directly verified. If all observation sentences implied by a theory were verified, then the theory as a whole was thought to be confirmed. The emphasis on direct verification is the reason that logical positivism is also known as 'verificationism'. In logical positivism, theoretical attributes, properties, and entities are logical constructions, which are implicitly defined through the observational vocabulary by means of correspondence rules. Theoretical attributes have no referents in reality.

Instrumentalism (Toulmin, 1953) also has an anti-realist orientation, but for different reasons. In contrast to logical positivists, instrumentalists do not see it as the task of science to give us verified or true theories. From an instrumentalist viewpoint, theories are instruments that allow us to predict future events and to exercise control over our environment. Theoretical attributes are part of the predictive machinery that science gives us. They allow us to make inferences to events that have not yet been observed. However, theoretical attributes need not refer to structures in the world. A theory may be useful without this being the case, and, according to instrumentalists, usefulness is the only appropriate criterion for scientific theories to satisfy. Thus, instrumentalists hold that the question whether theoretical attributes exist or not is both scientifically and philosophically unimportant.

Social constructivism (Gergen, 1985) is like instrumentalism in that it denies truth or verification to be a relevant criterion for theories to satisfy, and like logical positivism in that it views theoretical attributes as figments of the researcher's imagination. Researchers are not viewed as passive observers, but as actively involved in the construction of the world they study. Reality is thus seen not as a independent benchmark for scientific theories, but as a construction on part of the researcher, and so is truth. Social constructivists hold that theoretical attributes do not exist, but arise from a sort of negotiation or social exchange between researchers. The meaning of theoretical terms like 'intelligence' is actively constructed in this social exchange; in this respect, social constructivism is reminiscent of the ideas of the later Wittgenstein (1953) and of postmodern philosophy. However, it is unclear whether the word 'construction' is to be interpreted literally or metaphorically, especially because social constructivists do not tend to be very specific on how the construction process is carried out (Hacking, 1999). This contrasts sharply with logical positivism, in which the construction process is spelled out in detail.

Logical positivism, instrumentalism, and social constructivism differ in many respects. However, they share a fundamentally anti-realist view on the status of theoretical attributes or entities. In this view, one denies not only the existence of a theoretical attribute such as general intelligence, but also that the adequacy of the theory of general intelligence depends on its existence. This means that one is not merely an epistemological anti-realist (meaning that one does not know for sure whether, say, general intelligence exists; a position that, I think, every serious scientist should take) but that one is also a semantic anti-realist (meaning that one does not even think that whether general intelligence exists matters to the theory of general intelligence). I will generically indicate this line of reasoning as *constructivist*.

Like any philosopher of science, the constructivist needs an account of measurement. He cannot view the attributes measured in science as structures in reality that exist independently of our attempts to measure them. Thus, in order to remain consistent, the constructivist needs a measurement theory that squares with the idea that theoretical attributes, like general intelligence, are produced by the scientists who use intelligence tests. One way to achieve this is by conceptualizing general intelligence as a representation of empirically observable relations. A mathematically rigorous model that can be used for this purpose is the representational measurement model. Thus, representational measurement theory implements a constructivist philosophy of science at the level of measurement. In particular, it will be argued that representational measurement theory is an incarnation of the logical positivist doctrine on the relation between theoretical and observational terms.

Summarizing, the argument to be made in the following chapters is that latent variable theory is an implementation of realist thinking, while representationalist theory implements a constructivist philosophy. Where does this leave the most influential of theories, classical test theory? Is it an implementation of constructivist, or of realist philosophy? It turns out that classical test theory is highly ambiguous with respect to this issue. It can, however, be clearly coordinated with the semantic doctrine of operationalism, which holds that the meaning of theoretical concepts is synonymous with the operations used to measure them. This idea has well-known implausible consequences, and these will be shown to apply to classical test theory with equal force. Thus, the most influential and widely used test theory in psychology may rest on defective philosophical foundations.

1.4   Scope and outline of this book

Classical test theory, latent variable theory, and representational measurement theory are evaluated in chapters 2, 3, and 4, respectively. In chapter 5, I will enquire whether it is possible to integrate these different measurement models and the associated philosophical positions into a larger framework. It is argued that, at least as far as their statistical formulation is concerned, the models can be viewed from a unified perspective. However, even though the models are closely connected to each other under a suitable choice of model interpretation, the focus of each model remains different. In particular, true score theory deals with error structures, fundamental measurement concentrates on the representation of observed relations, and latent variable models address the sources of variation in the test scores. Because latent variable theory is the only model that explicitly addresses the question where variation in scores comes from, the question of test validity is best considered within this framework. Chapter 6 develops a concept of validity that is based on a realist interpretation of psychological attributes closely connected to latent variable theory.

2 True scores

> Nothing, not even real data, can contradict classical test theory...
> Philip Levy, 1969

2.1 Introduction

In September 1888, Francis Ysidro Edgeworth read a paper before Section F of the British Association at Bath, in which he unfolded some ideas that would profoundly influence psychology. In this paper, he suggested that the theory of errors, at that point mainly used in physics and astronomy, could also be applied to mental test scores. The paper's primary example concerned the evaluation of student essays. Specifically, Edgeworth (1888, p. 602) argued that '... it is intelligible to speak of the mean judgment of competent critics as the true judgment; and deviations from that mean as errors'. Edgeworth's suggestion, to decompose observed test scores into a 'true score' and an 'error' component, was destined to become the most famous equation in psychological measurement: $O_{bserved} = T_{rue} + E_{rror}$.

In the years that followed, the theory was refined, axiomatized, and extended in various ways, but the axiomatic system that is now generally presented as classical test theory was introduced by Novick (1966), and formed the basis of the most articulate exposition of the theory to date: the seminal work by Lord and Novick (1968). Their treatment of the classical test model, unrivalled in clarity, precision, and scope, is arguably the most influential treatise on psychological measurement in the history of psychology. To illustrate, few psychologists know about the other approaches to measurement that are discussed here: you may be able to find a handful of psychologists who know of latent variables analysis, and one or two who have heard about fundamental measurement theory, but every psychologist knows about true scores, random error, and reliability – the core concepts of classical test theory.

The main idea in classical test theory, that observed scores can be decomposed into a true score and an error component, has thus proved a very attractive one. Actually, what was once an idea seems to have been transformed into a fact: there is no psychological measurement without error. This seems to be a safe position to take when applying psychological tests – after all, who would be so overconfident to claim that he could measure perfectly – but it is also counterintuitive. That is, if I endorse the item 'I like to go to parties', why would there necessarily be measurement error involved? Could it not be that I truly like to go to parties? What, then, *is* measurement error? Now, this question is not as easily resolved as it may seem to be. It is seductive to conclude that random error, for example, represents the impact of unsystematic, transient, factors on the observations (e.g., the subject had a headache at the testing occasion, or she was distracted by noise, etc.). However, we will see that this interpretation is not without problems in the classical test theory framework. More generally, it is exceedingly difficult to reconcile the formal content of classical test theory with common interpretations of terms such as 'random error'. The friction between intuitive interpretations of terms, and the way they are formally conceptualized, is particularly salient in the interpretation of classical test theory's central concept, the true score.

The true score is commonly introduced by using phrases such as 'the true score is the construct we are attempting to measure' (Judd, Smith, and Kidder, 1991, p. 49), or by stressing the distinction 'between observed scores and construct scores (true scores)' (Schmidt and Hunter, 1999, p. 189). This interpretation of true scores, as 'valid' or 'construct' scores, has been called the *platonic true score* interpretation (Sutcliffe, 1965; Lord and Novick, 1968, pp. 39ff.). Of course, the use of the adjective 'true' strongly invites such an interpretation, and as a consequence it is endorsed by many researchers and students. However, problems with the platonic interpretation of true scores have been exposed by several authors (Klein and Cleary, 1967; Lord and Novick, 1968; Lumsden, 1976). In particular, cases can be constructed where equating the true score with the construct score leads to violations of basic theorems in classical test theory. In these cases, the identification of true and construct scores will, for example, lead to correlations between true and error scores (Lord and Novick, 1968; Lumsden, 1976), while in the classical test theory model, these correlations are zero by construction.

These observations point to the conclusion that the conjunction of the platonic true score interpretation with the axiomatic system of classical test theory is, at least for some cases, untenable. The implication of such a conclusion would be that, in general, the true score does not admit a realist interpretation. It is argued here that this is indeed the case. Further, the factors that preclude such an interpretation are elucidated. It is argued that the problems can be traced back to the fact that the true score is syntactically defined in terms of a series of observations. This severely restricts the interpretation of the concept; for instance, the true score does not lend itself to an identification with Loevinger's (1957) traits, which are presumed to exist independently of the test scores. The reason for this is that true scores are conceptualized in terms of observed scores, and, as a result of the way classical test theory is constructed, have a highly restricted domain of generalization – namely, the domain of parallel tests. It is, however, also argued in this chapter that the entire idea that two distinct tests could be parallel, is inconsistent. This essentially forces the conclusion that the true score can only apply to the test in terms of which it is defined. This, in turn, implies that a conceptualization of psychological constructs as true scores requires an operationalist position with regard to such constructs.

2.2   Three perspectives on true scores

The psychometric models discussed in this book are viewed from three perspectives: formal, empirical, and ontological. The formal perspective consists of two parts. First, the model formulation, or syntax, is discussed. Second, the interpretation of the formal terms in the model, i.e., the model semantics, is evaluated. After clarifying the syntax and semantics of the model, I discuss it from an empirical perspective, by examining the way the model handles data in actual research. Finally, the ontological stance evaluates whether psychometric concepts such as the true score can be taken to refer to an external, objective reality, or must be considered to be products of the imagination of the researcher.

In the context of classical test theory, the formal stance will focus mainly on the syntactical definitions of true and error scores, which form the basis of the theory. The semantic interpretation of these concepts immediately takes us into philosophical territory, because it must be framed in terms of counterfactual premises. Specifically, classical test theory must rely on a thought experiment to establish a version of probability theory that applies to the individual subject; this version of probability theory is needed for a consistent interpretation of the true score. From an empirical perspective, the thought experiment does heavy work in the interpretation of concepts such as reliability. But from an ontological perspective, the fact that the true score is defined in purely syntactic terms, and moreover requires an interpretation in terms of counterfactuals, severely limits the interpretation of the concept. It is argued here that the true score is better conceptualized as an instrumental concept that governs the interpretation of data analytic results in test analysis, rather than an entity that exists independently of the researcher's imagination.

2.2.1 The formal stance

Syntax Classical test theory is syntactically the simplest theory discussed in this book. Virtually all theorems follow from just two definitions. First, classical test theory defines the true score of person i, t_i, as the expectation of the observed score X_i over replications:

$$t_i \equiv \mathcal{E}(X_i). \tag{2.1}$$

Second, the error score E_i is defined as the difference between the observed score and the true score:

$$E_i \equiv X_i - t_i. \tag{2.2}$$

The notation emphasizes that, while X_i and E_i are considered random variables, the true score t_i is by definition a constant. Note that the error scores have zero expectation by construction, since $\mathcal{E}(E_i) = \mathcal{E}(X_i - t_i) = t_i - t_i = 0$.

An extra source of randomness is introduced by sampling from a population of subjects. As a result, the true score also becomes a random variable and the theory generalizes to the familiar equation

$$X = T + E. \tag{2.3}$$

Lord and Novick (1968, p. 34) note that no assumption concerning linearity needs to be made in order to derive equation 2.3. The linear relation between true scores and observed scores follows directly from the definitions of true and error scores. Novick (1966) showed that all other required assumptions follow from the definitions of true and error scores for the individual, as given in equations 2.1 and 2.2. For example, the above definitions ensure the independence of true and error scores, and imply that the error scores have zero expectation in the population (Mellenbergh, 1999).

Semantics The true score is defined as the expected value of the observed scores. However, the interpretation of the expectation operator immediately yields a problem, because the expected value of the observed score is conceived of at the level of the individual. This conceptualization is borrowed from the theory of errors (Edgeworth, 1888; see also Stigler, 1986, and Hacking, 1990), which has been fruitfully applied, for example, in astronomy. It is useful to summarize this theory briefly.

The theory of errors works as follows. Suppose that one wants to determine the position of a planet, and that the planet is sufficiently distant for its position to be considered a constant. Suppose further that multiple measurements of its position are made. These measurements, if made with sufficient precision, will not yield identical values (for most readers, this will not come as a surprise, but it was originally considered to be a tremendously shocking discovery; see Stigler, 1986). Now, the deviations from the true value may be interpreted as accidental disturbances, that is, as the aggregated effects of a large number of independent factors (e.g., weather conditions, unsystematic fluctuations in the measurement apparatus used, and the like). It is intuitively plausible that, if this is indeed the case, the observations will tend to produce a symmetrical, bell-shaped frequency distribution around the true value: because they are accidental, deviations to either side of the true value are equally likely, and, further, larger deviations are less likely than smaller ones. A formal justification for this idea can be given on the basis of the central limit theorem, which states that the sum of independently distributed variables approaches the normal distribution as the number of variables of which it is composed gets larger. Indeed, in the context of astronomical observations, the repeated measurements were often observed to follow such a bell-shaped frequency distribution. The theory of errors combines these ideas: it conceptualizes accidental disturbances as realizations of a random error variable, which will produce a normal distribution of the observations around the true value. If this conceptualization is adequate, then it follows that random errors will tend to average out as the number of observations increases. Thus, in such a case it is reasonable to assume that the expectation of the errors of measurement equals zero. This, in turn, supports the use of the arithmetic mean over a series of measurements as an estimate of the true position, because the mean is defined as the point for which the sum of the deviations from that point equals zero. It takes but a small step to conceptualize the true position of the planet as the expected value of the measurements, for which the arithmetic mean is a maximum likelihood estimator.

If classical test theory dealt with series of repeated measurements for which an analogous line of reasoning could be maintained, there would be few problems in the interpretation of the theory. However, classical test theory does not deal with such series of measurements, but with measurements on a single occasion. Moreover, series of measurements for which the theory holds are not to be expected in psychological measurement. Such series must satisfy the axioms of classical test theory, which require that the replications are parallel. This means that the true score must remain constant over replications. Thus, the true score should not change over time. In a realistic interpretation, this would mean that replicated observations should be considered to originate from a stationary random process; Molenaar (personal communication) has observed that, in the terminology of time series analysis, one would refer to the observed score as a 'white noise' variable with nonzero expectation. A procedure that would approximately satisfy the assumptions involved could, for example, consist in repeatedly throwing dice. That throwing dice would conform to the requirements of classical test theory is no coincidence, for what is in fact required is a procedure that allows for the application of the probability calculus in a frequentist sense. In the context of psychological measurement, the stated assumptions are unrealistic, because human beings will remember their previous response, learn, get fatigued, and will change in many other ways during a series of repeated administrations of the same test. Thus, even if the observed scores could be appropriately characterized as originating from a random process (which could be doubted in itself), this random process would not be stationary, which implies that the repeated measurements would not be parallel. It is clear, therefore, that classical test theory (a) is not concerned with series of measurements, and (b) could not concern itself with such series in the first place, because *actual* repeated measurements cannot be expected to conform to the assumptions of the theory. Still, the syntactical formulation of the theory uses the expectation operator at an essential point in the development of the theory – namely in the definition of its central concept, the true score. What is to be done about this awkward situation?

Introducing Mr Brown It is useful to put oneself in Lord and Novick's shoes in order to appreciate the problems at hand.[1] First, Lord and Novick want to use a probability model based on Kolmogorov's (1933) axioms, but are unable to give this model a strong frequentist interpretation, which would make it comply with the dominant view of probability at the time (e.g., Neyman and Pearson 1967), because no actual series of repeated measurements will allow for such an interpretation. A subjectivist interpretation (De Finetti, 1974) is conceptually difficult; of course, the true score of subject i could be conceptualized as the expected value of the researcher's degree-of-belief distribution over the possible responses of subject i, but this view will not match the average researcher's idea of what constitutes a true value. For example, in psychological testing, the researcher will often not have any knowledge of subject i prior to test administration. In such cases, the subjectivist view would motivate the use of a noninformative prior distribution, which would moreover be the same across subjects. But this would imply that every subject has the same true score prior to testing. This is not unreasonable within the subjectivist paradigm, but it is squarely opposed to the way the average researcher thinks of measurement. As a consequence, the application of the probability calculus has to be justified in a different manner.

[1] The development commented on can be found in Lord and Novick, 1968, chapter 2.

Second, Lord and Novick want to reason along the lines of the theory of errors, but they cannot do this because the *assumption* that errors will average out in an *actual* series of repeated observations, and that the arithmetic mean of that series will therefore be a reasonable estimate of the theoretical construct in question, is in flagrant contradiction with the basic fact that human beings, unlike coins and dice, are capable of learning and inclined to do so. Moreover, Lord and Novick do not want to restrict the theory to continuous variables with normally distributed error scores, which, in the theory of errors, are critical for motivating the interpretation of the expected value as the true score. On the contrary, they want to generalize the theory to categorical observed variables, because, in psychological testing, these are far more common than continuous observed variables. For example, intelligence tests work with items that are scored dichotomously (as correct or incorrect), and Lord and Novick surely want their theory to cover such situations.

Third, Lord and Novick need to do something with the individual, but this does not mean that they want to take such an undertaking seriously. Classical test theory has no business with the peculiar idiosyncratic processes taking place at the level of the individual: the probability model is merely needed to allow for the formulation of concepts such as reliability and validity, both of which are defined at the population level. A serious attempt at modelling individual subjects (e.g., through time series analysis) would, in all likelihood, not even yield results consistent with classical test theory. So, the individual subject must receive a probability distribution, but only in order to make him disappear from the analysis as smoothly as possible.

Lord and Novick's response to these problems may either be characterized as a brilliant solution, or as a deceptive evasion. In either case, their approach rigorously disposes of all problems in a single stroke: Lord and Novick simply delete subjects' memories by brainwashing them. Naturally, they have to rely on a thought experiment to achieve this. This thought experiment is taken from Lazarsfeld (1959):

> Suppose we ask an individual, Mr Brown, repeatedly whether he is in favour of the United Nations; suppose further that after each question we 'wash his brains' and ask him the same question again. Because Mr Brown is not certain as to how he feels about the United Nations, he will sometimes give a favorable and sometimes an unfavorable answer. Having gone through this procedure many times, we then compute the proportion of times Mr Brown was in favor of the United Nations. (Lazarsfeld, 1959; quoted in Lord and Novick, 1968, pp. 29–30)

Through the application of this thought experiment, the replications are rendered independent as a result of the brainwashing procedure. The resulting hypothetical series of observations allows for the application of standard probability theory, a quasi-frequentistic conception of probability, and a syntactical definition of the true score which has at least *a* semantic interpretation: in the particular case of Mr Brown, the true score equals the probability of him giving a favourable answer, which is estimated by the proportion of times he was in favour of the United Nations.

Propensities? Interestingly, Lord and Novick call the probability distribution characterizing this counterfactual series of replications a *propensity* distribution. This may be after Popper (1963), who proposed the propensity theory of probability as an objectivist alternative to Von Mises' conception of probability as relative frequency (Van Lambalgen, 1990). The propensity view holds that probability is not a relative long run frequency, but a physical characteristic of an object like a coin, or, more accurately, of the object and the chance experimental setup (Hacking, 1965). Lord and Novick's reference to the propensity view is remarkable because, in the thought experiment, they seem to introduce a limiting frequency view of probability. However, the limiting frequency and propensity interpretations of probability do not, in general, coincide. This is because propensities, by themselves, do not logically entail anything about relative frequencies. For example, a coin may have a propensity of 0.5 to fall heads; then it is possible, although perhaps unlikely, that it will forever fail to do so. In this case, the limiting relative frequency equals zero and thus deviates from the propensity. Because propensities are, in contrast to relative frequencies, logically disconnected from empirical observations, but are nevertheless supposed to conform to Kolmogorov's axioms, they have been said to operate under the 'conservation of mystery' (Kelly, 1996, p. 334). So, strictly speaking, the true score as a limiting frequency in the thought experiment is not logically connected to the true score as a propensity, because the propensity view and the relative frequency view are not logically connected.

Thus, Lord and Novick's reference to the propensity interpretation of probability is intriguing, especially in view of the fact that they are going through so much trouble in order to generate a relative frequency interpretation for the observed score distribution. One reason for their referencing the propensity view may be that it is the only objectivist theory of probability that allows one to ascribe probabilities to unique events. It is not improbable that Lord and Novick mention the term 'propensity' because they are aware of the fact that they are actually doing just this, and therefore cannot use a relative frequency account. But why, then, introduce the thought experiment in the first place? Why not settle for the propensity interpretation and let the relative frequencies be?

My guess is that the reason for this move is twofold. First, propensities are logically disconnected from relative frequencies (i.e., they are not defined in terms of such frequencies), but they are not fully disconnected either. It is in fact obvious that the propensity of a coin to fall heads is related to its behaviour in repeated coin tossing. One could say that propensities should be viewed as dispositions to behave in a certain way; a propensity of 0.5 to fall heads, as ascribed to a coin, could then be viewed as expressing the conditional 'if the coin were tossed a large number of times, the relative frequency of heads would be approximately 0.5'. Because ascribing a disposition generally involves a prediction of this kind, Ryle (1949) has called dispositional properties 'inference tickets'. So, if Mr Brown's true score is to be conceptualized in a similar way, the frequency behaviour for which it would be an inference ticket must involve replicated measurements. Actual replicated measurements, however, are not generated by stationary random processes, and so it is likely that the propensities will not predict the actual relative frequencies at all. This would render Ryle's inference ticket useless. The inference ticket would, however, apply to the replicated measurements with intermediate brainwashing.

Second, we must not forget that Lord and Novick are forging an account of psychological measurement; and although they know that they cannot follow the line of reasoning that is the basis for the theory of errors, they do want to stay close to it. The theory of errors is clearly based on an observation concerning the behaviour of scores in a long run of replicated measurements. Moreover, it is essential for these series themselves that they are unsystematic, i.e., that they are random. If they were not, there would be little reason to attribute the fact that repeated measurements are not identical, to unsystematic fluctuations, and to view such disturbances as random error. Again, actual replications are unlikely to produce such series; these will be neither stationary, nor random. Hence, the need for Mr Brown's being brainwashed between the replications.

The conclusion must be that Lord and Novick do not need the thought experiment for the application of the probability calculus itself; this could be done solely on the basis of the propensity view. Moreover, the propensity view seems more appropriate because classical test theory is largely concerned with probability statements concerning unique events. Lord and Novick need the thought experiment to maintain the connection between probability theory and the theory of errors, that is, to justify the definition of the true score as the expected value of the observed scores, and to defend the view that deviations from that value are to be interpreted as being due to random error.

Thought experiments The brainwashing thought experiment could be seen as successful, for it is used in many psychometric models. Models that use it are said to follow a *stochastic subject* interpretation (Holland, 1990; Ellis and Van den Wollenberg, 1993). A stochastic subject interpretation of psychometric models must, in general, rely upon a thought experiment like the above. The thought experiments are needed to provide an interpretation that is in line with both the probability calculus and the typical idea of random error, and could be said to function as a 'semantic bridge'. This property distinguishes them from other kinds of thought experiments, which are usually directed at a theory, rather than part of a theory (Brown, 1991; Sorensen, 1992). For this reason, it has been proposed to treat these thought experiments as a distinct class of 'functional' thought experiments (Borsboom, Mellenbergh, and Van Heerden, 2002a).

Classical test theory requires such a functional thought experiment, but this does not mean that it must take the particular form in which Lord and Novick present it. Any thought experiment that provides an interpretation consistent with the syntax of the theory could, in principle, be used. Rozeboom (1966a, p. 387) considers, for example, that 'we may fantasize an experiment in which each member i of P has been replicated p times and each replica (...) is tested (...), so that if p is large the frequency of a particular observed value X among i's replicas approaches the probability of this observed score for i'. This thought experiment thus considers a probability distribution over a very large number of replicas of Mr Brown, every one of whom is asked whether he is in favour of the United Nations. Still another form of the thought experiment is in terms of an infinite series of administrations of distinct parallel tests. In this case, we would not ask Mr Brown the same question repeatedly, but we would present him with different questions that are parallel to the original question, that is, with a series of questions that all have the same expected value and error variance as the original question. Probably, many other forms of the thought experiment could be imagined. These thought experiments have in common that, as Rozeboom (1966a, p. 385) puts it, they 'try to convey some feeling for how sense can be made of the notion that a given testing procedure determines a probability distribution over potential test scores specific to each individual who might so be tested'. It should be noted, however, that such thought experiments do little more than convey some feeling. Basically, the classical test theorist is trying to sell you shoes which are obviously three sizes too small.

How definitions replaced assumptions Lord and Novick swiftly go over the construction of true and error scores based on this thought experiment, and manage to dispose of the individual subject in exactly six pages (Lord and Novick, 1968, pp. 28–34). In the remainder of their treatment of classical test theory, the focus is on between-subjects results and techniques. At the basis of the theory, however, remains the true score, defined through this peculiar thought experiment.

It is illustrative to recapitulate what has happened here. Lord and Novick have managed to put the theory of errors on its head. Recall that this theory is based on the idea that accidental errors will average out in the long run. The statistical translation of this notion is that accidental error scores can be viewed as realizations of a random variable with zero expectation. The zero expectation of measurement errors must therefore be viewed as an empirical assumption (i.e., its truth is contingent upon the actual state of affairs in the world). On the basis of this assumption, the expectation of the measurements can be conceptualized as an estimate of the true score. Since Lord and Novick are not in a position to use anything resembling an actual series of replications, and therefore are not in possession of a suitable long run, they create one for themselves. However, because their long run is constructed on counterfactual premises, it must remain thought experimental. It is obvious that, upon this conceptualization, the zero expectation of error scores can no longer be taken seriously as an empirical assumption, because it applies to a counterfactual state of affairs. As a result, there is no empirical basis for taking the expected value of the measurements as an estimate of the true score. Lord and Novick's response to this problem is remarkable. Instead of taking the zero expectation of errors as an *assumption* on which one can base the *hypothesis* that the expectation of the observed scores is equal to the true score, they *define* the true score as the expected value of the observed scores and then *derive* the zero expectation of errors as a consequence. Where the theory of errors observes irregularities in measurement, and then proposes statistical machinery to deal with those, classical test theory proposes the statistical machinery, and then hypothesizes the irregularities that would conform to it. The identity of expected observed score and true score is thus transformed from a hypothesis into a definition; and the assumption that error scores have zero expectation becomes a necessary truth. Following these moves, one can see the circle close: the theory becomes a tautology. Thus, the theory is immune to falsification. The price that is paid for this consists in the fully syntactical definition of the true score.

2.2.2 *The empirical stance*

If the applications of classical test theory were as esoteric as its theoretical formulation, nothing could be done with it. However, classical test theory is without doubt the most extensively used model for test analysis. What, then, does it actually do in test analysis? How does it relate to empirical data?

At this point, it is important to distinguish between how the classical model could be used in test analysis, and how the model is typically used. The basic axioms of classical test theory imply nothing about the data, and are therefore permanently immune to falsification: the adequacy of the posited decomposition of observed scores in true and error scores cannot, for any given item, be checked. Thus, this part of the model is untestable. This does not mean, however, that classical test theory could not be used to formulate testable hypotheses at all. However, to formulate such hypotheses requires extending the model with additional assumptions. These additional assumptions concern relations between true scores on different test forms, or items. Three such relations are commonly distinguished: parallelism, tau-equivalence, and essential tau-equivalence. Two tests x and x' are parallel in a population if they yield the same expected value and the same observed score variance for every subpopulation (including subpopulations consisting of a single subject). If distinct tests are assumed to be parallel, they must have equal means and variances; in addition, all intercorrelations between tests must be the same. Two tests are tau-equivalent if they yield the same expected values, but different error variances; and they satisfy essential tau-equivalence if they yield neither identical expected values, nor identical observed score variances, but the expected values are linearly related through the equation $\mathcal{E}(X) = c + \mathcal{E}(X')$, where c is constant over persons. For a given set of items, all three of these relations can readily be tested. For example, as Jöreskog (1971) has observed, when the classical model is extended with any one of the above relations, the model can be formulated as an identified factor model, and the implied covariance matrix can be fitted to the observed covariance matrix. Thus, commonly invoked assumptions about relations between true scores do have testable consequences. At least some parts of the so-extended model could be tested.

This is how the model *could* be applied. It is safe to say, however, that classical test theory is never applied in this way. The common applications of classical test theory do not involve testing the model assumptions. The cause of this neglect is probably historical, but will not concern us here. Rather, we will be concerned with the function classical test theory fulfils in applications. The strategy that is followed is highly indirect, and works via the estimation of reliability. It is important to review this process extensively, for it contains the basis for many misinterpretations of what classical test theory is about.

Reliability

Reliability is a population dependent index of measurement precision (Mellenbergh, 1996). It indicates the fraction of observed variance that is systematic, as opposed to random, in a given population. In classical test theory, reliability is the squared population correlation, ρ^2_{XT}, between true and observed scores. This equals the ratio of true score variance to observed score variance:

$$\rho^2_{XT} = \frac{\sigma^2_T}{\sigma^2_X} = \frac{\sigma^2_T}{\sigma^2_T + \sigma^2_E}. \tag{2.4}$$

This equation has intuitive appeal: in a given population, the value of the reliability coefficient will decrease as the error variance increases. If there is no error variance, reliability is perfect and equals unity. Note that this definition of reliability is population dependent (Mellenbergh, 1996). The reason for this is that reliability is defined in terms of the population model in equation 2.3. This is reflected in the random variable notation for the true score in the definition of reliability, i.e., in equation 2.4 the true score is denoted as T and not as t. A well-known implication of this definition is that reliability becomes smaller, if the true score variance in a population approaches zero while the error variance remains constant. As a consequence, for any individual subject i the reliability of a test equals zero, because by definition $\sigma^2_{t_i}$ equals zero for all i. Because reliability is a population dependent concept, it can be meaningfully considered only when interpreted in terms of individual differences in a specific population. Therefore, it is meaningless to refer to *the* reliability of a test, without specifying a population; and general remarks like 'the reliability of test x has been shown to be satisfactory', dressed up with a value of Cronbach's α, are not in accordance with the logic of classical test theory – or, for that matter, with the logic of any other theory of psychological testing.

Of course, the formula for reliability contains the true score, which is unobservable. Thus, in practical applications equation 2.4 is of little use to the researcher. The concept of reliability needs to be somehow connected to observations. The conceptual strategy of classical test theory consists in rewriting the formula for reliability in terms of potentially observable terms. Lord and Novick (1968) discuss the matter on pp. 58–9; what follows here could be viewed as a conceptual reconstruction of this development.

First, suppose that we had the ability to brainwash subjects between measurements. In this case, determining reliability would pose no difficulties. The determination of true score variance would still be impossible at any given time point, but because replications would be parallel by definition, we could use the correlation between the observed scores on two administrations, X and X', as follows. Assume, without loss of generality, that the expected value of the test scores in the population is zero. The correlation between the observed scores at two time points would equal:

$$\rho_{XX'} = \frac{\sigma_{XX'}}{\sigma_X \sigma_{X'}} = \frac{\mathcal{E}(TT')}{\sigma_X \sigma_{X'}}. \tag{2.5}$$

See Lord and Novick, 1968, p. 58, for the details of the derivation. This almost equals equation 2.4, which defines reliability. All that remains to be done is to rewrite the term $\mathcal{E}(TT')$ as σ_T^2, and the term $\sigma_X \sigma_{X'}$ as σ_X^2. If this step can be justified, the quantity σ_T^2/σ_X^2, which is unobservable in principle, has been rewritten as the quantity $\rho_{XX'}$, which is observable in principle. This would create a possible connection to the analysis of empirical data. Thus, what we have to do is to interpret a covariance between two variables as the variance of a single variable, and the product of two standard deviations of different variables as the variance of a single variable. This requires that the two variables in question are one and the same. That is, we need to be able to say not only that $T = T'$, in the sense of being numerically equal, but that $T \equiv T'$, in the sense that T and T' are synonymous. The reason for this is not primarily syntactical: $\rho_{XX'}$ will be numerically equal to ρ_{XT}^2 as soon as the true scores and error variances on two tests x and x' are numerically equal for each subject, even if this is by accident. For a consistent interpretation of the theory, however, these quantities have to be equal by necessity.

As an illustration of this point, consider the following situation. Suppose that it were the case that height and weight correlated perfectly in a population of objects, and that these attributes were measured on such a scale that the expected value of the measurement of weight with a balance scale, and the expected value of the measurement of length with a tapemeasure, happened to always be numerically equal. One could then use the correlation between observed measures of height and weight as an estimate of the reliability of the balance scale. As a pragmatic empirical strategy, this could work. But theoretically, one cannot admit such a situation in definitions and derivations like the above, because it would not be a necessary, but a contingent fact that the expectations of the measurement procedures were equal; they might very well not have been. Thus, from a semantic perspective, equating the correlation between parallel tests with the reliability of a single test makes sense only if the two tests measure the same true score. This requires that the true scores on the first and second administration are not merely numerically equal, but synonymous.

Can we take the required step while retaining a consistent semantic interpretation of the theory? It is one of the intriguing aspects of classical test theory that this can be done. The reason for this is that the true scores in question are not only syntactically, but also semantically indistinguishable. This is because, for subject i, both t_i and t'_i are defined as the expected value on test x, where the expectation is interpreted in terms of repeated administrations with intermediate brainwashing. It may seem that, because t_i is the expected value of the observed scores on the first administration of test x, and t'_i is the expected value of the observed scores on the second administration of test x, t_i and t'_i are distinguishable with respect to their temporal position. But the role of time in the brainwashing thought experiment is a peculiar one. The thought experiment uses the term 'replications' in order to make the application of the expectation operator to the individual subject a little more digestible than it would otherwise be, but the idea that we are talking about replications in the actual temporal domain is an illusion. This may be illustrated through the classical test theory models for change (Mellenbergh and Van den Brink, 1998). In such models, the difference between subject i's observed scores on administrations 1 and 2 of the same test, $X_{i2} - X_{i1}$, must be considered to be an estimator of i's true gain score, defined as $t_{i2} - t_{i1}$. Each of the true scores is thus defined as the expected value at a single time point. Although the thought experiment creates the impression that the expectation can be interpreted in terms of temporally separated replications of the same test, the term 'brainwashing' must be taken to mean that the subject is restored to his original state – *not only with respect to memory, learning, and fatiguing effects, but with respect to time itself*. Otherwise, classical test theory concepts such as the true gain score would be completely uninterpretable. Within the brainwashing thought experiment, the true scores on replications must be considered synonymous. Thus, Lord and Novick are justified in stating that $T \equiv T'$, and are able to write

$$\rho_{XX'} = \frac{\mathcal{E}(TT')}{\sigma_X \sigma_{X'}} = \frac{\sigma_T^2}{\sigma_X^2} = \rho_{XT_X}^2, \tag{2.6}$$

which completes the first part of their mission.

Obviously, the development sketched above only takes us halfway in making the connection between classical test theory and the analysis of empirical data. What we want is not to express reliability in terms of counterfactual relations, which involve brainwashing entire populations, but to express it in terms of actual relations between observed variables in real data. So, Lord and Novick's brainwash has had its best time; it has been crucially important in deriving the main psychometric concepts in classical test theory, but now it has to go. Can we get rid of it? The answer is: yes and no. An exact estimate of reliability cannot be obtained from empirical data, so in this sense there is no way to get around the issue. We can, however, settle for lower bounds on reliability, which can be estimated from the data under rather mild conditions. In the final analysis, however, the true score must be invoked again to conceptualize what such a lower bound is a lower bound *for*.

Constructing empirical estimates of reliability

The first option for constructing estimates of reliability is to neglect the conditions that preclude the interpretation of actual repeated measurements as identical with the thought experimental replications by simply ignoring the problem. This can be done in two ways: either we may assume that two actual replications of the same test are parallel, or we may assume that two distinct tests are parallel. The first of these methods is known as the test–retest method, and the second forms the basis of the parallel test method, the split-halves method, and the internal consistency method.

Test–retest reliability The test–retest method is based on the idea that two administrations of the same test may be regarded as one administration of two parallel tests. If this were the case, the population correlation between the scores on these administrations would be equal to the reliability of the test scores. However, the assumption that repeated administrations are parallel introduces a substantive assumption into the technicalities of classical test theory, namely that the trait in question is stable. On the basis of this observation, it has been suggested that the test–retest correlation should be called a 'stability coefficient'. It should be noted, however, that the between-subjects correlation cannot distinguish between situations where individual true scores are stable and situations where they increase or decrease by the same amount. Therefore, the term 'stability' can only be taken to refer to the stability of the ordering of persons, not to the stability of the construct itself. Note also that the method necessarily confounds differential change trajectories and unreliability (McDonald, 1999). We do not know, for most constructs, whether change trajectories are homogeneous or heterogeneous across subjects. This, of course, poses a problem for the interpretation of the test–retest correlation as a reliability estimate.

A second problem is that, in contrast to the thought experimental replications, actual replications are temporally separated, which creates the problem of choosing an appropriate spacing of the replications. Is reliability to be estimated by test–retest correlations based on immediate retesting? Retesting after a day? A month? A year? Since classical test theory cannot provide an answer to these questions, the test–retest scheme must introduce decisions which are, from a methodological perspective, arbitrary. However, these arbitrary decisions concerning the spacing of the replications will generally influence the value of the test–retest correlation. Does this mean that there is a distinct reliability for each choice of temporal spacing? Or should we consider the approximation to reliability to be systematically affected by temporal spacing, so that, for example, the estimate becomes better as we wait longer before retesting? Or does the approximation decrease with the time elapsed since the first administration? Or is this relation curvilinear so that, for example, the approximation is optimal after 1.2 weeks? And should we consider the relation between the quality of the reliability estimate and elapsed time to be the same across testing situations? Across groups? Across constructs? Why? It seems that these issues cannot be satisfactorily addressed, either from a psychological, a philosophical, or a methodological perspective.

In view of these issues, it is interesting that the test–retest method has been defended by Brennan (2001), on the grounds that reliability is intelligible only when interpreted in terms of replications of full test forms. This is plausible, but the concept of reliability should be considered within the definitions of classical test theory. Classical test theory defines the true score in terms of a thought experiment, and since the syntactical notation of reliability contains the true score as one of its elements, this definitional issue carries over to the interpretation of reliability. Upon a consistent interpretation of classical test theory, reliability is the proportion of variance in observed scores that would be attributable to variance in true scores; for the test–retest correlation to be an estimate of this proportion, the entire population of subjects must be brainwashed between repeated administrations. Therefore, reliability must conceptually be interpreted in terms of the brainwashing thought experiment; it cannot be defined in terms of actual replications because these simply will not behave according to the axioms of classical test theory. Practically, of course, one may suppose that the actual test–retest correlation is an estimate of the thought experimental one, but in this case it has to be assumed that relevant characteristics of the thought experimental replication are retained in an actual replication. Unfortunately, the essential characteristics involve parallelism and independence of repeated measurements, i.e., the assumption that the replications could be viewed as realizations of a stationary random variable. This is extremely unrealistic. Thus, the interpretation of the test–retest correlation as reliability (i.e., as the concept is defined in classical test theory through equation 2.4) requires a substantial leap of faith.

Using correlations between distinct tests The second strategy, which encompasses the methods of parallel tests, split-halves, and internal consistency estimates, is based on the idea that two distinct tests could be parallel. First, consider the parallel test method. This method assumes that a simultaneous administration of two different tests could be viewed as approximating two thought experimental replications of a single test. In case we had distinct parallel tests, the correlation between them could then be taken to be a direct estimate of the reliability of the test scores. There are two problems with this method.

The first is a practical problem, namely that the search for parallel test forms has been unsuccessful to date; this is not surprising, because the empirical requirements for parallelism (equal means, variances, and covariances of observed scores) are rather demanding. Further, there is no substantive psychological reason for assuming that two tests for, say, spatial reasoning, should have equal means and variances; nor is there a reason for regarding such tests as theoretically superior to tests that are not parallel.

The second problem is of a theoretical nature, namely that the idea that two distinct tests could be parallel seems semantically inconsistent. We have seen, in section 2.2.1, that classical test theory interprets the true score on a test x as the expected value on a number of repeated independent administrations of that test. That is, the true score is explicitly defined in terms of the test in question. If we now turn to a distinct test, y, the true score on this test is semantically interpreted in terms of repeated independent administrations of test y. Earlier in this section, we have seen that, to interpret the correlation between parallel test scores as a reliability estimate, the covariance between the two true scores on these measures must be interpreted as the variance of one true score, that is, it must be assumed that $T \equiv T'$. This can be done within the counterfactual state of affairs, defined in Lord and Novick's brainwashing thought experiment, exactly because T and T' are synonymous. However, the true scores on distinct tests x and y are semantically distinguishable, simply because they are defined with respect to different tests. They may be empirically equal, but this does not make them logically identical. This is to say that the identity of the true scores on repeated administrations with intermediate brainwashing, as used in the derivation of equation 2.4, is a necessary truth; but the empirical equality of expected values on distinct tests is a contingent truth (if it is a truth at all). This may be illustrated by noting that the former equivalence will hold by definition (one does not even have to administer the test to find out), while the observation that the latter holds in the present testing occasion does not guarantee that it will hold tomorrow.

The problem here is not so much that, as a hypothesis formulated independently of the classical test theory model, two distinct tests could not be taken to measure the same attribute; this hypothesis could certainly be added, and would in effect specify a latent variable model. The problem is rather that classical test theory itself has insufficient conceptual power to do the trick. The syntax of classical test theory cannot express what it means for two distinct tests to measure the same attribute, if the attribute is identified with the true score. It is only possible to write down, syntactically, that two tests measure the same true score. However, semantically, this makes sense only if these two 'tests' are in fact replicated administrations of the same test, as they are in the brainwashing thought experiment. But of course the brainwashing thought experiment is completely unrealistic. This is why the theory must take recourse to the strange requirement of tests that are distinct and yet parallel. What the syntactical derivations, as well as the semantics, of classical test theory imply is that parallel measurements consist in two independent administrations of the same test. A procedure that could reasonably be said to conform to the requirement of parallelism is, for example, the replicated length measurement of a number of rods with the same ruler. With two distinct psychological items or test scores, however, this logic is, at best, artificial and contrived; at worst, it is inconsistent. Thus, it is difficult to see how the method could yield theoretically interesting results, since it seems built on a contradiction. It is also obvious that the method has little practical value, because tests that satisfy at least the empirical equivalence needed for exact reliability estimates to work are hard to come by. The parallel test method is thus useful for only one purpose, namely for the derivation of reliability formulae. It cannot be taken seriously as an empirical method.

In the pursuit of exact reliability estimates, two methods have been proposed that may serve as alternatives to the parallel test method. These are the split-halves and internal consistency methods. The split-halves method splits a test in two subtests of equal length, assumes that the subtests are parallel (or constructs them to be nearly so; Gulliksen, 1950; Mellenbergh, 1994), computes the correlation between the total scores on subtests, and yields an estimate of the reliability of total test scores by using the Spearman–Brown correction for test lengthening. Internal consistency formulae such as the KR_{20} and coefficient α extend this method. They can be interpreted as the average reliability coefficient as derived from the split-halves correlation, where the average is taken over all possible split-halves. If the split-halves are parallel, the resulting quantity yields an exact estimate of the reliability of the total test scores. Since parallelism is as troublesome for split-halves as it is for full test forms, these methods fail for the same reasons as the parallel test method.

Lower bounds The exact estimation of reliability from observed data is thus impractical and theoretically questionable. This has prompted classical test theorists to look at worst-case scenarios, and to search for lower bounds for reliability (Guttman, 1945; Jackson and Agunwamba, 1977). For instance, it can be proven that, if test forms are not parallel, but satisfy weaker assumptions such as essential tau-equivalence, reliability estimates like Cronbach's α provide a lower bound on reliability. Thus, if α equals 0.80 in the population, then the reliability of the test scores is at least 0.80. This is a clever strategy, and the researcher who follows it seems to be fairly safe. In essence, the reasoning which could be followed is: no matter how bad things may be, the reliability of my test is always higher than the (population) value of the lower bound that is computed. This is probably the most viable defence that could be given for the standard practice in test analysis.

Note, however, that the true score does not do any work in the computation of any of the statistics discussed. The test–retest correlation is, well, a test–retest correlation, and internal consistency is just a transformation of the average split-half correlation. Both could be used in test analysis, and judged for their merits, without recourse to classical test theory as a theory of measurement. The statistical machinery will do just fine. However, this does not mean that classical test theory is irrelevant to the way the analyses are used. For the *interpretation* of test–retest correlations or average split-halves correlations as reliability estimates does involve classical test theory. What is obtained in the analysis is a test–retest or average split-halves correlation, but when these are interpreted in terms of reliability, they are interpreted as estimates of, or lower bounds for, the quantity denoted as $\rho^2_{XT_X}$, and this quantity does involve the true score as defined in classical test theory. Thus, what we observe here is an inference from empirical relations (involving only observables) to theoretical relations (involving observables and unobservables). This type of inference is, of course, nothing new, for it is the gist of science. What is typical and unusual here is that the inference does not come at a price. The researcher gets the theoretical interpretation in terms of unobservable true scores for free. The question, however, is what this theoretical interpretation is worth: what is it exactly, that we are informed about? What is the status of the true score?

2.2.3 The ontological stance

Of all psychometric concepts, reliability plays the most important role in practical test analysis. Of course, all researchers pay lip service to validity, but if one reads empirical research reports, reliability estimates are more often than not used as a primary criterion for judging and defending the adequacy of a test. In this sense, reliability is the poor man's validity coefficient, as Rozeboom (1966a) has observed. I think that the analysis presented above casts doubt on whether reliability deserves this status. The theoretical acrobatics necessary to couple empirical quantities, like test–retest correlations, to reliability, as defined in classical test theory, are disconcerting. Coupled with the fact that these coefficients are used and interpreted rather uncritically, the observation that 'classical measurement theory [is] the measurement model used in probably 95 per cent of the research in differential psychology' (Schmidt and Hunter, 1999, p. 185) seems to be a cause for concern, not for celebration. The problems grow even deeper when one considers that 95 per cent of the researchers involved in research in differential psychology are probably not doing what they think they are doing. For no concept in test theory has been so prone to misinterpretation as the true score.

As has been noted earlier in this chapter, it is tempting to think that the distinction between true scores and observed scores is the same as the distinction 'between observed scores and construct scores' (Schmidt and Hunter, 1999, p. 189), or that 'the true score is the construct we are attempting to measure' (Judd, Smith, and Kidder, 1991, p. 49), or that it is the score 'that would be obtained if there were no errors of measurement' (Nunnally, 1978, p. 110). This is the way the matter is often explained to students, and it is the way many researchers think about psychological measurement. However, the identification of the psychological construct with the true score of classical test theory is not without problems.

There are two problematic assumptions underlying the platonic interpretation of the true score. The first assumption underlying the idea that the true score is the real score on a psychological construct is the result of a confounding of unreliability and invalidity. This is a recognized fallacy, but it is so common and persuasive that it deserves a thorough treatment. The second assumption concerns the ontological status of the true score itself. It will be argued here that the entire idea that a person has a true score, as defined in classical test theory, is unintelligible – except when interpreted in a thought experimental sense. So interpreted, it has the status of a dispositional concept, but, oddly enough, it specifies dispositional properties with respect to an impossible sequence of situations; namely, the thought experimental replications. The true score is therefore best thought of as a fiction. Finally, in contrast to psychological constructs, the true score cannot be conceptualized independently of the test in question. This is why the true score must be seen as a concept that is best interpreted in an operationalist sense.

True scores as construct scores

The idea that true scores are valid construct scores can be seen as a confounding of reliability and validity. These are qualitatively different concepts: reliability has to do with the precision of the measurement procedure, while validity involves the question whether the intended attribute is indeed being measured. For the simple reason that no formal model can contain its own meaning (it cannot itself say what it is a model for), it seems obvious that this interpretation is incorrect from the outset. However, although various authors have warned against it, the platonic true score interpretation is like an alien in a B-movie: no matter how hard you beat it up, it keeps coming back. A recent revival has, for example, been attempted by Schmidt and Hunter (1999). True scores are not valid construct scores, and neither do they necessarily reflect construct scores.

At the present point in the discussion, the concept of validity is introduced, and therefore the relation of measurement has become important. In itself, it is interesting that, in the entire discussion so far, the term 'measurement' has remained unanalysed. We have been able to review the assumptions, semantics, and empirical applications of classical test theory without making the meaning of this concept explicit. This is typical of classical test theory and contains an important clue as to why the identification of true scores with psychological constructs is so problematic. To see this, take it as given that the objective of psychological testing is to measure constructs, or, if you like, the phenomena to which constructs refer. If true scores could be taken to be identical to construct scores, then it should be possible for classical test theory to rewrite the relation of measurement, interpreted as a relation between observed scores and construct scores, as a relation between observed scores and true scores. It turns out that classical test theory cannot do this. The reason for this is that, because the theory is statistical in nature, it is natural to conceive of the relation between observed scores and construct scores statistically. This is also the position taken by Lord and Novick (1968, p. 20), who say that '... an observable variable is a measure of a theoretical construct if its expected value is presumed to increase monotonically with the construct' and '... to be primarily related to construct being defined'. This is similar to the measurement relation as conceived in item response models, where the expected value on items is related to the position on the latent variable. It follows from this conceptualization, however, that true scores cannot play the role of construct scores. This is because the true score is itself defined as the expected value on a test, so that identifying true scores with construct scores and substituting this in Lord and Novick's conception of measurement leads to the following definition: '... an observable variable is a measure of a [true score] if its [true score] is presumed to increase monotonically with the [true score]'. This can hardly be considered enlightening.

In contrast to, for example, latent variable models, classical test theory does not have the conceptual power to represent the construct in the model. The relation of measurement must thus be seen as a relation between true scores and something else. This is in perfect accordance with the way validity is treated in classical test theory, namely as the correlation between the true scores on the test in question and an external criterion. However, it is inconsistent with the idea that true scores are construct scores. It is actually rather strange that this misconception occurs at all, because classical test theory defines the true score without ever referring to psychological constructs or a measurement relation. The theory does not contain the identity of true scores and construct scores – either by definition, by assumption, or by hypothesis. Moreover, it is obvious from the definition of the true score that classical test theory does not assume that there is a construct underlying the measurements at all. In fact, from the point of view of classical test theory, literally every test has a true score associated with it. For example, suppose we constructed a test consisting of the items 'I would like to be a military leader', '$0.10\sqrt{0.05 + 0.05} = ..$', and 'I am over six feet tall'. After arbitrary – but consistent – scoring of a person's item responses and adding them up, we multiply the resulting number by the number of letters in the person's name, which gives the test score. This test score has an expectation over a hypothetical long run of independent observations, and so the person has a true score on the test. The test will probably even be highly reliable in the general population, because the variation in true scores will be large relative to the variation in random error (see also Mellenbergh, 1996). The true score on this test, however, presumably does not reflect an attribute of interest.

It is also very easy to construct situations in which there is a valid construct score, while that score differs from the true score as classical test theory defines it. Consider, for example, the following example, which is based on an example by Lord and Novick (1968, pp. 39ff.; this example is in turn based on a paper by Sutcliffe, 1965). At present, whether a patient has Alzheimer's disease or not cannot be determined with certainty until the patient is deceased and an autopsy can be performed. In other words, the diagnostic process, taking place while the patient is still alive, is subject to error. We can conceptualize the diagnostic process as a test, designed to measure a nominal variable with two levels ('having the disease' and 'not having the disease'). Because this variable is nominal, we may assign an arbitrary number to each of its levels. Let us assign the number '1' to a patient who actually has Alzheimer's, and the number '0' to a patient who does not. This number represents patient i's construct score c_i on the nominal variable 'having Alzheimer's'. Thus, a patient who actually has Alzheimer's has construct score $c_i = 1$, and a patient who does not have Alzheimer's has construct score $c_i = 0$.

In practice, the construct score cannot be directly determined. Instead, we obtain an observed score, namely the outcome of the diagnostic process. This observed score is also nominal, so we may again assign an arbitrary number to each of its levels. Let us code patient i's observed score x_i as follows. The value $x_i = 1$ indicates the diagnosis 'having Alzheimer's', and the value $x_i = 0$ indicates the diagnosis 'not having Alzheimer's'.

The diagnostic process is imperfect and therefore the test scores are subject to error. Now suppose that the test is valid, so that misclassifications are due solely to random error, for example, to equipment failures that occur at random points in time. This renders the observed score a random variable X. What is the true score on the test? It is tempting to think that a patient's i's true score, t_i, on the diagnostic test is equal to the construct score (i.e., $t_i = c_i$). Specifically, the infelicitous use of the adjective 'true' suggests that a patient who actually has Alzheimer's, i.e., a patient with construct score $c_i = 1$, also has a true score of $t_i = 1$ on the test. For this indicates the diagnosis 'having Alzheimer's', and it is, after all, true that the patient has that disease.

This interpretation of the true score is not, in general, consistent with classical test theory. For suppose that the sensitivity of the diagnostic test is 0.80. This means that the probability that a patient who actually has Alzheimer's will be correctly diagnosed as such is 0.80. Now consider the true score of a patient who has Alzheimer's, i.e., a patient with construct score $c_i = 1$. This patient's true score is not $t_i = 1$, because the true score of classical test theory is equal to the expectation of the observed score, which is $t_i = E(X_i | c_i = 1) = 0.80$. Suppose further that the sensitivity of the test is 0.70. This means that the probability that a patient who does not have Alzheimer's will be correctly diagnosed is 0.70. For a patient who does not have Alzheimer's (i.e., a patient whose construct score is $c_i = 0$), the true score is equal to $t_i = E(X_i | c_i = 0) = 0.30$. In both cases the true score and construct score yield different values.[2]

It can now be seen why the identification of true scores with construct scores is logically inconsistent with classical test theory in general. If the test in the example contains error, this means that there is misclassification; and if there is misclassification, the expected value of the observed score can never be equal to the construct score. So, if measurements

---

[2] Note that the argument implicitly uses a latent class formulation, where the construct score indicates class membership; this suggests that latent variables can be used to extend the model in the required direction. It will be argued in the next chapter that this is indeed the case.

contain random error, the identification of true scores with construct scores is logically inconsistent with classical test theory in general. It should be noted that Lord and Novick (1968) themselves were thoroughly aware of this, since they explicitly state that 'in general the two concepts and definitions [of true scores and construct scores] do not agree' (p. 41).

It is clear that the identification of construct scores with true scores is fundamentally incorrect. The objective of psychological measurement is to measure psychological constructs, but classical test theory cannot express the relation of measurement as a relation between observed and true scores. Rather, the theory must conceptualize the measurement relation as a relation between true scores and psychological constructs, which shows that these should not be considered identical. This conclusion is strengthened by the observation that we can easily construct cases where a true score 'exists', but where it is invalid in that it does not have substantial meaning in terms of a theory. We can also construct cases where there is a valid score, but where that score is not the true score.

In view of these problems, it is interesting and elucidating to enquire under what conditions the true score and the construct score could be taken to coincide. It seems that the situation in which this would be the case is exactly the situation as the theory of errors portrays it. Namely, if the validity of the test has been ascertained, the observations are continuous, the attribute in question is stable, and deviations from the true value over actual replications are produced by a large number of independent factors. In this case, the axioms of classical test theory will be satisfied by actual, rather than thought experimental, replications – in fact, there would be no need for a thought experiment. It also seems that the number of psychological measurement procedures, for which these assumptions could be taken to hold, equals zero. Thus, it is safe to conclude that, in psychological measurement, the true score cannot be taken to coincide with the construct score.

Do true scores exist?

The identification of true scores with constructs is a serious mistake that, unfortunately, permeates much of the literature on psychological measurement. The fact that true scores cannot be considered in this way does not, however, entail that true scores cannot exist. We may suppose that true scores and construct scores both exist, but are not identical; for example, we could imagine true scores to exist quite independently of the construct, but to be systematically related to that construct. This is the way Lord and Novick construct the relation of measurement, as we have seen, and it is also the way that latent variable models sometimes formulate the situation. The question then becomes how the existence of true scores could be interpreted. Is there a plausible interpretation that could locate the true score in reality, i.e., conceive of it as an objectively existing entity, without becoming inconsistent or downright absurd? It is argued in this section that such a realist interpretation is unreasonable. When the classical test theorist invites us to imagine the existence of a true score, most of us will be inclined to grant him this much. We will see, however, that it is not entirely clear what we are supposed to imagine. The reason for this is that it is difficult to give a plausible account of the distribution of observed scores, on which the true score is defined. The problem is that the thought experiment, that is supposed to define this distribution, does not specify sources of random error, and that the almost universally endorsed interpretation of random error is circular. Moreover, the assumption that true scores exist in reality does not lead to testable predictions, which strongly invites the application of Occam's razor – especially because the true score leads to a needless multiplication of theoretical entities, which is undesirable.

Where does error come from? The conceptualization of the true score as an expected value is ill-defined. For it is entirely unclear under what circumstances the replications mentioned in Lord and Novick's brainwashing thought experiment should occur. The primary problem is that it is unclear where the random variation is supposed to come from. This issue is usually circumvented in treatises on psychological measurement. These suggest that random error is due to unsystematic factors affecting the observations. For example, the typical examples of unsystematic errors are: Mr Brown had a headache at the particular testing occasion; Mr Brown accidentally filled in 'yes', while he intended to fill in 'no'; Mr Brown was distracted by the noise of schoolchildren playing nearby, etc. However, identifying this, in itself reasonable, conceptualization of random error with the formal term indicated by E_i is circular.

To see this, first recall that the true score cannot be conceptualized as the average score over *actual* replications. This would violate the basic assumptions of the model, especially those concerning independence and parallelism of repeated measurements. For the same reason, error cannot be conceptualized as the lump sum of all variables that cause variation in the observed scores over actual replications: the true score is defined through a thought experiment, and so is the error score. Further, we have seen that the semantics of classical test theory do not only require that Mr Brown is brainwashed in between measurements, but also that Mr Brown takes a trip in a time-machine in between measurements, because the true score must be conceptualized as being instantiated at a particular time point. What, then, is supposed to cause the fluctuations that might generate the probability distribution on which the true score is defined, at this particular time point? In other words: what varies in the replications under consideration?

There are three possible answers to this question. The first is: nothing. In this interpretation, we have a quite mysterious source of randomness, which is supposedly inherent to Mr Brown himself. Test theorists holding this interpretation should definitely have a chat with people working in quantum mechanics, for it would follow that human beings and quarks have more in common than one might think. But certainly, the random error would not come from variations in 'irrelevant' variables, because there would not be variation at all. This interpretation does therefore not return the typical idea of random error as discussed above.

The second answer to the question is: everything. Now we imagine Mr Brown taking his United Nations test not only in the original testing situation, but also in the jungle, in space, under water, while playing a game of tennis, and so on. This interpretation, however, neither returns the typical idea of random error. For nothing prohibits Mr Brown's constitution from being changed in such a way that, say, his social desirability level goes down, or, more drastically, he becomes deaf, or, still more dramatically, he becomes identical to a different person (say, Kofi Annan). Therefore, this interpretation forces us to include under the header 'random error' factors that we do not usually view as such – social desirability, for instance, is the classic example of a variable that is supposed to influence test scores systematically, not randomly.

The third answer that we may give is: some things will change, and some will not. This, however, requires that we distinguish between factors that are variable across replications and factors that are constant. Doing this allows us to create the desired interpretation of random error, but at the price of circularity. For which things are supposed to change in order to return the desired interpretation of random error? Well, those things that are supposed to be unsystematic. Which things are they? Supposedly, Mr Brown's headache, schoolchildren playing nearby, etc. But why these things? Because they are influential and change across replications. And why do they change? Because we have included them as varying in the thought experiment. Now we are back at square one. Thus, a platonic conception of error, as reflecting unsystematic influences on the observed testscore, involves a circularity in reasoning. It actually allows us to create any interpretation of random error we desire, by incorporating the factors we want to subsume under that header as variable in the thought experimental replications. Nothing is gained in this interpretation.

Clearly, the true score is ill-defined as an expected value, because the distribution that is supposed to generate it cannot be characterized – not even roughly. The thought experiment that should do this does not specify the conditions under which replications should occur, except for the fact that these should be statistically independent, which, ironically, is exactly the reason that such replications cannot in general be equated with actual replications. Moreover, there is a serious problem in the interpretation of the thought experimental replications. Not only does classical test theory fail to provide grounds for choosing between the above accounts of random error, but the available accounts are either mysterious, inadequate, or circular. The thought experiment does not elucidate the situation. Mr Brown's brainwash adds little to the syntactic formula $t_i = \mathcal{E}(X_i)$, but rather obscures the fact that taking the expectation of a distribution, which is defined at a particular moment on a particular person, is a doubtful move. Thus, when Lord and Novick invite the reader to assume the existence of a true score, it is not at all clear what the reader is supposed to believe in.

The multiplication of true scores The true score is ill-defined, but this, in itself, is not sufficient reason for rejecting the realist interpretation. Many concepts lack an unambiguous definition; surely, most psychological constructs do. The inability to define a construct unambiguously does not force us to the conclusion that the phenomena denoted by that construct therefore cannot exist. In many cases, definitions are the result of doing research, not a prerequisite for it. Indeed, much scientific progress can be described in terms of a continuous redefining of scientific constructs.

However, what we may require from a realist interpretation of true scores is some kind of testability. This does not mean that theories must be falsifiable in the strict sense of Popper (1959) – in psychology, this would probably leave us with no theories at all – but there must be some kind of connection to observations that takes the form of a prediction. In theories of psychological measurement, this connection usually takes the form of discriminative hypotheses. For example, the intelligence tester may concede that he cannot give a definition of intelligence, but he can formulate the hypothesis that the number series '1, 1, 2, 3, 5, 8, ...' does measure intelligence (in a population of normal adults), while the item 'I like to go to parties' does not. This is, for example, the way that constructs are related to testable predictions in latent variable modelling. In the case of true score theory, no such connection can be made. There are two reasons for this. First, according to the classical test model, a distinct true score exists for literally every distinct test. Second, the theory cannot say what it means for two distinct tests to measure the same true score, except through the awkward requirement of parallelism. Therefore, the true score hypothesis does not yield testable predictions in the discriminative sense discussed above.

Consider the first point. The definition of the true score as an expected value leaves no room for saying that some tests do measure a true score, and some do not: we may always imagine a series of thought experimental replications and define the true score as the expected value of the resulting distribution. This means that every imaginable test has an associated true score, as has been illustrated in the previous section. Admitting the true score into reality thus forces the conclusion that every person is a walking collection of infinitely many true scores – one for every imaginable testing procedure. It would seem that, in this way, reality gets rather crowded.

Second, classical test theory cannot posit the true score as a hypothesis generating entity. This could, in principle, be done if it were reasonable for, say, the intelligence tester, to say that a number series item measures the same true score as a Raven item, similar to the way different items can be related to a single latent variable in item response models. Within true score theory, the only way to say that two tests measure the same true score is by saying that the tests are parallel. However, there is absolutely no reason to suppose that two distinct items that measure the same construct should be empirically parallel. Moreover, it has been shown in section 2.2.2 that the very idea that two items that are empirically parallel measure the same true score is inconsistent in its own right: the only item that could be said to measure the same true score as the number series item '1, 1, 2, 3, 5, 8, . . . ' is the number series item '1, 1, 2, 3, 5, 8, . . . ' itself. Of course, one could reason that two items that measure the same construct should have, for example, perfectly correlated true scores. This does yield testable predictions, but these do not result from the true score hypothesis itself. Rather, they result from a hypothesis concerning relations between true scores; a hypothesis that, in turn, is based on the idea that the items measure the same construct – in fact, it is based on a latent variable hypothesis and specifies Jöreskog's (1971) congeneric model. The construct theory can specify testable discriminative hypotheses ('these items measure intelligence, but those do not'), but the hypothesis that there exists a true score for a given measurement procedure cannot.

Thus, upon a realist interpretation, the true score is a metaphysical entity of the worst kind: posing its existence does not lead to a single testable hypothesis. This does not mean that true scores, or classical test theory, are useless; obviously, the true score may figure in a set of hypotheses based on substantive theory, as it does in the congeneric model. It means that the true score hypothesis in itself is not capable of generating testable predictions.

Can true scores be constructed?
The realist interpretation of true scores borders on absurdity. This does not mean, however, that true score theory is inconsistent with a realist interpretation. If one is prepared to overpopulate his universe with an infinite number of true scores, each corresponding to a particular imaginable testing procedure, then one can maintain a realist interpretation. However, it is clear that such an interpretation is neither required by the theory, nor particularly elegant. This means that we should search for other interpretations.

A constructivist interpretation suggests itself. However, although the phrase 'concept x is a construction' seems, for some authors (e.g., Gergen, 1985), to mean a free ticket to impose one's own philosophical interpretation on that concept, it would seem helpful if a constructivist interpretation would also indicate just *how* the involved entities or attributes are to be constructed. An example of a theory that can be used for this purpose is the representationalist theory to be discussed in chapter 4; this theory specifies exactly how relations between measured objects can be represented in a numerical system, thereby offering a sensible account of how scales can be constructed.

Does classical test theory suggest such a way of constructing true scores from the data? It does not. If one were to be serious about constructing true scores, then that would involve obtaining the replications hypothesized in the brainwashing experiment. That is, *if* we were in a position to test Mr Brown repeatedly with intermediate brainwashing, *then* we could construct his true score by simply averaging the observed scores so obtained. However, we cannot obtain this series of observations. A constructivist interpretation of true scores is thus about as informative as an Operation Manual for a Perpetuum Mobile. It has a merely metaphorical value: the true score is *like* a construction in that it *could* be constructed on the basis of observations *if* an impossible state of affairs were to obtain. This just piles up one thought experiment on the other, and very little is gained in terms of making sense of classical test theory. It seems that a constructivist interpretation of true scores is no more feasible than a realist interpretation.

I conclude that both realism and constructivism are compatible with classical test theory in the sense that the theory does not suggest an obvious choice between these frameworks. An optimistic interpretation of this situation would be that classical test theory is 'neutral' with respect to such philosophical issues. However, it seems that both constructivist and realist interpretations are rather far-fetched, to say the least. This makes one wonder whether there exist any interpretations of classical test theory that do make sense.

In the next paragraph, it is argued that such an interpretation does exist, although it is semantic rather than ontological in character. Unfortunately for classical test theory, the interpretation that the theory lines up with is a rather implausible philosophical doctrine that was discredited over half a century ago: operationalism.

Operationalism and true score theory

Operationalism is a theory on the relation between scientific concepts and observations that was introduced by Bridgman (1927). In one sentence, the theory holds that the meaning of a theoretical term is synonymous with the operations by which it is measured. Thus, the concept of length is synonymous with the operations associated with the use of a measuring stick, the concept of weight is synonymous with the operations associated with the use of a balance scale, etc. Interestingly, we have seen that the true score is defined without reference to anything but a measurement process. The true score is thus completely defined in terms of a series of operations: it is the proportion of times Mr Brown would be in favour of the United Nations if he were tested infinitely many times. That the operations in question are hypothetical, and cannot be carried out, is a peculiar feature of the true score, but it does not preclude the conclusion that the true score is defined in terms of these operations, which is consistent with operationalism.

The true score also has some typical problematic aspects that are essentially identical to those faced by the operationalist philosophy of measurement. It has been argued against that view, for example, that it leads to a multiplication of theoretical terms (Suppe, 1977). For example, suppose that the meaning of the theoretical term 'intelligence' is equated with the set of operations that lead to an IQ-score on the Stanford-Binet. It immediately follows that the WAIS, the Raven, or any other intelligence test cannot also measure intelligence, because each test specifies a distinct set of operations. So, each measurement procedure generates a distinct theoretical concept. It is therefore conceptually difficult, if not impossible, for an operationalist to say what it means for two tests to measure the same construct. Philosophers have, in general, objected to this thesis because it seems plainly absurd to say that no two measurement instruments can measure the same attribute; wavelength shifts and measuring sticks are both used to calculate distance, and a philosophical viewpoint that automatically renders this statement false seems rather implausible.

In classical test theory, however, we face exactly this problem. The true score is defined in terms of the expected value on a particular test, and since each test generates a distinct expected value, it generates a distinct true score. Moreover, when the classical test theorist tries to express the idea that two tests measure the same true score, he runs into troubles that are comparable to those facing the operationalist. The only option, that comes close to saying that two tests measure the same true score, is to invoke the idea of distinct yet parallel tests. This is not only a highly contrived and unnecessarily strict requirement that in no way matches the intended meaning of the proposition that the Stanford-Binet and the WAIS measure the same construct; it is essentially a concealed way of saying that the only test that measures the same construct as test x is test x itself. The same conclusion would be reached by an operationalist.

The operationalist view also resolves some of the problems surrounding the true score, as exposed in previous sections. For instance, the operationalist need not refer to a construct or attribute as something that exists independently of the measurement process. In operationalism, we cannot speak of length without mentioning a centimetre; we cannot speak of weight without referring to a balance scale; and we cannot consider intelligence apart from the IQ-test. To do this is, in the eyes of the operationalist, to indulge in intolerable metaphysical speculation. A difficulty for operationalism may be created by countering that objects would still have a definite length if there were nobody to measure it, and that people already possessed intelligence before the advent of IQ-tests. This argument, which of course invites realism about such attributes, can be deflected by invoking scores on attributes as dispositional properties. Rather than accepting my height, which is about 185 cm, as a property which I have independent of any measurement apparatus used, the proposed solution is that height is a dispositional property with respect to a measurement procedure: *if* I were measured with a centimetre rule, *then* the indicated height would be about 185 cm.

It is interesting to enquire whether the true score could also be interpreted as a disposition, and, if so, what kind of disposition it is. In this context, Van Heerden and Smolenaars (1989) propose a taxonomy of dispositions by cross-classifying them with respect to the question whether they concern heterogeneous or homogeneous behaviour, and whether this behaviour is recurrent or unique. An example of a disposition that refers to the unique, non-recurrent, presentation of a specific piece of homogeneous behaviour is 'being mortal'. Saying that John is mortal expresses the fact that, upon the appropriate operations (e.g., poisoning him), John will decease. Dispositions may also refer to the recurrent presentation of homogeneous behaviour. For example, the proposition 'Professor G.

likes to go out with his PhD students at conferences' refers to professor G.'s tendency to end up in a bar, in the company of his PhD students, at conferences – usually at closing time. A proposition that refers to the recurrent presentation of a heterogeneous set of behaviours is 'Professor J. is forgetful.' This proposition refers to Professor J.'s tendency to display a wide variety of behaviours recurrently; for example, Professor J. regularly finds himself in the secretary's office without remembering what he went there for, he forgets to remove the keys from his bicycle, etc. Finally, a disposition can refer to the unique presentation of a heterogeneous set behaviours. Van Heerden and Smolenaars (1989) give the example of 'being intelligent', which can be viewed as a disposition that may manifest itself once by completing the different (heterogeneous) tasks of an intelligence test.

The latter example is interesting, because Rozeboom (1966a) treats test scores in a similar manner. He observes that, in order to conceptualize the idea that 'every person has an IQ-score', we must not interpret this sentence realistically (in which case it is obviously false), but in terms of the dispositional 'for every person it is true that, if that person were tested, he or she would obtain an IQ-score'. In a similar vein, we can interpret the sentence 'every person has a true IQ-score' as 'for every person it is true that, if he or she were tested infinitely many times (with intermediate brainwashing and time-travel), the resulting observed score distribution would have an expected value'. In the terminology of Van Heerden and Smolenaars (1989), the behaviour under consideration could be heterogeneous (if it refers to total test scores) or homogeneous (if it refers to item scores), but it would certainly be recurrent, although with respect to thought experimental replications.[3] The true score, as classical test theory defines it, may thus be considered to be a disposition, which specifies how a person will behave in a counterfactual state of affairs.

The overburdening of reality, which follows from the realist interpretation of true scores, dissolves upon this view. I am not a walking collection of true scores on all imaginable tests; but it is the case that, *if* I were repeatedly administered an arbitrary test (with the appropriate brainwashing and time travel), *then* my true score on that test would take on a definite value. Such dispositions are thus not located in reality, but rather specify characteristics of subjunctive, or in our case counterfactual, conditionals (Rozeboom, 1966a). It is certainly the case that the true score, with its thought experimental character, must be considered

---

[3] It is interesting to observe that, upon a dispositional interpretation of true scores, the stochastic aspect of classical test theory may receive a new interpretation. For instance, the value of the observed score variance for a given subject (normally interpreted as an index of measurement precision) would in this case reflect the strength of the disposition.

an oddball among recognized dispositional properties (e.g., solubility, fragility), because these usually specify responses, of the object to which the dispositional property is ascribed, in situations that could actually occur. The concept of fragility is considered to be dispositional, because it is characterized by conditionals such as 'this vase is fragile, for if it were dropped, it would break'; and we may check this by actually dropping the vase. Similarly, all of the examples of Van Heerden and Smolenaars (1989) refer to actually realizable behaviours in realistic situations. This is the reason that Ryle (1949) characterizes dispositions as inference tickets. Rozeboom (1973) argues that such dispositional properties involve a realist commitment to underlying characteristics that generate the dispositions, and Van Heerden and Smolenaars (1989) interpret dispositions as promissory notes (i.e., they involve a promise that, if one looks into dispositional properties, one could discover more fundamental laws that govern dispositional behaviour).

The true score is not open to such an interpretation as long as the thought experiment is retained. For it refers to what would happen in an impossible state of affairs, namely to the observed score distribution that Mr Brown would generate in the brainwashing thought experiment. So, the thought experimental character of the true score makes it quite useless as an inference ticket in the common interpretation of that term. A possible response to this problem is to dispose of the thought experiment and to interpret true scores as propensities, without reference to limiting frequencies. I have already discussed this possibility in 2.2.1. Doing this, however, would preclude an interpretation of true score theory as a theory of measurement, for the only remaining connection to the theory of errors would disappear. In fact, classical test theory would become a statistical theory of dispositions; interpretations of observed score variance as 'random error', for example, would be out of the question, and the interpretation of the squared correlation between observed and true scores as 'reliability' would hardly make sense. Certainly, the founders of the theory did not intend classical test theory in this way, and its users do not interpret it so; in fact, it is likely that, interpreted as a statistical theory of dispositions for unique events, classical test theory would not appeal to those involved in psychological testing at all.

2.3   Discussion

Classical test theory was either one of the best ideas in twentieth-century psychology, or one of the worst mistakes. The theory is mathematically elegant and conceptually simple, and in terms of its acceptance by psychologists, it is a psychometric success story. However, as is typical of popular statistical procedures, classical test theory is prone to misinterpretation. One reason for this is the terminology used: if a competition for the misnomer of the century existed, the term 'true score' would be a serious contestant. The infelicitous use of the adjective 'true' invites the mistaken idea that the true score on a test must somehow be identical to the 'real', 'valid', or 'construct' score. This chapter has hopefully proved the inadequacy of this view beyond reasonable doubt.

The problems with the platonic true score interpretation were, however, seen to run deeper than a confounding of validity and unreliability. Classical test theory is, ontologically speaking, ambiguous. In principle, it allows for both realist and constructivist interpretations, but sits well with neither. The constructivist interpretation of classical test theory is vacuous: although it is possible to specify how a true score could be constructed on the basis of observations (namely by averaging), the observations that are necessary for doing this are exactly the repeated measurements with intermediate brainwashing. The constructivist account of true scores can only be interpreted metaphorically, and it is not at all clear what such a metaphorical interpretation adds to the theory. On the other hand, a realist interpretation of true scores leads to a metaphysical explosion of reality: a new true score has to be invoked for every thinkable testing procedure.

Although it does not seem possible to clearly coordinate classical test theory with an ontological doctrines like realism or constructivism, it is possible to relate the theory to a semantic doctrine, namely that of operationalism. The operationalist defines theoretical concepts in terms of the operations used to measure them. Likewise, the classical test theorist defines the true score in terms of a hypothetical series of operations; namely, the repeated test administrations with intermediate brainwashing. As a result, classical test theory runs into problems that are highly similar to those of operationalism, such as the unlimited multiplication of theoretical terms. However, the classical test theorist can also use some of the operationalist defensive techniques; in particular, he can invoke a dispositional interpretation of theoretical terms.

Upon a dispositional interpretation of true scores, the true score is viewed as the disposition of a person to generate a particular kind of score. This does not require realism: just as we do not say that every person has an IQ-score, but rather that every person would receive an IQ-score if tested, we have to refrain from saying that every person has a true score. Rather, we should say that every person would have a true score, if he or she were repeatedly tested in a long run of testing occasions with intermediate brainwashing and time travel. The true score can thus be considered to be a dispositional concept, in particular as a disposition to generate specific long run frequencies. However, the fact that not even such frequencies can be granted a place in reality, but must be considered in terms of a thought experiment, further degenerates the connection that the true score may bear to the real world.

An operationalist interpretation could also restore the identity of constructs and true scores; this time, however, not by upgrading true scores, but by degrading constructs. Such an interpretation should therefore not be considered a platonic true score interpretation, but rather a non-platonic construct interpretation. That is, if one is willing to conceive of psychological constructs such as intelligence, extraversion, or attitudes, in an operationalist fashion (with a touch of fictionalism to accommodate for the thought experimental character of the true score), then the true score could be a candidate for representing these constructs in a measurement model. The fictionalist element, which must be introduced because the true score, as a disposition, generalizes over a domain of impossible replications, precludes the interpretation of the true score as an inference ticket (Ryle, 1949), or a promissory note (Van Heerden and Smolenaars, 1989). It also deprives the concept of the possible realist semantics that may be introduced for dispositions (Rozeboom, 1973), unless the entire idea that we are dealing with a theory of measurement is given up, by dismissing the thought experiment and disconnecting the theory from the theory of errors. I suspect that no classical test theorist will be willing to do this; classical test theory is intended, formulated, and used as a theory of measurement, and I do not expect classical test theorists to revert their self-image from 'expert in measurement theory' to 'expert in dispositional psychology'. However, retaining the idea that we are dealing with a theory of measurement requires one to take an operationalist perspective.

Of course, since the true score is appropriately characterized as a product of the test theorist's imagination, and therefore does not obtain a realist ontology, this is not a particularly pressing philosophical problem. At least, it is better than the kind of realism needed to localize the true score in the world. It is a pressing theoretical problem for psychology, however, because I do not think that many researchers in psychology are particularly interested in a true score, which specifies a disposition with respect to a set of impossible situations. So, once again we see the fundamental tension that Lord and Novick have introduced through their axiomatic treatment of test theory: the theory is constructed in such a way that it always works, but at the price of losing the natural interpretation of its central concepts. A psychologically meaningful interpretation of true scores and random error, as reflecting a stable characteristic and unsystematic variation respectively, is philosophically untenable. A philosophically acceptable interpretation of these concepts, as products of the imagination which refer to recurrent dispositions in a counterfactual state of affairs, is psychologically unattractive. Classical test theory systematically falls between these two stools.

It is my understanding that few, if any, researchers in psychology conceive of psychological constructs in a way that would justify the use of classical test theory as an appropriate measurement model. Why, then, is the classical test theory model so immensely successful? Why is it that virtually every empirical study in psychology reports values of Cronbach's α as the main justification for test use? I am afraid that the reason for this is entirely pragmatic, and has been given in section 2.2.2: the common use of classical test theory does not involve testing the model assumptions. The lower bound strategy always returns a value for the internal consistency coefficient. In fact, this value can be obtained through a mindless mouse-click. Inserting the lower bound into formulae for disattenuating correlations between test scores, as advocated by Schmidt and Hunter (1999), will further allow one to boost validity coefficients to whatever level is desired. All this will come at no additional costs, for it does not require any of the tedious work involved in latent variable models, which moreover have a tendency to prove many of the commonly held interpretations of test scores illusory.

Applying classical test theory is easy, and a commonly accepted escape route to avoid notorious problems in psychological testing, such as constructing unidimensional tests. The model is, however, so enormously detached from common interpretations of psychological constructs, that the statistics based on it appear to have very little relevance for psychological measurement. Coupled with the unfortunate misinterpretations of the true score as the construct score, of random error as irrelevant variation, and of reliability as some kind of fixed characteristic of tests, instead of as a population dependent property of scores, it would seem that large parts of the psychological community are involved in self-deception. Wishful thinking, however, is not a particularly constructive scientific procedure. I therefore hope that the analysis reported here has added to the understanding and demystification of classical test theory concepts, and has made clear that much more is needed for an adequate treatment of psychological test scores.

3 Latent variables

> Once you have formed the noun 'ability' from the adjective 'able', you are in trouble.
>
> B. F. Skinner, 1987

3.1 Introduction

In the previous chapter, I have argued that the classical test theory model is unsatisfying for a number of reasons. Most important is the fact that the attribute to be measured is not adequately represented in the model. The reason for this is that the true score is an operationalist concept, and can only represent a psychological attribute if this attribute is similarly defined in an operationalist fashion. In fact, unless one holds a strongly operationalist view of the measurement process, it is difficult to maintain even that classical test theory is a theory of measurement in the first place.

A view of measurement that does represent the attribute explicitly in the model formulation can be based on latent variable theory. In latent variable models, one sets up a formal structure that relates test scores to the hypothesized attribute, deduces empirical implications of the model, and evaluates the adequacy of the model by examining the goodness of fit with respect to empirical data. Because the latent variable model has to be restricted to make empirical tests possible, a theoretical justification of the model structure is, in general, required. Latent variable theory thus goes beyond classical test theory in that it attempts to construct a hypothesis about the data-generating mechanism in which the attribute is explicitly represented as a latent variable.

Historically, the conceptual framework originates with the work of Spearman (1904), who developed factor analytic models for continuous variables in the context of intelligence testing. In the twentieth century, the development of the latent variable paradigm has been spectacular. The factor analytic tradition continued with the work of Lawley (1943), Thurstone (1947) and Lawley and Maxwell (1963), and entered into the conceptual framework of confirmatory factor analysis (CFA) with

Jöreskog (1971), Wiley, Schmidt, and Bramble (1973), and Sörbom (1974). In subsequent years, CFA became a very popular technique, largely because of the LISREL program by Jöreskog and Sörbom (1993). In a research program that developed mostly parallel to the factor analytic tradition, the idea of latent variables analysis with continuous latent variables was applied to dichotomous observed variables by Guttman (1950), Lord (1952, 1980), Rasch (1960), Birnbaum (1968) and Mokken (1970). These measurement models, primarily used in educational testing, came to be known as Item Response Theory (IRT) models. The IRT framework was extended to deal with polytomous observed variables by Samejima (1969), Bock (1972), and Thissen and Steinberg (1984). Meanwhile, in yet another parallel research program, methods were developed to deal with categorical latent variables. In this context, Lazarsfeld (1950), Lazarsfeld and Henry (1968), and Goodman (1974) developed latent structure analysis. Latent structure models may involve categorical observed variables, in which case we speak of latent class analysis, or metrical observed variables, giving rise to latent profile analysis (Bartholomew, 1987). After boundary-crossing investigations by McDonald (1982), Thissen and Steinberg (1986), Takane and De Leeuw (1987), and Goldstein and Wood (1989), Mellenbergh (1994) connected some of the parallel research programs by showing that most of the parametric measurement models could be formulated in a common framework.

At present, there are various developments that emphasize this common framework for latent variables analysis, cases in point being the work of Muthén and Muthén (1998), McDonald (1999), and Moustaki and Knott (2000). Different terms are used to indicate the general latent variable model. For example, Goldstein and Wood (1989) use the term Generalized Linear Item Response Model (GLIRM), while Mellenbergh (1994) speaks of Generalized Linear Item Response Theory (GLIRT), and Moustaki and Knott (2000) follow McCullagh and Nelder (1989) in using the term Generalized Linear Model (GLIM). I will adopt Mellenbergh's terminology and use the term GLIRT, because it emphasizes the connection with IRT, and, in doing so, the fact that the model contains at least one latent variable. Now, at the beginning of the twenty-first century, it would hardly be an overstatement to say that the GLIRT model, at least among psychometricians and methodologists, has come to be the received view in the theory of psychological measurement – notwithstanding the fact that classical test theory is still the most commonly used theory in test analysis.

The growing use of latent variables analysis in psychological research is interesting from a philosophical point of view, exactly because latent variable theory, in contrast to classical test theory, is typically aimed at constructing an explanatory model to account for relations in the data.

This means that explanations that make use of unobservable theoretical entities are increasingly entertained in psychology. As a consequence, the latent variable has come to play a substantial role in the explanatory structure of psychological theories. Concepts closely related to the latent variable have been discussed extensively. These concepts include the meaning of the arrows in diagrams of structural equation modelling (see, for example, Sobel, 1994; Pearl, 1999; Edwards and Bagozzi, 2000), the status of true scores (Klein and Cleary, 1967; Lord and Novick, 1968; Lumsden, 1976), definitions of latent variables (Bentler, 1982; Bollen, 2002), specific instances of latent variables such as the Big Five Factors in personality research (Lamiell, 1987; Pervin, 1994), and the trait approach in general (Mischel, 1968, 1973). Also, the status of unobservable entities is one of the major recurrent themes in the philosophy of science of the twentieth century, where battles were fought over the conceptual status of unobservable entities such as electrons (see Cartwright, 1983; Hacking, 1983; Van Fraassen, 1980; and Devitt, 1991, for some contrasting views). However, the theoretical status of the latent variable as it appears in models for psychological measurement has not received a thorough and general analysis as yet.

Questions that are relevant, but seldom addressed in detail, are similar to the questions addressed in the previous chapter. For instance, should we assume that the latent variable signifies a real entity, or conceive of it as a useful fiction, constructed by the human mind? Should we say that we measure a latent variable in the sense that it underlies and determines our observations, or is it more appropriately considered to be constructed out of the observed scores? What exactly constitutes the relation between latent variables and observed scores? Is this relation of a causal nature? If so, in what sense? And, most importantly, is latent variable theory neutral with respect to these issues? In the course of discussing these questions, we will see that latent variable theory is not philosophically neutral; specifically, it will be argued that, without a realist interpretation of latent variables, the use of latent variables analysis is hard to justify. At the same time, however, the relation between latent variables and individual processes proves to be too weak to defend causal interpretations of latent variables at the level of the individual. This observation leads to a distinction between several kinds of latent variables, based on their relations with individual processes.

3.2 Three perspectives on latent variables

The syntax, semantics, and ontology of latent variable models are substantially different from those used in classical test theory. Syntactically, the model relates expected item responses to a latent variable by specifying an appropriate item response function. This function formulates a regression of the item score on a latent variable. Semantically, the expected item response may be interpreted in two ways: as a true score, in which case we follow a stochastic subject interpretation, or as a subpopulation mean, in which case we follow a repeated sampling interpretation. From an ontological viewpoint, the model is most naturally interpreted in a realist fashion. This probes the question what constitutes the nature of the relation between latent variables and observed scores. It is argued that this relation can be constructed as a causal one, but only when the latent variable is interpreted as the cause of differences between subpopulations.

3.2.1 The formal stance

Syntax In modern test theory models, such as the various IRT-models or confirmatory factor models, the relation between the latent variable and the observed scores is mathematically explicit. In GLIRT, the form for this relation is a generalized regression function of the observed scores on the latent variable, although this regression may differ in form. The model relates an observed item response variable U to a latent variable θ via a function of the form

$$g[\mathcal{E}(U_{ij})] = \beta_j + \alpha_j \theta_i, \tag{3.1}$$

where g is a link function, $\mathcal{E}(U_{ij})$ is interpreted either as the expected item response of subject i on item j, or as the expectation of the item response in a population of subjects with position θ_i on the latent variable, and α_j and β_j are an item-specific regression weight and intercept term, respectively.

Some specific forms of the model will be relevant in the following chapters. First, in item response theory for dichotomous items and continuous latent variables, the link function is often taken to be the logit transformation (the natural logarithm of the odds ratio). In this case we have a model of the form

$$\ln\left[\frac{\mathcal{E}(U_{ij})}{1 - \mathcal{E}(U_{ij})}\right] = \beta_j + \alpha_j \theta_i. \tag{3.2}$$

The intercept term β is then usually interpreted as item difficulty, because it refers to the location of the item response function on the θ-scale, and α is interpreted as item discrimination, because it refers to the slope of the item response function. If all item discrimination parameters are assumed equal, then we have an additive model, because item and subject effects are independent (i.e., they do not interact, where the interpretation of 'interact' is the same as in analysis of variance). This form of the model is known as the Rasch model (Rasch, 1960). Allowing the discrimination parameters to vary gives the less restrictive two-parameter logistic model introduced by Birnbaum (1968). This model can be viewed as incorporating a person × item interaction term.

If item responses are continuous, and the function g is taken to be the identity link, we arrive at Jöreskog's (1971) congeneric model, better known as the common factor model:

$$\mathcal{E}(U_{ij}) = \beta_j + \alpha_j \theta_i. \tag{3.3}$$

Finally, if the latent variable is categorical, we can formulate the latent class model (if item responses are dichotomous) or the latent profile model (if item responses are continuous) by dummy coding the latent variable. Various other models can be arrived at by introducing appropriate restrictions and transformations (Mellenbergh, 1994), but the models discussed above are the most important ones for the present discussion.

It is important to realize that, despite the intricate mathematics that sometimes accompany the literature on latent variable theory, the basic form of the model is very simple. For instance, in a factor model for general intelligence, the model says that an increase of n units in the latent variable leads to an increase of n times the factor loading in the expected value of a given item. So, formally, the model is just a regression model, but the independent variable is latent rather than manifest. The ingenious idea in latent variable modelling is that, while the model cannot be tested directly for any given item because the independent variable is latent, it can be tested indirectly through its implications for the joint probability distribution of the item responses for a number of items. Specifically, in the standard latent variable model the item responses will be independent, conditional on the latent variable, which means that the items satisfy local independence.

Now there are two things we can do on the basis of our set of assumptions. First, we can determine how observed scores would behave if they were generated under our model (this applies not only to mathematical derivations but also to simulation studies). Second, we can develop plausible procedures to estimate parameters in the model on the basis of manifest scores, given the assumption that these scores were generated by our model. It is sometimes implicitly suggested that the formal derivations tell us something about reality, but this is not the case. Each supposition 'inside' the formal system is a tautology, and tautologies in themselves cannot tell us anything about the world. So this is all in the syntactic domain, that is, it has no meaning outside the formal theory. Let us denote the latent variable as it appears in this formal stance (that is, the concept indicated by θ, in the IRT literature, or by ξ, in the SEM literature) as the formal latent variable.

Semantics The syntax of latent variable theory specifies a regression of the observed scores on the latent variable. What are the semantics associated with this relation? In other words: how do we interpret this regression?

Of course, as is the case for classical test theory, the syntax of latent variables analysis is taken from statistics, and so are its semantics. And, like classical test theory, latent variable theory needs an interpretation for the use of the expectation operator in the model formulation. Because it is not at all clear why a response to an item, say, the item '2 + 2 = ...', should be considered a random variable, it is important to interpret the item response in such a way as to justify this approach. The problem faced here is similar to that faced by the classical test theorist in the definition of the true score, but the latent variable theorist has a considerably greater freedom of interpretation.

The first interpretation, known as the stochastic subject interpretation, uses the same line of reasoning as classical test theory, and views the expectation as applying to the individual subject. This implies a series of hypotheticals of the form 'given that subject i has value θ_i on the latent variable, i's expected item response equals $\mathcal{E}(U_{ij}|\theta_i)$', where $\mathcal{E}(U_{ij}|\theta_i)$ is the expectation of the item response as given by the item response function. Supposing that the imaginary subject John takes an intelligence test item, this would become something like 'given that John's level of intelligence is two standard deviations below the population mean, he has a probability of 0.70 to answer the item '2 + 2 = ...' correctly'. For subjects with different positions on the latent variable, different parameters for the probability distribution in question are specified. So, for John's brighter sister Jane we could get 'given that Jane's level of intelligence is one standard deviation above the population mean, Jane has a probability of 0.99 to answer the item correctly'. The item response function (i.e., the regression of the item response on the latent variable) then specifies how the probability of a correct answer changes with the position on the latent variable. The stochastic subject interpretation requires a thought experiment similar to that used in classical test theory, and in this interpretation the expected value of subject i on item j, $\mathcal{E}(U_{ij})$, can be considered to be identical to subject i's true score on item j if the latent variable model is true.

In contrast to classical test theory, however, the model can also be formulated without the brainwashing thought experiment. This requires conceptualizing the model in terms of a repeated sampling interpretation, which is more common in the literature on factor analysis (see, for example, Meredith, 1993) than in the literature on IRT. This is a between-subjects formulation of latent variables analysis. It focuses on characteristics of populations, instead of on characteristics of individual subjects. The probability distribution of the item responses, conditional on the latent variable, is conceived of as a probability distribution that arises from repeated sampling from a population of subjects with the same position on the latent variable. In particular, parameters of these population distributions are related to the latent variable in question.

Thus, the repeated sampling interpretation is in terms of a series of sentences of the form 'the population of subjects with position θ_i on the latent variable follows distribution f over the possible item responses u_{ij}; the expected item response $\mathcal{E}(U_{ij}|\theta_i)$ is the expectation of the item responses in the subpopulation of subjects with position θ_i on the latent variable'. Now, the probability distribution over the item responses that pertains to a specific position θ_i on the latent variable arises from repeated sampling from the population of subjects taking this position; the expectation may then be interpreted as a subpopulation mean. In this interpretation, the probability that John answers the item correctly does not play a role. Rather, the focus is on the probability of drawing a person that answers the item correctly from a population of people with John's level of intelligence, and this probability is 0.70. In other words, 70 per cent of the population of people with John's level of intelligence (i.e., a level of intelligence that is two standard deviations below the population mean) will answer the item correctly; and 30 per cent of those people will answer the item incorrectly. There is no random variation located within the person.

The difference between the stochastic subject and repeated sampling interpretations is substantial, for it concerns the very subject of the theory. The two interpretations entertain different conceptions of what it is we are modelling: in the stochastic subject formulation, we are modelling characteristics of individuals, while in the repeated sampling interpretation, we are modelling subpopulation means. However, if we follow the stochastic subject interpretation and assume that everybody with John's level of intelligence has probability 0.70 of answering the item correctly, then the expected proportion of subjects with this level of intelligence that will answer the item correctly (repeated sampling interpretation) is also 0.70. The assumption that the measurement model has the same form within and between subjects has been identified as the local homogeneity assumption (Ellis and Van den Wollenberg, 1993). Via this assumption, the stochastic subject formulation suggests a link between characteristics of the individual and between-subjects variables. Ellis and

Van den Wollenberg (1993) have shown, however, that the local homogeneity assumption is an independent assumption that in no way follows from the other assumptions of the latent variable model. Also, the assumption is not testable, because it specifies what the probability of an item response would be in a series of independent replications with intermediate brainwashing in the Lord and Novick (1968, p. 29) sense. Basically, this renders the connection between within-subject processes and between-subjects variables speculative (in the best case). In fact, it will be argued later on that the connection is little more than an article of faith: the standard measurement model has virtually nothing to say about characteristics of individuals, and even less about item response processes. This will prove crucially important for the ontology of latent variables, to be discussed later in this chapter.

3.2.2 The empirical stance

Because a latent variable model has testable consequences at the level of the joint distribution of the item responses, it is possible to test the adequacy of the model against the data. In contrast to classical test theory applications, such model tests are commonly carried out in latent variables analysis. Like many testing procedures throughout science, however, such model fit tests suffer from the problem of underdetermination of theory by data. This means that many data generating mechanisms can produce the same structure in the data as the hypothesized model. So, if observed variables behave in the right way, a latent variable model will fit, but this does not imply that the model is correct.

The issue that is called underdetermination in the philosophy of science is called statistical equivalence in the modelling literature (see, for example, Hershberger, 1994). In this context it has, for instance, been shown by Bartholomew (1987; see also Molenaar and Von Eye, 1994) that a latent profile model with p latent profiles generates the same first and second order moments (means, variances, and covariances) for the observed data as a factor model with $p - 1$ continuous latent variables. These models are conceptually different: the factor model posits continuous latent variables (i.e., it specifies that subjects vary in degree, but not in kind), while the latent profile model posits categorical latent variables at the nominal level (i.e., it specifies that subjects vary in kind, but not in degree). This suggests, for example, that the five factor model in the personality literature corresponds to a typology with six types. Moreover, on the basis of the covariances used in factor analysis, the Big Five Factors would be indistinguishable from the Big Six Types. The fact that theoretically distinct models are practically equivalent in an empirical sense urges a strong distinction between the formal and empirical structure of latent variables analysis.

This point is important because it emphasizes that the attachment of theoretical content to a latent variable requires an inferential step, and is not in any way 'given' in empirical data, just as it is not 'given' in the mathematical formulation of a model. The latent variable as it is viewed from the empirical stance, i.e., the empirical entity that is generally presented as an estimate of the latent variable, will be denoted here as the operational latent variable. Note that there is nothing latent about the operational latent variable. It is simply a function of the observed variables, usually a weighted sumscore (that the weights are determined via the theory of the formal latent variable does not make a difference in this respect). Note also that such a weighted sumscore will always be obtained, and will in general be judged interpretable if the corresponding model fits the data adequately. The foregoing discussion shows, however, that the fit of a model does not entail the existence of a latent variable. A nice example in this context is given by Wood (1978), who showed that letting people toss a number of coins (interpreting the outcome of the tosses as item responses) yields an item response pattern that is in perfect agreement with the Rasch model. A more general treatment is given in Suppes and Zanotti (1981) who show that, for three dichotomous observed variables, a latent variable can be found if and only if the observed scores have a joint distribution. The developments in Bartholomew (1987) and Molenaar and Von Eye (1994) further show that model fit does not entail the form (e.g., categorical or continuous) of the latent variable, even if its existence is assumed a priori.

The above discussion shows that the connection between the formal and operational latent variable is not self-evident. In order to make that connection, we need an interpretation of the use of formal theory in empirical applications. This, in turn, requires an ontology for the latent variable.

3.2.3 *The ontological stance*

The formal latent variable is a mathematical entity. It figures in mathematical formulae and statistical theories. Latent variable theory tells us how parameters that relate the latent variable to the data could be estimated, if the data were generated under the model in question. The 'if' in the preceding sentence is very important. It points the way to the kind of ontology we have to invoke. The assumption, that it was this particular model that generated the data, must precede the estimation process. In other words, if we consider the weighted sumscore as an estimate of the position of a given subject on a latent variable, we do so under the model specified. Now this weighted sumscore is not an estimate of the formal latent variable: we do not use an IQ-score to estimate the general concept usually indicated by the Greek letter θ, but to estimate intelligence. Thus, we use the formal side of the model to acquire knowledge about some part of the world; then it follows that we estimate something which is also in that part of the world. What is that something?

It will be clear that the answer to this question must consider the ontology of the latent variable, which is, in quite a crucial way, connected to its theoretical status. An ontological view is needed to connect the operational latent variable to its formal counterpart, but at first sight there seems to be a considerable freedom of choice regarding this ontology. I will argue that this is not the case.

There are basically three positions one can take with respect to this issue. The first position adheres to a form of entity realism, in that it ascribes an ontological status to the latent variable in the sense that it is assumed to exist independent of measurement. The second position could be coined 'constructivist' in that it regards the latent variable as a construction of the human mind, which need not be ascribed existence independent of measurement. The third position maintains that the latent variable is nothing more than the empirical content it carries – a 'numerical trick' used to simplify our observations: this position holds that there is nothing beyond the operational latent variable and could be called operationalist. Strictly taken, operationalism is a kind of constructivism, but the latter term is intended to cover a broader class of views (for example, the more sophisticated empiricist view of Van Fraassen, 1980). In fact, only the first of these views can be consistently attached to the formal content of latent variable theory.

Operationalism and the numerical trick

It is sometimes heard that the latent variable is nothing but the result of a numerical trick to simplify our observations. In this view, the latent variable is a (possibly weighted) sumscore and nothing more. There are several objections that can be raised against this view. A simple way to see that it is deficient is to take any standard textbook on latent variable theory and to replace the term 'latent variable' by 'weighted sumscore'. This will immediately render the text incomprehensible. It is, for example, absurd to assert that there is a sumscore underlying the item responses. The obvious response to this argument is that we should not take such texts literally; or, worse, that we should maintain an operationalist point of view. Such a move, however, raises more serious objections.

If the latent variable is to be conceived of in an operationalist sense, then it follows that there is a distinct latent variable for every single test we construct. This is consistent with the operationalist view of measurement (Bridgman, 1927) but not with latent variable theory. To see this, consider a simple test consisting of three items j, k, and l. Upon the operationalist view, the latent variable that accounts for the item responses on the subtest consisting of items j and k is different from the latent variable that accounts for the item response pattern on the subtest consisting of items k and l. So, the test consisting of items j, k, and l does not measure the same latent variable and therefore cannot be unidimensional. In fact, upon the operationalist view, it is impossible even to formulate the requirement of unidimensionality; consequently, an operationalist would have a very hard time making sense of procedures commonly used in latent variable theory, such as adaptive testing, where different tests are administered to different subjects with the objective to measure a single latent variable. Note the striking difference with classical test theory, which suffers from exactly the opposite problem, because it cannot say what it means for two tests to measure the same attribute. Where classical test theory and operationalism go hand in hand, operationalism and latent variable theory are fundamentally incompatible.

In a line of reasoning that is closely related to operationalism, it can be argued that the use of latent variable theory is merely instrumental, a means to an end. This would yield an instrumentalist point of view (Toulmin, 1953). In this view, the latent variable is a pragmatic concept, a 'tool', that is merely useful for its purpose (the purpose being prediction or data reduction, for example). No doubt, methods such as exploratory factor analysis may be used as data reduction techniques and, although principal components analysis seems more suited as a descriptive technique, are often used in this spirit. Also, such models can be used for prediction, although it has been forcefully argued by several authors (e.g., Maxwell, 1962) that the instrumentalist view leaves us entirely in the dark when confronted with the question why our predictive machinery (i.e., the model) works. We do not have to address such issues in detail, however, because the instrumentalist view simply fails to provide us with a structural connection between the formal and operational latent variable. In fact, the instrumental interpretation begs the question. For suppose that we interpret latent variable models as data reduction devices. Why, then, are the factor loadings determined via formal latent variable theory in the first place? Obviously, upon this view, no weighting of the sumscore tructurally defended over any other. Any defence of this position refore be as ad hoc as the use of latent variables analysis for data itself.[1]

Realism and constructivism

So, if there is more to the latent variable than just a calculation, used to simplify our observations, what is it? We are left with a choice between realism, maintaining that latent variable theory should be taken literally – the latent variable signifying a real entity – and constructivism, stating that it is a fiction, constructed by the human mind.

The difference between realism and constructivism resides mainly in the constructivist's denial of one or more of the realist claims. Realism exists in a number of forms, but a realist will in general maintain one or several of the following theses (Hacking, 1983; Devitt, 1991). First, there is realism about theories: the core thesis of this view is that theories are either true or false. Second, one can be a realist about the entities that figure in scientific theories: the core thesis of this view is that at least some theoretical entities exist. Third, realism is typically associated with causality: theoretical entities are causally responsible for observed phenomena. These three ingredients of realism offer a simple explanation for the success of science: we learn about entities in the world through a causal interaction with them, the effect of this being that our theories get closer to the truth. The constructivist, however, typically denies both realism about theories and about entities. The question is whether a realist commitment is implied in latent variables analysis. It will be argued that this is the case: latent variable theory maintains both theses in the set of assumptions underlying the theory.

Entity realism is weaker than theory realism. For example, one may be a realist about electrons, in which case one would maintain that the theoretical entities we call 'electrons' correspond to particles in reality. This does not imply a full-blown realism about theories: for example, one may view theories about electrons as abstractions, describing the behaviour of such particles in idealized terms (so that these theories are, literally taken, false). Cartwright (1983) takes such a position. Theory realism without entity realism is much harder to defend, for a true theory that refers to nonexistent entities is difficult to conceive of. I will first discuss entity realism, before turning to the subject of theory realism.

---

[1] This should not be read as a value judgment. Data reduction techniques are very important, especially in the exploratory phases of research. The fact that these techniques are important, however, does not entail that they are not ad hoc.

Entity realism

Latent variable theory adheres to entity realism, because this form of realism is needed to motivate the choice of model in psychological measurement. The model that is customary in psychological measurement is the model in the left panel of figure 3.1. (The symbolic language is borrowed from the structural equation modelling literature, but the structure of the model generalizes to IRT and other latent variable models.) The model specifies that the pattern of covariation between the indicators can be fully explained by a regression of the indicators on the latent variable, which implies that the indicators are independent after conditioning on the latent variable (this is the assumption of local independence). An example of the model in the left panel of the figure would be a measurement model for, say, dominance, where the indicators are item responses on items like 'I would like a job where I have power over others', 'I would make a good military leader', and 'I try to control others.' Such a model is called a reflective model model (Edwards and Bagozzi, 2000), and it is the standard latent variable model in psychology – employed in prominent models such as the general intelligence and Big Five models. An alternative model, that is more customary in sociological and economical modelling, is the model in the right panel of figure 3.1. In this model, called a formative model, the latent variable is regressed on its indicators. An example of a formative model is the measurement model for social economic status (SES). In such a model a researcher would, for example,

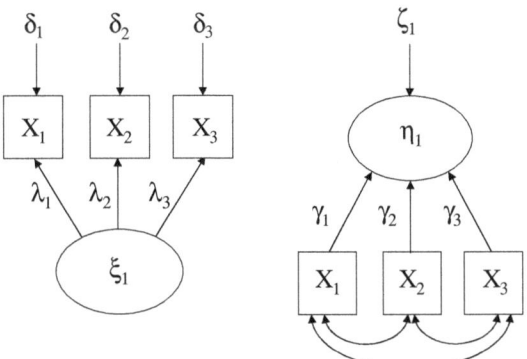

Figure 3.1. Two models for measurement. The figure in the left panel is the reflective measurement model. The X's are observed variables, ξ is the latent variable, λ's are factor loadings and the δ's are error terms. The right panel shows the formative model. The latent variable is denoted η, the γ's are the weights of the indicators, and ζ is a residual term.

record the variables income, educational level, and neighbourhood as indicators of SES.

The models in figure 3.1 are psychometrically and conceptually different (Bollen and Lennox, 1991). There is, however, no a priori reason why, in psychological measurement, one should prefer one type of measurement model to the other.[2] The measurement models that psychologists employ are typically of the reflective model kind. Why is this?

The obvious answer is that the choice of model depends on the ontology of the latent variables it invokes. A realist point of view motivates the reflective model, because the response on the questionnaire items is thought to vary as a function of the latent variable. In this case, variation in the latent variable precedes variation in the indicators. In ordinary language: dominant people will be more inclined to answer the questions affirmatively than submissive people. In this interpretation, dominance comes first and 'leads to' the item responses. This position implies a regression of the indicators on the latent variable, and thus motivates the choice of model. In the SES example, however, the relationship between indicators and latent variable is reversed. Variation in the indicators now precedes variation in the latent variable: SES changes as a result of a raise in salary, and not the other way around.

Latent variables of the formative kind are not conceptualized as determining our measurements, but as a summary of these measurements. These measurements may very well be thought to be determined by a number of underlying latent variables (which would give rise to the spurious model with multiple common causes of Edwards and Bagozzi, 2000), but we are not forced in any way to make such an assumption. Now, if we wanted to know how to weight the relative importance of each of the measurements comprising SES in predicting, say, health, we could use a formative model like that in the right panel of figure 3.1. In such a model, we could also test whether SES acts as a single variable in predicting health. In fact, this predictive value would be the main motivation for conceptualizing SES as a single latent variable. However, nowhere in this development have we been forced to admit that SES exists independent of our measurements.

The formative model thus does not necessarily require a realist interpretation of the latent variable that it invokes. In fact, if a realist interpretation were to be given, it would be natural to conceptualize this as a spurious model with multiple common causes in the sense of Edwards and

---

[2] It is in itself an interesting (and neglected) question where to draw the line separating these classes of models at a content-level. For example, which of the formal models should be applied to the relation between diagnostic criteria and mental disorders in the DSM?

Bagozzi (2000). This would again introduce a reflective model part in the model, which would correspond to that part of the model that has a realist interpretation. Thus, the realist interpretation of a latent variable implies a reflective model, whereas constructivist, operationalist, or instrumentalist interpretations are more compatible with a formative model.

In conclusion, the standard model in psychological measurement is a reflective model that specifies that the latent variable is more fundamental than the item responses. This implies entity realism about the latent variable, at least in the hypothetical side of the argument (the assumptions of the model). Maybe more important than this is the fact that psychologists use the model in this spirit. In this context, Hacking's (1983) remark that 'the final arbitrator in philosophy is not how we think but what we do' (p. 31) is relevant: the choice for the reflective measurement model in psychology expresses realism with respect to the latent variable.

Theory realism

Theory realism is different from entity realism in that it concerns the status of the theory, over and above the status of the entities that figure in the theory. It is therefore a stronger philosophical position. The realist interpretation of theories is naturally tied to a correspondence view of truth (O'Connor, 1975). This theory constructs truth as a 'match' between the state of affairs as posed by the theory and the state of affairs in reality, and is the theory generally endorsed by realists (Devitt, 1991). The reason why such a view is connected to realism is that, in order to have a match between theoretical relations and relations in reality, these relations in reality have to exist quite independent of what we say about them. For the constructivist, of course, this option is not open. Therefore, the constructivist will either deny the correspondence theory of truth and claim that truth is coherence between sentences (this is the so-called coherence theory of truth), or deny the relevance of the notion of truth altogether, for example by posing that not truth, but empirical adequacy (consistency of observations with predictions) is to be taken as the central aim of science (Van Fraassen, 1980).

The formal side of latent variable theory, of course, does not claim correspondence truth; it is a system of tautologies and has no empirical content. The question, however, is whether a correspondence type of assumption is formulated in the application of latent variable theory. There are three points in the application where this may occur. First, in the evaluation of the position of a subject on the latent variable; second, in the estimation of parameters; and third, in conditional reasoning based on the assumption that a model is true.

In the evaluation of the position of a subject on the latent variable, correspondence truth sentences are natural. The simple reason for this is that the formal theory implies that one could be wrong about the position of a given subject on the latent variable, which is only possible upon the assumption that there is a true position. To see this, consider the following. Suppose you have administered an intelligence test and you successfully fit a unidimensional latent variable model to the data. Suppose that the single latent variable in the model represents general intelligence. Now you determine the position on the latent variable for two subjects, say John and Jane Doe. You find that the weighted sum-score (i.e. the operational latent variable) is higher for John than for Jane, and you tentatively conclude that John has a higher position on the trait in question than Jane (i.e., you conclude that John is more intelligent). Now could it be that you have made a mistake, in that John actually has a lower score on the trait than Jane? The formal theory certainly implies that this is possible (in fact, this is what much of the theory is about; the theory will even be able to specify the probability of such a mistake, given the positions of John and Jane on the latent variable), so that the answer to this question must be affirmative. This forces commitment to a realist position because there must be something to be wrong about. That is, there must be something like a true (relative) position of the subjects on the latent trait in order for your assessment to be false. You can, as a matter of fact, never be wrong about a position on the latent variable if there is no true position on that variable. Messick (1989) concisely expressed this point when he wrote that 'one must be an ontological realist in order to be an epistemological fallibilist' (p. 26).

This argument is related to the second point in the application where we find a realist commitment, namely in the estimation of parameters. Here, we find essentially the same situation, but in a more general sense. Estimation is a realist concept: roughly speaking, one could say that the idea of estimation is only meaningful if there is something to be estimated. Again, this requires the existence of a true value: in a seriously constructivist view of latent variable analysis, the term 'parameter estimation' should be replaced by the term 'parameter determination'. For it is impossible to be wrong about something if it is not possible to be right about it. And estimation theory is largely concerned with being wrong: it is a theory about the errors one makes in the estimation process. At this point, one may object here that this is only a problem within a frequentist framework, because the idea of a true parameter value is typically associated with frequentism (Fisher, 1925; Hacking, 1965; Neyman and Pearson, 1967). It may further be argued that using Bayesian statistics (Novick and Jackson, 1974; Lee, 1997) could evade the problem. Within a Bayesian framework, however, the realist commitment becomes even more articulated. A Bayesian conception of parameter estimation requires one to specify a prior probability distribution over a set of parameter values. This probability distribution reflects one's degree of belief over that set of parameter values (De Finetti, 1974). Because it is a probability distribution, however, the total probability over the set of parameter values must be equal to one. This means that, in specifying a prior, one explicitly acknowledges that the probability (i.e., one's degree of belief) that the parameter actually has a value in the particular set is equal to one. In other words, one states that one is certain about that. The statement that one is certain that the parameter has a value in the set implies that one can be wrong about that value. And now we are back in the original situation: it is very difficult to be wrong about something if one cannot be right about it. In parameter estimation, this requires the existence of a true value.

The third point in the application of latent variables analysis where we encounter correspondence truth is in conditionals that are based on the assumption that a model is true. In the evaluation of model fit, statistical formulations use the term 'true model'; for example, the p-value resulting from a likelihood ratio difference test between two nested models with a differing number of parameters is interpreted as the probability of finding this (or a more extreme) value for the corresponding chi-square, assuming that the most restricted model (i.e., the model that uses less parameters) is true. Psychometricians are, of course, aware of the fact that this is a very stringent condition for psychological measurement models to fulfil. So, in discussions on this topic, one often hears that there is no such thing as a true model (Cudeck and Browne, 1983; Browne and Cudeck, 1992). For example, McDonald and Marsh (1990) state that '... it is commonly recognized, although perhaps not explicitly stated, that in real applications no restrictive model fits the population, and all fitted restrictive models are approximations and not hypotheses that are possibly true' (p. 247). It would seem as if such a supposition, which is in itself not unreasonable, expresses a move away from realism. This is not necessarily the case. The supposition that there is no true model actually leaves two options: either all models are false or truth is not relevant at all. The realist, who adheres to a correspondence view of truth, must take the first option. The constructivist will take the second, and replace the requirement of truth with one of empirical adequacy.

If the first option is taken, the natural question to ask is: in what sense is the model false? Is it false, for example, because it assumes that the latent variable follows a normal distribution while this is not the case? So interpreted, we are still realists: there is a true model, but it is a different model from the one we specified, i.e., one in which the latent variable is not normally distributed. The fact that the model is false is, in this sense, contingent upon the state of affairs in reality. The model is false, but not necessarily false (i.e., it might be correct in some cases, but it is false in the present application). One could, upon this view, reformulate the statement that there is no such thing as a true model as the statement that all models are misspecified. That this interpretation of the sentence 'all models are false' is not contrary to, but in fact parasitic on realism, can be seen from the fact that the whole notion of misspecification requires the existence of a true model: for how can we misspecify if there is no true model? Now, we may say that we judge the (misspecified) model close enough to reality to warrant our estimation procedures. We then interpret the model as 'approximately true'. So, upon this interpretation, we are firmly in the realist camp, even though we acknowledge that we have not succeeded in formulating the true model. This is as far as a realist could go in the acknowledgment that our models are usually wrong. Popper (1963) was a realist who held such a view concerning theories.

The constructivist must take the second option and move away from the truth concept. The constructivist will argue that we should not interpret the statement that the model is true literally, but weaken the requirement to one of empirical adequacy. The whole concept of truth is thus judged irrelevant. The assumption that the model is true could then be restated as the assumption that the model fits the observable item response patterns perfectly at the population level. This renders the statistical assumption that a model is true (now interpreted as 'empirically adequate') meaningful, because it allows for disturbances in the observed fit due to random sampling, without assuming a realist view of truth. However, so interpreted, underdetermination rears up its ugly head.

For example, take a simple case of statistically equivalent covariance structure models such as the ones graphically represented in figure 3.2. (taken from Hershberger, 1994). These models are empirically equivalent. This means that, if one of them fits the data, the other will fit the data equally well. If the assumption that model A is true is restated as the assumption that it is empirically adequate (i.e., it fits the item responses perfectly at the population level), the assumption that model A is true is fully equivalent to the assumption that model B is true.

Now try to reconstruct the estimation procedure. The estimation of the correlation between the latent variables ξ_1 and ξ_2 takes place under the assumption that model B is true. Under the empirical adequacy interpretation, however, this assumption is equivalent to the assumption that model A is true, for the adjective 'true' as it is used in statistical theory now merely refers to empirical adequacy at the population level. This

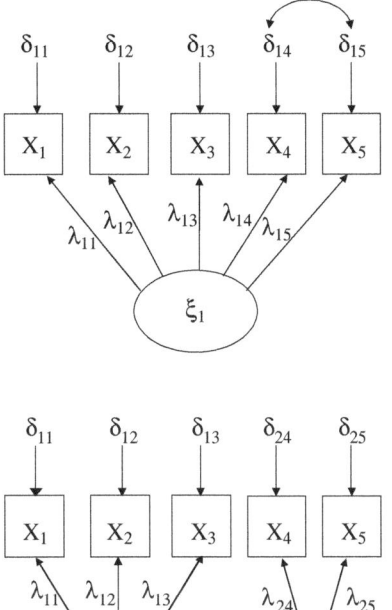

Figure 3.2. Two equivalent models. The SEM-models in the figure predict the same variance-covariance matrix and are thus empirically equivalent. X's indicate observed variables, ξ's latent variables, λ's are factor loadings, δ's error terms, and ϕ is the correlation between latent variables.

implies that the assumption that model B is true may be replaced by the assumption that model A is true, for these assumptions are the same. However, this would mean that the correlation between the latent variables ξ_1 and ξ_2 can be estimated under the assumption that model A is true. In model A, however, there is only one latent variable. It follows that, upon the empirical adequacy view, the correlation between two latent variables can be estimated under the assumption that there is only one latent variable underlying the measurements. In my view, this is not particularly enlightening. But it must be said that the situation need not necessarily bother the constructivist, since the constructivist did not entertain a realist interpretation of these latent variables in the first place. However, it would take some ingenious arguments to defend this interpretation.

In sum, the evaluation of the position of a subject on the latent variable, the process of estimating parameters, and the conditional reasoning based on the assumption that a model is true, are characterized by realist commitments. It is difficult to interpret these procedures without an appeal to some sort of correspondence truth. This requires a substantial degree of theory realism. However, what I have shown is only that the natural interpretation of what we are doing in latent variables analysis is a realist one; not that it is the only interpretation. It may be that the constructivist could make sense of these procedures without recourse to truth. For now, however, I leave this task to the constructivist, and contend that theory realism is required to make sense of latent variables analysis.

Causality

The connection between the formal and the operational latent variable requires a realist ontology. The question then becomes what constitutes the relation between the latent variable and its indicators. Note that this question is not pressing for the operationalist, who argues that the latent variable does not signify anything beyond the data, which implies that the relation between the latent variable and its indicators is purely logical. Nor need it bother the constructivist, who argues that we construct this relation ourselves; it is not an actual but a mental relation, revealing the structure of our theories rather than a structure in reality. The realist will have to come up with something different, for the realist cannot maintain either of these interpretations.

The natural candidate, of course, is causality. That a causal interpretation may be formulated for the relation between latent variables and their indicators has been argued by several authors (e.g., Pearl, 1999, 2000; Edwards and Bagozzi, 2000; Glymour, 2001), and I will not repeat these arguments. The structure of the causal relation is known as a common cause relation (the latent variable is the common cause of its indicators) and has been formulated by Reichenbach (1956). Here, I will concentrate on the form of the relation in a standard measurement model. Specifically, I will argue that a causal connection can be defended in a between-subjects sense, but not in a within-subject sense.

For this purpose, we must distinguish between two types of causal statements that one can make about latent variable models. First, one can say that population differences in position on the latent variable cause population differences in the expectation of the item responses. In accordance with the repeated sampling interpretation, this interpretation posits no stochastic aspects within persons: the expectation of the item response is defined purely in terms of repeated sampling from a population of subjects with a particular position on the latent variable. Second, one can say that a particular subject's position on the latent variable causes his or her item response probabilities. This interpretation corresponds to the stochastic subject interpretation and does pose probabilities at the level of the individual. The first of these views can be defended, but the second is very problematic.

Between-subjects causal accounts To start with the least problematic, consider the statement that differences in the latent variable positions (between populations of subjects) causes the difference in expected item responses (between populations of subjects). This posits the causal relation at a between-subjects level. The statement would fit most accounts of causality, for example the three criteria of J. S. Mill (1843). These hold that X can be considered a cause of Y if (a) X and Y covary, (b) X precedes Y, and (c) ceteris paribus, Y does not occur if X does not occur. In the present situation, we have (a) covariation between the difference in position on the latent variable and the difference in expected item responses, (b) upon the realist viewpoint, the difference in position on the latent variable precedes the difference in expected item responses, and (c) if there is no difference in position on the latent variable, there is no difference in expected item responses. The between-subjects causal statement can also be framed in a way consistent with other accounts of causality, for example the counterfactual account of Lewis (1973), or the related graph-theoretical account of Pearl (1999, 2000). I conclude that a causal relation can be maintained in a between-subjects form. Of course, many problems remain. For example, most latent variables cannot be identified independent of their indicators. As a result, the causal account violates the criterion of separate identifiability of effects and causes, so that circularity looms. However, this is a problem for any causal account of measurement (Trout, 1999); and the main point is that the relation between the latent variable and its indicators can at least be formulated as a causal one.

Within-subject causal accounts The individual account of causality is problematic. Consider the statement that subject i's position on the latent variable causes subject i's item response. The main problem here is the following. One of the essential ingredients of causality is covariation. All theories of causality use this concept, be it in a real or in a counterfactual manner. If X is to cause Y, X and Y should covary. If there is no covariation, there cannot be causation (the reverse is of course not the case). One can say, for example, that striking a match caused the house to burn down. One of the reasons that this is possible, is that a change in X (the condition of the match) precedes a change in Y (the condition of the house). One cannot say, however, that subject i's latent variable value caused his item responses, because there is no covariation between his position on the latent variable and his item responses. An individual's position on the latent variable is, in a standard measurement model, conceptualized as a constant, and a constant cannot be a cause. The same point is made in a more general context by Holland (1986) when he says that an attribute cannot be a cause.

Counterfactuals The obvious way out of this issue is to invoke a counterfactual account of causation (see, for example, Lewis, 1973; Sobel, 1994). On this account, one analyses causality using counterfactual alternatives. This is done by constructing arguments such as 'X caused Y, because if X had not happened, ceteris paribus, Y would not have happened.' This is called a counterfactual account because X did in fact happen. For the previous example, one would have to say that 'the striking of the match caused the house to burn down, because the house would not have burned down if the match had not been struck'. For our problem, however, this account of causality does not really help. Of course, we could construct sentences like 'if subject i had had a different position on the latent variable, subject i would have produced different item responses', but this raises some difficult problems.

Suppose, for example, that one has administered Einstein a number of IQ-items. Consider the counterfactual 'if Einstein had been less intelligent, he would have scored lower on the IQ-items'. This seems like a plausible formulation of the hypothesis tested in a between-subjects model, and it also seems as if it adequately expresses the causal efficacy of Einstein's intelligence, but there are strong reasons for doubting whether this is the case. For example, we may reformulate the above counterfactual as 'if Einstein had had John's level of intelligence, he would have scored lower on the IQ-items'. But does this counterfactual express the causal efficacy of intelligence within Einstein? It seems to me that what we express here is not a within-subject causal statement at all, but a between-subjects conclusion in disguise, namely, the conclusion that Einstein scored higher than John because he is more intelligent than John. Similarly, 'if Einstein had had the intelligence of a fruitfly, he would not have been able to answer the IQ-items correctly' does not express the causal efficacy of Einstein's intelligence, but the difference between the population of humans and the population of fruitflies. We know that fruitflies act rather stupidly, and so are inclined to agree that Einstein would act equally stupidly if he had the intelligence of a fruitfly. And it seems as if this line of reasoning conveys the idea that Einstein's intelligence has some kind of causal efficacy. However, the counterfactual is completely unintelligible except when interpreted as expressing knowledge concerning the difference between human beings (a population) and fruitflies (another population). It does not contain information on the structure of Einstein's intellect, and much less on the alleged causal power of Einstein's intelligence. It only contains the information that Einstein will score higher on an IQ-test than a fruitfly because he is more intelligent than a fruitfly – but this is exactly the between-subjects formulation of the causal account. Clearly, the individual causal account transfers knowledge of between-subjects differences to the individual, and posits a variable that is defined between-subjects as a causal force within-subjects.

In other words, the within-subjects causal interpretation of between-subjects latent variables rests on a logical fallacy (the fallacy of division; Rorer, 1990). Once you think about it, this is not surprising. What between-subjects latent variables models do is to specify sources of between-subjects differences, but because they are silent with respect to the question of how individual scores are produced, they cannot be interpreted as posing intelligence as a causal force within Einstein. Thus, the right counterfactual (which is actually the one implied by the repeated sampling formulation of the measurement model) is between-subjects: the IQ-score we obtained from the i-th subject (who happened to be Einstein) would have been lower, had we drawn another subject with a lower position on the latent variable from the population. Note, however, that the present argument does not establish that it is impossible that some other conceptualization of intelligence may be given a causal within-subject interpretation. It establishes that such an interpretation is not formulated in a between subjects model, and therefore cannot be extracted from such a model: a thousand clean replications of the general intelligence model on between-subjects data would not establish that general intelligence plays a causal role in producing Einstein's item responses.

Exchangeability and local homogeneity But what about variables like, for example, height? Is it so unreasonable to say that 'if Einstein had been taller, he would have been able to reach the upper shelves in the library'? No, this is not unreasonable, but it is unreasonable to assume a priori that intelligence, as a between-subjects latent variable, applies in the same way as height does. The concept of height is not defined in terms of between-subjects differences, but in terms of an empirical concatenation operation (Krantz, Luce, Suppes, and Tversky, 1971; Michell, 1999; see also chapter 4). Roughly, this means that we know how to move Einstein around in the height dimension (for example by giving him platform shoes), and that the effect of doing this is tractable (namely, wearing platform shoes will enable Einstein to reach the upper shelves). Moreover, it can be assumed that the height dimension applies to within-subject differences in the same way that it applies to between-subject differences. This is to say that the statements 'if Einstein had been taller, he would have been able to reach the upper shelves in the library' and 'if we had replaced Einstein with a taller person, this person would have been able to reach the upper shelves in the library' are equivalent with respect to the dimension under consideration. They are equivalent in this sense, exactly because the dimensions pertaining to within and to between subjects variability are qualitatively the same: if we give Einstein platform shoes which make him taller, he is, in all relevant respects, exchangeable with the taller person in the example. I do not object to introducing height in a causal account of this kind, because variations in height have demonstrably the same effect within and between subjects. But it remains to be shown that the same holds for psychological variables like intelligence.

The analogy does, however, provide an opening: the individual causal account could be defended on the assumption that intelligence is like height, in that the within-subjects and between-subjects dimensions are equivalent. However, the between-subjects model does not contain this equivalence as an assumption. Therefore, such an argument would have to rest on the idea that, by necessity, there has to be a strong relation between models for within-subjects variability and models for between-subjects variability. It turns out that this idea is untenable. The reason for this is that there is a surprising lack of relation between within-subjects models and between-subjects models.

To discuss within-subject models, we now need to extend our discussion to the time domain. This is necessary, because to model within-subjects variability, there has to be variability, and variability requires replications of some kind; and if variability cannot result from sampling across subjects, it has to come from sampling within subjects. In this paradigm, one could, for example, administer Einstein a number of IQ-items repeatedly over time, and analyse the within-subject covariation between item responses. The first technique of this kind was Cattell's so called P-technique (Cattell and Cross, 1952), and the dynamic factor analysis of repeated measurements of an individual subject has been refined, for example, by Molenaar (1985). The exact details of such models need not concern us here; what is important is that, in this kind of analysis, systematic covariation over time is explained on the basis of within-subject latent variables. So, instead of between-subjects dimensions that explain between-subjects covariation, we now have within-subject dimensions that explain within-subject covariation. One could imagine that, if the within-subject model for Einstein had the same structure as the between-subjects model, then the individual causal account would make sense despite all the difficulties we encountered above.

In essence, such a situation would imply that the way in which Einstein differs from himself over time is qualitatively the same as the way in which he differs from other subjects at one single time point. This way, the clause 'if Einstein were less intelligent' would refer to a possible state of Einstein at a different time point, however hypothetical. More importantly, this state would, in all relevant respects, be identical to the state of a different subject, say John, who is less intelligent at this time point. In such a state of affairs, Einstein and John would be exchangeable, like a child and a dwarf are exchangeable with respect to the variable height. It would be advantageous, if not truly magnificent, if a between-subjects model would imply or even test such exchangeability. This would mean, for example, that the between-subjects five factor model of personality would imply a five factor model for each individual subject. If this were to be shown, the case against the individual causal account would reduce from a substantial objection to a case of philosophical hairsplitting. However, the required equivalence has not been shown, and the following reasons lead me to expect that it will not, in general, be a tenable assumption.

The link connecting between-subjects variables to characteristics of individuals is similar to the link discussed in the stochastic subject formulation of latent variable models, where the model for the individual is counterfactually defined in terms of repeated measurements with intermediate brainwashing. I have already mentioned that Ellis and Van den Wollenberg (1993) have shown that the assumption that the measurement model holds for each individual subject (local homogeneity) has to be added to and is in no way implied by the model. One may, however, suppose that, while finding a particular structure in between-subjects data may not imply that the model holds for each subject, it would at least render this likely. Even this is not the case. It is known that if a model fits in a given population, this does not entail the fit of the same model for any given element from a population, or even for the majority of elements from that population (Molenaar, 1999; Molenaar, Huizenga, and Nesselroade, 2003).

So, the five factors in personality research are between subjects; but if a within-subjects time series analysis would be performed on each of these subjects, we could get a different model for each of the subjects. In fact, Molenaar et al. (2003) have performed simulations in which they had different models for each individual (so, one individual followed a one factor model, another a two factor model, etc.). It turned out that, when a between-subjects model was fitted to between-subjects data at any specific time point, a factor model with low dimensionality (i.e., a model with one or two latent variables) provided an excellent fit to the data, even if the majority of subjects had a different latent variable structure.

With regard to the five factor model in personality, substantial discrepancies between intraindividual and interindividual structures have been empirically demonstrated in Borkenau and Ostendorf (1998). Mischel and Shoda (1998), Feldman (1995), and Cervone (1997, 2004) have illustrated similar discrepancies between intraindividual and interindividual structures. This shows that between-subjects models and within-subject models bear no obvious relation to each other, at least not in the simple sense discussed above. This is problematic for the individual causal account of between-subjects models, because it shows that the premise 'if Einstein were less intelligent...' cannot be supplemented with the conclusion '...then his expected item response pattern would be identical to John's expected item response pattern'. It cannot be assumed that Einstein and John (or any other subject, for that matter) are exchangeable in this respect, because, at the individual level, Einstein's intelligence structure may differ from John's in such a way that the premise of the argument cannot be fulfilled without changing essential components of Einstein's intellect. Thus, the data generating mechanisms at the level of the individual are not captured, not implied, and not tested by between-subjects analyses without heavy theoretical background assumptions which, in psychology, are simply not available.

The individual causal account is not merely implausible for philosophical or mathematical reasons; for most psychological variables, there is also no good theoretical reason for supposing that between-subjects variables do causal work at the level of the individual. For example, what causal work could the between-subjects latent variable we call general intelligence do in the process leading to Einstein's answer to an IQ-item? Let us reconstruct the procedure. Einstein enters the testing situation, sits down, and takes a look at the test. He then perceives the item. This means that the bottom-up and top-down processes in his visual system generate a conscious perception of the task to be fulfilled: it happens to be a number series problem. Einstein has to complete the series 1, 1, 2, 3, 5, 8,...? Now he starts working on the problem; this takes place in working memory, but he also draws information from long-term memory (for example, he probably applies the concept of addition, although he may also be trying to remember the name of a famous Italian mathematician of whom this series reminds him). Einstein goes through some hypotheses concerning the rules that may account for the pattern in the number series. Suddenly he has the insight that each number is the sum of the previous two (and simultaneously remembers that it was Fibonacci!).

Now he applies that rule and concludes that the next number must be 13. Einstein then goes through various motorical processes which result in the appearance of the number 13 on the piece of paper, which is coded as '1' by the person hired to do the typing. Einstein now has a 1 in his response pattern, indicating that he gave a correct response to the item. This account has used various psychological concepts, such as working memory, long-term memory, perception, consciousness, and insight. But, where, in this account of the processes leading to Einstein's item response, did intelligence enter? The answer is: nowhere. Intelligence is a concept that is intended to account for individual differences; and the model that we apply is to be interpreted as such. Again, this implies that the causal statement drawn from such a measurement model retains this between-subjects form.

Elliptical accounts The last resort for anyone willing to endorse the individual causal account of between-subjects models is to view the causal statement as an elliptical (i.e., a shorthand) explanation. The explanation for which it is a shorthand would, in this case, be one in terms of processes taking place at the individual level. This requires stepping down from the macro-level of repeated testing (as conceptualized in the within subjects modelling approach) to the micro-level of the processes leading up to the item response in this particular situation. I will argue in the next paragraph that there is merit to this approach in several respects, but it does not really help in the individual causal account as discussed in this section. The main reason for this is that the between-subjects latent variable will not indicate the same process in each subject. Therefore, the causal agent (i.e., the position on the latent variable) that is posited within subjects based on a between-subjects model does not refer to the same process in all subjects.

This is a problem for an elliptical account. For instance, one can say that the *Titanic* has rusted after so many years on the bottom of the sea, because it was made of iron. This explanation is elliptical, because it does not specify all processes that actually lead to the phenomenon we call rust. The reason why the explanation works, however, is that the explanation subsumes the *Titanic* under the category of iron things, and this category is homogeneous with respect to the processes that will occur when such things are left on the bottom of the ocean. Thus, one may look up the details of the reaction between Fe and H_2O that leads to rust, and unproblematically take these processes to apply to the *Titanic*. One could say that the category of iron things displays *process homogeneity* with respect to the situation at hand.

In psychological measurement, such process homogeneity is not to be expected in most cases. This is a particularly pressing problem for models that posit continuous latent variables. The reason for this is that an elliptical explanation would probably refer to a qualitatively different process for different positions on the latent variable; probably even to different processes for different people with the same position on the latent variable. Jane, high on the between-subjects dimension general intelligence, will in all likelihood approach many IQ-items using a strategy that is qualitatively different from her brother John's. John and his nephew Peter, equally intelligent, may both fail to answer an item correctly, but for different reasons (e.g., John has difficulties remembering series of patterns in the Raven task, while Peter has difficulties in imagining spatial rotations). It is obvious that this problem is even more serious in personality testing, where we generally do not even have the faintest idea of what happens between item administration and item response. For this reason, it would be difficult to conceive of a meaningful interpretation of such an elliptical causal statement without rendering it completely vacuous, in the sense that the position on the latent variable is a shorthand for whatever process leads to person's response. In such an interpretation, the within-subject causal account would be trivially true, but uninformative.

However, it must be said that in this case latent class models could have an advantage. For instance, in the models used to model children's responses on the balance scale task (Jansen and Van der Maas, 1997), latent classes are considered to be homogeneous with respect to the strategy used to solve the items. In this case, the classes do have process homogeneity, and an elliptical explanation could be defended. The line of reasoning followed in such models could, of course, be extended and could lead to valid elliptical explanations of respondent behaviour. Unfortunately, at present such cases of theoretically inspired modelling are rare.

On the basis of this analysis, we must conclude that the within-subject causal statement, that subject i's position on the latent variable causes his item responses, does not sit well with existing accounts of causality. A between-subjects causal relation can be defended, although it is certainly not without problems. Such an interpretation conceives of latent variables as sources of individual differences, but explicitly abstracts away from the processes taking place at the level of the individual. The main reason for the failure of the within-subjects causal account seems to be that it rests on the misinterpretation of a measurement model as a process model, that is, as a mechanism that operates at the level of the individual.

This fallacy is quite pervasive in the behavioural sciences. For instance, part of the nature–nurture controversy, as well as controversies surrounding the heritability coefficients used in genetics, may also be due to this misconception. The fallacious idea, that a heritability coefficient of 0.50 for IQ-scores means that 50 per cent of an individual's intelligence is genetically determined, remains one of the more pervasive misunderstandings in the nature–nurture discussion. Ninety per cent of variations in height may be due to genetic factors, but this does not imply that my height is 90 per cent genetically determined. Similarly, a linear model for interindividual variations in height does not imply that individual growth curves are linear; that 30 per cent of the interindividual variation in success in college may be predicted from the grade point average in high school, does not mean that 30 per cent of the exams you passed were predictable from your high school grades; and that there is a sex difference in verbal ability does not mean that your verbal ability will change if you undergo a sex change operation. It will be clear to all that these interpretations are fallacious. Still, for some reason, such misinterpretations are very common in the interpretation of results obtained in latent variables analysis. However, they can all be considered to be specific violations of the general statistical maxim, that between-subjects conclusions should not be interpreted in a within-subjects sense.

3.3 Implications for psychology

It is clear that between-subjects models do not imply, test, or support causal accounts that are valid at the individual level. In turn, the causal accounts that can be formulated and supported in a between-subjects model do not address individuals. However, connecting psychological processes to the latent variables that are so prominent in psychology is of obvious importance. It is essential that such efforts be made, because the between-subjects account in itself does not correspond to the kind of hypotheses that many psychological theories would imply, as these theories are often formulated at the level of individual processes. The relation (or relations) that may exist between latent variables and individual processes should therefore be studied in greater detail, and preferably within a formalized framework, than has so far been done. In this section, I provide an outline of the different ways in which the relation between individual processes and between-subject latent variables can be conceptualized. These different conceptualizations correspond to different kinds of psychological constructs. They also generate different kinds of research questions and require different research strategies in order to substantiate conclusions concerning these constructs.

Locally homogeneous constructs First, theoretical considerations may suggest that a latent variable is at the appropriate level of explanation for both between-subjects and within-subjects differences. Examples of psychological constructs that could be conceptualized in this manner are various types of state-variables such as mood, arousal, or anxiety, and maybe some attitudes. That is, it may be hypothesized, for differences in the state variable 'arousal', that the dimension on which I differ from myself over time, and the dimension on which I differ from other people at a given time point, are the same. If this is the case, the latent variable model that explains within-subjects differences over time must be the same model as the model that explains between-subjects differences. Fitting latent variable models to time series data for a single subject is possible with dynamic factor models (Molenaar, 1985), and such techniques suggest exploring statistical analyses of case studies in order to see whether the structure of the within-subject latent variable model matches between-subjects latent variables models. If this is the case, there is support for the idea that we are talking about a dimension that pertains both to variability within a subject and between-subjects variability. Possible states of a given individual would then match possible states of different individuals, which means that, in relevant respects, the exchangeability condition discussed in the previous section holds. Thus, in this situation we may say that a latent variable does explanatory work both at the within-subject and the between-subjects level, and a causal account may be set up at both of these. Following the terminology introduced by Ellis and Van den Wollenberg (1993) I propose to call this type of construct *locally homogeneous*, where 'locally' indicates that the latent variable structure pertains to the level of the individual, and 'homogeneous' refers to the fact that this structure is the same for each individual.

Locally heterogeneous constructs Locally homogeneous constructs will not often be encountered in psychology, where myriads of individual differences can be expected to be the rule rather than the exception. I would not be surprised if, for the majority of constructs, time series analyses on individual subjects would indicate that different people exhibit different patterns of change over time, which are governed by different latent variable structures. So, for some people, psychological distress may be unidimensional, while for others it may be multidimensional. If this is the case, it would seem that we cannot lump these people together in between-subjects models to test hypotheses concerning psychological processes, for they would constitute a heterogeneous population in a theoretically important sense. At present, however, we do not know how often and to what degree such a situation occurs, which makes this one of the big unknowns in psychology. This is because there is an almost universal – but surprisingly silent – reliance on what may be called a uniformity of nature assumption in doing between-subjects analyses; the relation between mechanisms that operate at the level of the individual and models that explain variation between individuals is often taken for granted, rather than investigated. For example, in the attitude literature (Cacioppo and Berntson, 1999; Russell and Carroll, 1999) there is currently a debate on whether the affective component of attitudes is produced by a singular mechanism, which would produce a bipolar attitude structure (with positive and negative affect as two ends of a single continuum), or should be conceptualized as consisting of two relatively independent mechanisms (one for positive, and one for negative affect).

This debate is characterized by a strong uniformity assumption: it either is a singular dimension (for everyone), or we have two relatively independent subsystems (for everyone). It is, however, not obvious that the affect system should be the same for all individuals; for it may turn out that the affective component in attitudes is unidimensional for some people but not for others. It must be emphasized that such a finding would not render the concept of attitude obsolete; but clearly, a construct governed by different latent variable models within different individuals will have to play a different role in psychological theories than a locally homogeneous construct. I propose to call such constructs *locally heterogeneous*. Locally heterogeneous constructs may have a clear dimensional structure between subjects, but they pertain to different structures at the level of individuals. Thus, we now have a distinction between two types of constructs: locally homogeneous constructs, for which the latent dimension is the same within and between subjects, and locally heterogeneous constructs, for which this is not the case. In applications, it is imperative that we find out about which of the two we are talking, especially when we are testing hypotheses concerning processes at the individual level with between-subjects models.

Locally irrelevant constructs It will be immediately obvious that constructs which are hypothesized as relatively stable traits, such as the factors in the Big Five, will not exhibit either of these structures. If a trait is stable, covariation of repeated measurements will not obey a latent variable model at all. All variance of the observed variables will be error variance, so that this implies that these observed variables will be independent over time. This hypothesis could, and should, be tested using time series analysis. If it holds, the latent variable in question would be one that produces between-subjects variability, but does no work at the individual level. I propose to call this type of construct a *locally irrelevant* construct. This terminology should not be misread as implying a value judgment, as locally irrelevant constructs have played, and will probably continue to play, an important role in psychology. However, the terminology should be read unambiguously as indicating the enormous degree to which such constructs abstract from the level of the individual. They should, for this reason, not be conceptualized as explaining behaviour at the level of the individual. In the personality literature, this has been argued on independent grounds by authors such as Lamiell (1987), Pervin (1994), and Epstein (1994).

It is disturbing, and slightly embarrassing for psychology, that we cannot say with sufficient certainty in which of these classes particular psychological constructs (e.g., personality traits, intelligence, attitudes) fall. This is the result of a century of operating on silent uniformity of nature assumptions by focusing almost exclusively on between-subjects models. It seems that psychological research has adapted to the limitations of common statistical procedures (for example, by abandoning case studies because analysis of variance requires sample sizes larger than one), instead of inventing new procedures that allow for the testing of theories at the proper level, which is often the level of the individual, or at the very least exploiting time series techniques that have been around in other disciplines (e.g., econometrics) for a very long time. Clearly, extending measurements into the time domain is essential, and fortunately the statistical tools for doing this are rapidly becoming available. Models that are suited for this task have seen substantial developments over the last two decades (see, for example, Molenaar, 1985; McArdle, 1987; Wilson, 1989; Fischer and Parzer, 1991; Hamaker, Dolan and Molenaar, in press), and powerful, user friendly software for estimating and testing them has been developed (Jöreskog and Sörbom, 1993; Muthén and Muthén, 1998; Neale, Boker, Xie, and Maes, 1999). Especially, it would be worthwhile to try latent variable analyses at the level of the individual, which would bring the all but abandoned case study back into scientific psychology – be it, perhaps, from an unexpected angle.

Ontology revisited There remains an open question pertaining to the ontological status of latent variables, and especially those that fall into the class of locally irrelevant constructs. It has been argued here that latent variables, at least those of the reflective model kind, imply a realist ontology. How should we conceptualize the existence of such latent variables, if they cannot be found at the level of the individual? It seems that the proper conceptualization of the latent variable (if its reality is maintained) is as an emergent property, in the sense that it is a characteristic of an aggregate (the population) which is absent at the level of the constituents of this aggregate (individuals). Of course, this does not mean that there is no relation between the processes taking place at the level of the individual and between-subjects latent variables. In fact, the between-subjects latent variable must be parasitic on individual processes, because these must be the source of between-subjects variability. If it is shown that a given set of cognitive processes leads to a particular latent variable structure, we could therefore say that this set of processes realizes the latent variables in question. The relevant research question for scientists should then be: which processes generate which latent variable structures? What types of individual processes, for example in intelligence testing, are compatible with the general intelligence model?

Obviously, time series analyses will not provide an answer to this question in the case of constructs that are hypothesized to be temporally stable, such as general intelligence. In this case, we need to connect between subjects models to models of processes taking place at the level of the individual. This may involve a detailed analysis of cognitive processes that are involved in solving IQ-test items, for example. Such inquiries have already been carried out by those at the forefront of quantitative psychology. Embretson (1994), for example, has shown how to build latent variable models based on theories of cognitive processes; and one of the interesting features of such inquiries is that they show clearly how a single latent variable can originate, or emerge, out of a substantial number of distinct cognitive processes. This kind of research is promising and may lead to important results in psychology. I would not be surprised, for example, if it turned out that Sternberg's (1985) triarchic theory of intelligence, which is largely a theory about cognitive processes and modules at the level of the individual, is not necessarily in conflict with the between-subjects conceptualization of general intelligence. Finally, I note that the connection of cognitive processes and between-subjects latent variables requires the use of results from both experimental and correlational psychological research traditions, which Cronbach (1957) has called the two disciplines of scientific psychology. This section may therefore be read as a restatement of his call for integration of these schools.

3.4 Discussion

Latent variable models introduce a hypothetical attribute to account for relations among observable variables. In a measurement context, they assert that a number of items measure the same latent variable. This requires a realist ontology for the latent variable, and a good deal of theory realism for the postulated model. In comparison to classical test theory, latent variable theory is certainly a substantial improvement. It specifies a relation between item responses and the attribute measured, which means that it can be properly considered to give a theory of measurement. Specifically, measurement is conceptualized in terms of a common cause relation. Upon closer examination, however, the specific interpretation of the causal relation is not without problems. When formulated in terms of subpopulation distributions, a causal account can indeed be defended. The within-subject interpretation of the model, however, is extremely problematic.

Before I discuss some implications of these results, there are two important asides to make concerning what I am not saying. First, it is not suggested here that one cannot use a standard measurement model, and still think of the latent variable as constructed out of the observed variables or as a fiction. But I do insist that this is an inconsistent position, in that it cannot be used to connect the operational latent variable to its formal counterpart in a consistent way. Whether one should or should not allow such an inconsistency in one's reasoning is a different question that is beyond the scope of this chapter. Second, if one succeeds in fitting a latent variable model in a given situation, the present discussion does not imply that one is forced to believe in the reality of the latent variable. In fact, this would require a logical strategy known as 'inference to the best explanation' or 'abduction', which is especially problematic in the light of underdetermination. So I am not saying that, for example, the fit of a factor model with one higher order factor to a set of IQ measurements implies the existence of a general intelligence factor: what I am saying is that the consistent connection between the empirical and formal side of a factor model requires a realist position. Whether realism about specific instances of latent variables, such as general intelligence, can be defended is an epistemological issue that is the topic of heated discussion in the philosophy of science (see, for example Van Fraassen, 1980; Cartwright, 1983; Hacking, 1983; Devitt, 1991). Probably, on the epistemological side of the problem, there are few latent entities in psychology that fulfil the epistemological demands of realists such as Hacking (1983).

It will be felt that there are certain tensions in the application of latent variable models to psychological measurement. I have not tried to cover these up, because I think they are indicative of some fundamental problems in psychological measurement and require a clear articulation. The realist interpretation of latent variable theory leads to conclusions that will seem too strong for many psychologists. Psychology has a strong empiricist tradition and psychologists often do not want to go beyond the observations – at least, no further than strictly necessary. As a result, there is a feeling that realism about latent variables takes us too far into metaphysical speculations. At the same time, we would probably like latent variable models to yield conclusions of a causal nature (the model should at the very least allow for the formulation of such relations). But we cannot defend any sort of causal structure invoking latent variables, if we are not realists about these latent variables, in the sense that they exist independent of our measurements: one cannot claim that A causes B, and at the same time maintain that A is constructed out of B. If we then reluctantly accept realism, invoking perhaps more metaphysics than we would like, it appears that the type of causal conclusions available are not the ones we desired. Namely, the causality in our measurement models is only consistently formulated at the between-subjects level. And although the boxes, circles, and arrows in the graphical representation of the model suggest that the model is dynamic and applies to the individual, upon closer scrutiny no such dynamics are to be found. Indeed, this has been pinpointed as one of the major problems of mathematical psychology by Luce (1997): our theories are formulated in a within-subjects sense, but the models we apply are often based solely on between-subjects comparisons.

What are the consequences of this problem for the conception of psychological measurement that latent variable theory offers? It depends on how you look at it. If one accepts the possibility that a causal account can apply to characteristics of populations, without applying to each element of these populations, the problems are relatively small. Such causal accounts are not uncommon: variation in the variable 'smoking' causes variation in the variable 'cancer', but it does not do so for each person. Still, I think that causality can be meaningfully applied in this case, be it with the understanding that its validity at the population level does not imply that the causal relation holds for each individual. Upon such a view, one does have to settle for a measurement relation that is solely expressed in terms of variation: variation on the latent variable causes variation on the observables, but for a single person the latent variable does not have to play a role in this respect. One could argue against this view by saying that, if a causal model is invalid for each individual, then it cannot be valid in the population. Upon this view, a causal account of the measurement process is impossible in the locally heterogeneous and locally irrelevant cases. I think such a view is too restrictive, because it would imply that it is impossible to measure between-subjects differences in attributes, if these attributes are inherently stable within-subjects. This would mean, for instance, that genotypic differences cannot be measured through phenotypic effects. However, if the purpose of a measurement procedure is to measure differences between subjects, then one cannot hold it against the procedure that its results do not apply to differences within subjects. It does seem that these are radically different levels of explanation, and therefore they should not be mixed up.

The same causal account of measurement can be set up within persons, of course, and in the special case that the between-subjects and the within-subjects accounts are both valid, one is in the lucky position to draw within-subject conclusions on the basis of between-subjects data. Whether this assumption applies, how one could gather evidence for it, and which constructs are supposed to be candidates for it in the first place, are important but neglected questions in psychology, as has been argued in this chapter. However, if one takes the position that measurement can apply to sources of variation in a population, without applying directly to the individuals that make up this population, then latent variable theory does not necessarily disqualify as a theory of measurement in the locally heterogeneous and locally irrelevant cases. It may be that the analysis given suggests that we are not measuring the right things, i.e., that we are not investigating what we would want to investigate, but this is not a conceptual problem for latent variable theory. It is a conceptual problem for psychology and for the way it utilizes latent variable models.

For now, I contend that latent variable theory can offer a quite elegant account of the measurement process. The theory has several notable benefits. First, it places the attribute in the measurement model in a way that seems very plausible: differences in the attribute (either within or between subjects) lead to differences in the observations. It is clear that such a view requires both realism about the attribute and a causal interpretation of the measurement process. Second, although this view introduces some heavy metaphysics, the metaphysics are clearly necessary, serve a clear purpose, and in fact lead to some interesting research questions. This is a substantial improvement over the classical test theory model, which has metaphysics wandering all over the place for no clear purpose except to be able to construct mathematically simple equations. Third, the latent variable view seems to align closely with the way many working researchers think about measurement. This property cannot be ascribed to the classical test model, and neither to the fundamental measurement model, as will be argued in the next chapter. The latent variable model is, of course, in danger of misinterpretation. However, if the fact that a technique is easily misinterpreted were to be held against it, methodology and statistics would probably be empty within a day. Latent variable theory must be considered to formulate a plausible philosophy of measurement.

4 Scales

> It may be that the task of the new psychometrics is impossible; that fundamental measures will never be constructed. If this is the case, then the truth must be faced that perhaps psychology can never be a science...
>
> Paul Kline, 1998

4.1 Introduction

In the 1930s, the British Association for the Advancement of Science installed a number of its members with a most peculiar task: to decide whether or not there was such a thing as measurement in psychology. The commission, consisting of psychologists and physicists (among the latter was Norman Campbell, famous for his philosophical work on measurement), was unable to reach unanimous agreement. However, a majority of its members concluded that measurement in psychology was impossible; Campbell (cited in Narens and Luce, 1986, p. 186), for example, asked 'why do not psychologists accept the natural and obvious conclusion that subjective measurements (...) cannot be the basis of measurement'. Similarly, Guild (cited in Reese, 1943, p. 6) stated that 'to insist on calling these other processes [i.e., attempts at psychological measurement] measurement adds nothing to their actual significance, but merely debases the coinage of verbal intercourse. Measurement is not a term with some mysterious inherent meaning, part of which may be overlooked by the physicists and may be in course of discovery by psychologists.' For this reason, Guild concluded that using the term 'measurement' to cover quantitative practices in psychology 'does not broaden its meaning but destroys it'. Reese (1943, p. 6) summarized the ultimate position of the commission: they [the members of the commission] argue that psychologists must then do one of two things. They must either say that the logical requirements for measurement in physics, as laid down by the logicians and other experts in the field of measurement, do not hold for psychology, and then develop other principles that are logically sound; or they must admit that their attempts at measurement do not meet the criteria and both cease calling these manipulations by the word "measurement" and stop treating the results obtained as if they were the products of true measurement.'

It would seem that the members of the commission anticipated that the alternative 'logically sound' principles for 'true measurement' in psychology would probably never be discovered. But perhaps they did anticipate their report to have the desired impact in the sense that psychologists would finally recognize their errors, and would stop the unauthorized use of terms like measurement and quantity. Interestingly, exactly the opposite has happened: psychologists *have* developed an alternative, but generally use the term 'measurement' to denote every procedure of assigning numbers *except* the logically 'correct' one. That is, the theory of fundamental measurement (the 'true' measurement theory to which Guild refers) has been extended in such a manner that 'logically sound' principles have become available for psychological measurement situations, primarily through the development of conjoint measurement structures (Luce and Tukey, 1964; Krantz, Suppes, Luce, and Tversky, 1971). Ironically, however, not a soul uses that theory in the practice of psychological measurement: every year there appears an enormous number of books that consider psychological measurement, but few of them even contain a reference to this work. The logical foundation for psychological measurement has thus become available, only to be neglected by its presumed audience – and psychologists have continued to use the term measurement for everything else.

The gist of what has been called the 'axiomatic' approach to measurement (Cliff, 1992), of which the theory of fundamental measurement can be considered a special case, is that measurement is an essentially *representational* activity, i.e., a process of assigning numbers in such a manner as to preserve basic qualitative relations observed in the world (Narens and Luce, 1986). The result of this activity is called a measurement scale. Psychologists are familiar with this concept mainly through Stevens' (1946) famous typology of 'levels of measurement' in terms of nominal, ordinal, interval, and ratio scales. The scale type is often deemed very important for determining what kind of statistics may be used, and in this manner it exerts considerable influence on the practice of data analysis in psychology (or, in any event, on the conscience of psychologists doing the analyses). The prescriptive aspect of scales has been the subject of enduring controversies between measurement theoreticians and statisticians (Lord, 1953; Stevens, 1968; Gaito, 1980; Townshend and Ashby, 1984; Michell, 1986; Velleman and Wilkinson, 1993), mainly because statisticians refuse to be told what is admissible and what not by what they seem to perceive as an utterly impractical theory (Lord, 1953; Gaito, 1980). However, apart from generating such controversies and acting on the psychologist's statistical conscience, scales and the associated theory of measurement have not entered mainstream psychology at all (Cliff, 1992).

This does not mean that nobody works with representationalism in psychology. The original developers of the theory, such as Luce, Suppes, and Narens, continue to work out the mathematical basis of measurement theory, joined by a group of researchers united in the Society for Mathematical Psychology. In a completely different corner of psychology, the advocates of Rasch measurement frequently allude to the fundamental measurement properties of the Rasch model; notable in this context are Wright (1997), Roskam and Jansen (1984), and Bond and Fox (2001). Finally, at a more conceptual level Michell (1990; 1997) has attacked the common practice in psychology and psychometrics using a line of reasoning based on the axiomatic theory of measurement. His efforts have had impact on at least one psychometrician (Kline, 1998), and may well influence more. These researchers look to the future, and some of them seem to regard the coming of the 'revolution that never happened' (Cliff, 1992) as the only road to a truly scientific psychology (Kline, 1998; Bond and Fox, 2001). Or, like Luce (1996, p. 95), they view such developments as simply 'inevitable', so that 'the only question is the speed with which they are carried out'.

The axiomatic theory of measurement thus has a certain apologetic quality about it. It is also strongly normative, or even prescriptive, as is evidenced by terminology such as 'admissible transformations', and the idea that performing an inadmissible transformation destroys the 'meaningfulness' of conclusions based on the data (see Michell, 1986, for a discussion of this view). Now, methodology is in a sense always normative, but there is no approach in psychological measurement – not even in latent variables analysis – that so pertinently presents itself as the gatekeeper of rationality. Treatises based on the approach also insist on empirical testability of hypotheses in a manner that almost suggests that, if a hypothesis cannot be directly tested, it is meaningless, or at the very least suspect. For example, Michell (2000) has characterized the a priori assumption that psychological attributes are quantitative, which indeed is a strong metaphysical assumption in many latent variable models, as a methodological thought disorder, and this leads him to label the entire field of psychometrics as pathological. The reason for this disqualification seems to be that the hypothesis is not directly testable in commonly used models like the factor model. Those familiar with the philosophy of science may see a parallel with a historical movement that shared both the strong normativity, the desire to demarcate between meaningful and meaningless propositions, and the emphasis on the dangers of metaphysics – namely, the Vienna Circle. There seems to be a certain similarity between, on the one hand, the divide between the verificationist orientation of logical positivism and the robust realist, falsificationist philosophy of Popper (1959), and, on the other hand, the schism between representational measurement theory and the latent variables approach.

This chapter develops this intuition by inquiring into the status of the measurement scale, the central concept of representational measurement theory. It is argued that the theory of representationalism implements a constructivist philosophy of measurement most closely related to logical positivism. Like the logical positivists envisioned, representationalism departs from observable relations between objects, and then build its theoretical concept, the scale, up from these relations in a rigorous axiomatic fashion. When compared to the approach as it is taken in latent variable models, representationalism is almost devoid of metaphysics. However, the theory runs into problems that are similar to those of logical positivism. Although representational measurement theory elucidates the measurement process, it is difficult to view it as a literal description of how measurement works in practice, and therefore it is best viewed as a rational reconstruction of the measurement process – much like logical positivism offered a rational reconstruction of scientific progress. Moreover, a prescriptive reading of the theory is hard to take seriously, because representationalism has great difficulties dealing with noisy data or measurement error. This is because, where latent variable theory takes the data as noisy, and idealizes the underlying structures, representationalism instead idealizes the data in order to make its rigorous axiomatic approach work. When data do not conform to the axioms laid down by representationalists, one must either choose ad hoc solutions, or formulate the model probabilistically. In the latter case, realist metaphysics have to be introduced, and one ends up with a structure that is almost indistinguishable from a latent variable model.

4.2 Three perspectives on measurement scales

Representational measurement theory is aimed at specifying the conditions necessary for the construction of an adequate representation of empirical relations in a numerical system. From a formal perspective, this is conceptualized in terms of a mapping of one set of relations into another. The resulting representation is considered adequate if it preserves the observed, empirical relations. Semantically, the interpretation of the measurement process is in terms of a reconstruction of the measurement process. For example, numerical operations are conceptualized as corresponding to empirical operations, even though no scientist ever carried out these operations in the manner described by the theory. From an ontological perspective, scales cannot be considered anything but a construction. It could, of course, be held that these scales have referents in reality, for example objective magnitudes. However, such a realist interpretation, if endorsed, is external to the model, in contrast to the inherent realism in latent variables analysis.

4.2.1 The formal stance

Syntax Representational measurement theory constructs measurement as the mapping of objects and relations between objects from an empirical domain into a numerical domain. Both are characterized in terms of set theory (Scott and Suppes, 1958; Suppes and Zinnes, 1963). We imagine a set of objects, which is is denoted A, and a set of n relations holding between these objects, denoted $R_1, R_2, \ldots, R_n$. A relation between objects may, for example, be one of dominance between objects (e.g., John is larger than Jane), between objects and stimuli (e.g., John 'dominated' an IQ-test item by solving it), or between stimuli (e.g. item 1 is more difficult than item 2). It may also be one of proximity or similarity (e.g., John's political orientation is more similar to Jane's than to Peter's), which may again be considered in terms of similarity between objects, between stimuli, or between objects and stimuli (Coombs, 1964). Still other relations may be based on preference orderings, as is common in subjective expected utility theory.

Whatever the precise nature of the relations is taken to be, they are always taken to be purely qualitative (representationalism takes 'larger than' to be a qualitative comparison). Often, there is some operation that can be interpreted as 'combining' two objects to create a new one. This combining operation is denoted $\oplus$. Sometimes this operation is empirical, such as laying two rods end-to-end to create a new one, and in this case we speak of extensive measurement. Such an empirical operation of combining is known as a concatenation operation. Campbell (1920) believed that fundamental measurement must be extensive, that is, there must exist an empirical concatenation operation, and treated all other measurement as 'derived' from these fundamental measures. However, this position was severely criticized by Rozeboom (1966b) and it was later shown that there are cases where representational measurement works without there being an empirical concatenation operation (Luce and Tukey, 1964; Krantz, Luce, Suppes, and Tversky, 1971).

Taken together, the set of objects, the relation between them, and the combining operation form what is called an empirical relational system which we will call $\mathcal{O}$, which may be read as a shorthand for 'observed'. This system is denoted as $\mathcal{O} = \langle A, R, \oplus \rangle$. Now it is the business of representationalism to construct, entirely on the basis of the observed relations between objects in the set and the combinations of these objects, a numerical representation which preserves the information in the empirical system. This basically comes down to assigning to each object in A a number from some numerical domain N, to find a mathematical relation S that represents the empirical relation $\mathcal{R}$, and to find a mathematical operation $\star$ that matches the combining operation $\oplus$. The resulting representational system, call it $\mathcal{R}$, a shorthand for 'representation', is then denoted $\mathcal{R} = \langle N, S, \star \rangle$. Because the representation preserves all the information that was present in the empirical system, the relation between these systems is one of homomorphism (it is not isomorphic because more than one of the elements in the empirical system may map to the same number in the representational system). The combination of $\mathcal{O}$ and $\mathcal{R}$ is called a measurement structure. Measurement, in the representationalist view, is thus essentially a homomorphic representation of objects and relations between them in a numerical system.

Representational measurement is called axiomatic, because its main theoretical strategy is (1) to specify certain axioms with respect to objects and relations between them, (2) to prove mathematically that, given these relations, a homomorphic representation is possible (this is done in a *representation* theorem), and (3) to show under which transformations of the scale values this homomorphism is preserved (this is done in a *uniqueness* theorem). The latter proof characterizes the transformations of the assigned scale values under which the representation is preserved. Uniqueness results form the basis for the well-known 'levels of measurement' introduced by Stevens (1946). If the structure of the representation is invariant up to all one-one transformations, we have a nominal scale; if it is invariant up to all monotonic transformations, we have an ordinal scale; if it is invariant up to all linear transformations, we have an interval scale; and if it is invariant up to all affine transformations, we have a ratio scale. These four scale types do not exhaust the possible scale types (Krantz, Luce, Suppes, and Tversky, 1971), but will do for the present exposition.

Semantics The semantics of representationalism vary somewhat depending on whether one considers extensive measurement, for which a concatenation operation exists, or other forms of measurement. In the extensive case, the semantics can be based on a rather concrete connection of the measurement process and the manipulation of the assigned numbers through the concatenation operation, which is itself mapped into a numerical operation. In cases of measurement that are not characterized by concatenation, the semantics of the theory are limited to representation itself. Here, the discussion will be limited to extensive measurement and one particularly important nonextensive case, namely additive conjoint measurement.

Extensive measurement The semantics of representationalism, and especially of extensive fundamental measurement as envisioned by Campbell (1920), are exquisite. The typical example for which the construction of representational scales is illustrative is the measurement of length. In this case, one may consider a set of objects, say, people, to form the set A. Further, a qualitative relation can be constructed as 'not noticeably longer than', denoted by $\preceq$, where 'Jane $\preceq$ John' means 'Jane is not noticeably longer than John'. Finally, a concatenation operation $\oplus$ is available, namely we can lay Jane and John head-to-feet and compare the resulting combined entity, 'Jane$\oplus$John' to other people, or concatenations of other people, in the set. This gives the empirical relational system $\mathcal{O} = \langle A, \preceq, \oplus \rangle$. Now, we can map the relations in the empirical relational system into a numerical system in such a manner that all relations, holding between the objects in the empirical set, continue to hold between the numbers representing these objects. So, if Jane is is not noticeably longer than John, then the number representing Jane must be smaller than or equal to the number representing John. We can, as is usual among representational measurement theorists as well as carpenters, construct the representation in the set of positive real numbers, Re+, so that each person is represented by a number in this set. A common way to do this is by comparing an object to a unit of measurement, such as a centimetre, by counting the number of units that must be concatenated in order to match the object. This is done through the construction of a so-called standard sequence of equal intervals (Krantz, Luce, Suppes, and Tversky, 1971). A ruler with centimetre marks is an instantiation of such a standard sequence.

Next, we choose the empirical relation $\preceq$ to be represented by the numerical relation $\leq$, and the concatenation operation $\oplus$ by the numerical operation $+$. Suppose that John is assigned the value $\phi(\text{John}) = 1.85$ in the metre scale, and Jane the value $\phi(\text{Jane}) = 1.75$, so that $\phi(\text{Jane}) \leq \phi(\text{John})$. Now a comparison between John and Jane, with the unaided eye, will reveal that Jane is not noticeably longer than John, i.e., Jane$\preceq$John. So, it is indeed the case that $\leq$ does a good job of representing $\preceq$. The representation will hold for all people $a, b, \ldots$ in the set A, and the technical way of expressing this is to say that $a \preceq b$ if and only if $\phi(a) \leq \phi(b)$. Also, we will find that the value assigned to the combined object Jane$\oplus$John will be $\phi(\text{Jane} \oplus \text{John}) = 3.60$, which is equal to $\phi(\text{Jane}) + \phi(\text{John}) = 1.75 + 1.85 = 3.60$. The representation of $\oplus$ by $+$ is therefore also adequate. It can furthermore be shown that the representation preserves all relevant relations in the empirical system, such as transitivity (if Jane$\preceq$John, and John$\preceq$Peter, then Jane$\preceq$Peter).

Thus, the mappings of the objects in A into numbers in Re^+, of $\preceq$ into $\leq$, and of $\oplus$ into $+$ have succeeded. Moreover, it can be proven that the scale is invariant up to the choice for a unit of measurement (this is to say that it does not matter whether we express someone's height in centimetres or in metres, as long as we do this consistently). Thus, the scale is insensitive to transformations of the form $\phi'(a) = c\phi(a)$, where $\phi(a)$ is the original scale value, c represents a change in unit of measurement, and $\phi'(a)$ is the resulting transformed value. This means that, if John and Jane are measured in centimetres rather than metres (so that $c = 100$), all relations will continue to hold. For example, $\phi'(\text{Jane}) + \phi'(\text{John}) = 175 + 185 = 360$ will continue to match $\phi'(\text{Jane} \oplus \text{John}) = 360$. However, if we use a centimetre instead of a metre *and* give each measured object a bonus length of 100 centimetres (so that we are in fact performing a linear transformation of the form $\phi''(a) = 100 \times \phi(a) + 100$), the mapping is destroyed. For now we would get, for Jane separately, $\phi''(\text{Jane}) = 100 \times 1.75 + 100 = 275$, and, for John separately, $\phi''(\text{John}) = 100 \times 1.85 + 100 = 285$. So, the sum of their scale values equals 560. But the concatenated object Jane $\oplus$ John, when measured with this bonus centimetre, would receive a scale value of $\phi''(\text{Jane} \oplus \text{John}) = 100 \times \phi(\text{Jane} \oplus \text{John}) + 100 = 360 + 100 = 460$. Thus, the mathematical operation $+$ ceases to be an adequate representation of the empirical operation $\oplus$. The scale values may be multiplied, but not translated, because this destroys the homomorphism between the empirical and numerical systems. This is one way of saying that the measurement of length is on a ratio scale.

Campbell (1920) held that measures that are extensive are the only genuine cases of fundamental measurement. However, Michell (2000; 2001) has noted the interesting fact that the German mathematician Hölder had already shown in 1901 that Campbell's demands were overly restrictive; he had axiomatically proven that distance was quantitative without invoking a concatenation operation. Campbell and his contemporaries were apparently unaware of Hölder's work (Michell, 2001), and fervently defended the thesis that measurement without concatenation was not really measurement at all. This was the basis of the critique of the commission installed by the British Association for the Advancement of Science; for in psychology, it is generally difficult to identify an empirical concatenation operation. What this would require is something like the following. Suppose that I were to administer an intelligence test to a number of people (objects). Suppose further that John scores 100, and Jane scores 120. Now if I could concatenate (combine) the objects (Jane and John) in a suitable way, and this combination were shown to produce a score of $100 + 120 = 220$, and if this were true not only for John and Jane but for all combinations of people, then I would have shown that an empirical concatenation operation exists and matches the numerical operation of addition. In psychology, such concatenation operations are usually unavailable. For this reason, the hardliners in the committee stood by their opinion that psychological measurement is impossible.

Additive conjoint measurement Although the viewpoints of the commission of the British Association for the Advancement of Science were, at the very least, overly restrictive, the discussion of psychological measurement that followed the publication of the commission's report was instrumental in the development of measurement theory. In fact, the mathematical psychologists who took up the challenge ended up with a formalization of measurement that was far more powerful than Campbell's own, and has perhaps even been more important for physics than for psychology. The response of psychologists started with the explicit articulation of representationalism by Stevens (1946). Stevens' representationalism leaned heavily towards operationalism, because he defined measurement as 'the assignment of numerals according to rule', where the nature of the rule involved is left unspecified, and Stevens was quite clear that this can be any rule. So, in Stevens' version, measurement occurs more or less by fiat; consequently, it is meaningless to ask whether something is 'really' being measured, because the fact that numerals are assigned according to rule is the sole defining feature of measurement. There is neither a need nor a place for postulating attributes which are prior to the measurement operation, as is explicitly done in latent variable theory. Representationalism, as it developed in the work of Krantz, Luce, Suppes, and Tversky (1971), followed Stevens in dropping the concatenation operation, and also retained the idea that measurement theory is a theory about numerical assignments. However, not any rule of assignment will do, because the assignment rule used must preserve the empirical relations as laid down in the empirical relational system.

The broadening of the semantics associated with representationalism, which was a direct result of dropping the demand for empirical concatenation operations, provided an opening for constructing psychological measurement systems. For in this more liberal approach, measurement does no longer require the representation of concrete empirical *operations*; any representation that mirrors empirical *relations* will do, if it complies with the demand that it forms a homomorphic representation. This follows directly from Stevens' move, which for a large part consisted in drawing attention away from the manner in which measurements are obtained (i.e., through concatenation), and towards their relations-preserving character. It also avoids the pitfall of degrading into operationalism, however, because it is possible that the empirical relations between objects are determined in different ways for different parts of the system. This is important, for while it may be possible to concatenate rigid rods of manageable length, it is arguably difficult to concatenate objects to match interstellar distances, or to place Jupiter on a balance scale. Still, my encyclopedia mentions the fact that the average distance between the earth and the sun is about 149,597,890 kilometres, and that the mass of Jupiter is approximately 1.967×10^{27} kilograms; and I strongly suspect that the writers of my encyclopedia mean these statements to refer to qualitatively the same dimensions as, say, the distance between my cup of coffee and my telephone, and the mass of the computer I am now working on. In the rigid version of measurement theory, which leads directly to Bridgman's (1927) operationalism, these interpretations are not warranted; but in the more liberal representationalist interpretation, they are. Moreover, any imaginable structure that allows for a homomorphic representation can be subsumed under the general category of measurement. This includes structures observed in psychological measurement.

The class of structures most important to the present discussion is the class of additive conjoint structures (Luce and Tukey, 1964; Krantz, Luce, Suppes, and Tversky, 1971; Narens and Luce, 1986). Additive conjoint structures pertain to relations between at least three variables. Two of these variables are considered 'independent' variables and one is 'dependent'. The meaning of these terms is similar to that used in analysis of variance. The measurement relation is then defined on all three variables simultaneously. Call the independent variables A and B, and the dependent variable Y; their levels are denoted a, b, and y, respectively. What is represented in conjoint measurement is the Cartesian product $A \times B$, which consists of all ordered pairs (a, b), and the relation that is mapped in $\geq$ is the effect of these combinations on the dependent variable Y. Denote the levels of the independent variable A by i, j, k and the levels of the independent variable B by l, m, n. The idea is that, if the joint effect of (a_i, b_l) exceeds that of (a_j, b_m), so that $(a_i, b_l) \succeq (a_j, b_m)$, where $\succeq$ again is a qualitative relation and not a quantitative one, then the combination (a_i, b_l) must be assigned a higher number than the combination (a_j, b_m). The process of quantification (i.e., representing qualitative relations in the real numbers) now applies to all three variables simultaneously, but it does not require an empirical concatenation operation. What happens is that the variables A, B, and Y are scaled at once through a quantitative representation of the trade-off between A

and B in producing Y (Narens and Luce, 1986). The representation theorem for conjoint measurement axiomatically states the conditions under which this can be done. If these conditions are satisfied, then mappings f and g of the independent variables A and B into the real numbers can be found so that $(a_i, b_l) \succeq (a_j, b_m)$ if and only if $f(a_i) + g(b_l) \geq f(a_j) + g(b_m)$. The representational structure for the Cartesian product terms (a, b) is for any combination of levels i of A and l of B then given by $\phi(a_i, b_l) = f(a_i) + g(b_l)$. The representation is on an interval scale, because it is unique up to linear transformations of the assigned scale values.

It is important to consider why conjoint measurement gives an interval scale, i.e., what the meaning of the measurement unit is. This comes down to the question what it is, exactly, that is being measured. Basically, what is represented in the model is a trade-off. The meaning of the measurement unit is in terms of this trade-off. For instance, suppose that we have a given combination (a_i, b_l), and increase the level of A from a_i to a_j, thereby constructing a new combination (a_j, b_l) that is $\succ$ to the original one. The conjoint model then says by how many units the factor B has to be decreased in order to produce a new combination (a_j, b_k) that is not noticeably different from (i.e., that is both $\succeq$ and $\preceq$ to) the original combination (a_i, b_l). Thus, the model states how effects resulting from variations in A can be undone by variations in B, and vice versa. The measurement unit is explicitly defined in terms of this trade-off. The reason for this is that any two distances $a_i - a_j$ and $a_j - a_k$ on the factor A are defined to be equal to each other if they can be matched to the same distance $b_l - b_k$ on the factor B. The measurement unit on the factor A is thus defined as the change in A necessary to match an arbitrary change on the factor B, and the measurement unit on the factor B is defined as the change in B necessary to match an arbitrary change in the factor A. This is the reason why it is crucial to have two factors; one cannot define a unit of measurement on one factor without reference to the other. Because the method does not match levels in A by levels in B, but rather differences between levels of A by differences in levels of B, it can be expected to yield an interval scale. This is formally the case because the representation is invariant up to linear transformations of the assigned scale values. Additive conjoint measurement represents the variables on interval scales with a common unit.

4.2.2 The empirical stance

Representational measurement is, as has been stated before, concerned with formulating the conditions that must be fulfilled in order to be able to construct a representation. These conditions, which are formulated as axioms, thus describe the relations that must hold in the data at hand for a representation to be possible. They are of an empirical nature; in Krantz, Luce, Suppes, and Tversky (1971) they are even called empirical laws. For extensive measurement, the axioms involved are rather simple (see Narens and Luce, 1986, for a lucid description). For conjoint measurement, they are more complicated. Basically, if one knew a priori that the effects of the independent variables were additive, there would be no need for the specification of the axioms involved, and an additive representation could be readily constructed. The strategy of representationalism, however, is not to posit variables and relations between them in reality and to look at whether the data structure is more or less consistent with these (i.e., the model fitting approach as used in latent variable modelling). It always starts with the data, never with the metaphysics. So, the axioms of conjoint measurement describe characteristics that the data must exhibit for us to be able to *construct* an additive representation. Several of such axiom systems exist; here I follow the system proposed by Luce and Tukey (1964).

As is common in fundamental measurement theory, the point of departure is a set of purely qualitative relations. In the case of conjoint measurement the elements on which these relations are defined are the combinations (a, b). These combinations are assumed to be ordered. This ordering is in a sense 'induced' by Y. For example, suppose that a subject must judge, for a tone generated by a given combination (a, b) of intensity (A) and frequency (B) whether its loudness (Y) noticeably exceeds ($\succeq$) that of a tone generated by a different combination. The first axiom of conjoint measurement states that the ordering so produced must be a weak order. A weak order is an order that is transitive and connected. Transitivity means that for each combination of levels i, j, k of A and l, m, n of B, if $(a_i, b_l) \succeq (a_j, b_m)$ and $(a_j, b_m) \succeq (a_k, b_n)$, then $(a_i, b_l) \succeq (a_k, b_n)$. Connectedness means that each comparison is made, and for all comparisons either $(a_i, b_l) \succeq (a_j, b_m)$, or $(a_j, b_m) \succeq (a_i, b_l)$, or both. Two combinations (a_i, b_l) and (a_j, b_m) are $\sim$ to each other (not noticeably different) if both $(a_i, b_l) \succeq (a_j, b_m)$ and $(a_j, b_m) \succeq (a_i, b_l)$ hold.

The second axiom is called solvability. Consider the combinations (a_i, b_l) and (a_j, b_m). In these combinations we have the terms a_i, b_l, a_j, and b_m. Suppose we leave the position taken by the term a_i blank, so that we have $(\cdot, b_l)$ and (a_j, b_m). The solvability axiom states that, regardless of the choice of levels b_l, a_j, and b_m, it is always possible to fill up this blank spot with a level a_i of A such that $(a_i, b_l) \sim (a_j, b_m)$. In general, for any combination of three entries, a fourth must exist that makes the two combinations $\sim$ to each other. For instance, suppose that we have selected a given frequency and amplitude for one tone, but we have only selected a frequency for a second. Then it must always be possible to select an amplitude for this second tone that yields a tone that is not noticeably different from the first in its subjective loudness. This requires that both factors are sufficiently dense that a solution of the equations always exists.

The third axiom is the axiom of double cancellation. This axiom tests a consequence of additivity. In order to explain it, it is useful to first consider a property called independence. This is is not strictly taken to be an axiom, because it is a consequence of the other axioms, but a discussion is useful because it brings out the similarity between additive conjoint measurement and the Rasch model, where the independence condition is also important (it is similar to what Rasch (1960) called parameter separability).

Independence means that the ordering of the levels in A, which is induced by the ordering in Y, must be unaffected by which particular value of B is chosen to assess this ordering; the converse must also hold. So, if we assess the ordering of perceived loudness as produced by varying levels of intensity, we have to do this while holding the frequency of the presented tones constant. The independence condition says that it must not make a difference for the ordering whether we set the frequency at 100Hz or at 1000Hz. Higher intensities must in either case produce either an unnoticeable difference or a higher perceived loudness. This means that, if there is an interaction effect of the independent variables, no additive conjoint measurement representation can be formed. However, the restriction this poses is less serious than it may seem. This is because the original observations on the Y variable are assumed to be merely ordinal. Thus, any monotonic, order-preserving transformation on these observations is permissible. The restriction posed is therefore relatively mild: there must exist a monotonic transformation of the dependent variable that renders the effects of the independent variables additive. It is possible to remove a wide class of interaction effects by transforming the dependent variable. A real problem occurs, however, in the presence of disordinal interactions, i.e., when effects 'cross'. This would be the case, for example, if for tones with a frequency below 1000Hz a higher amplitude would produce a higher perceived loudness, but for tones with a frequency above 1000Hz, a higher amplitude would produce a lower perceived loudness. If this happens, the very ordering on A, as induced by the ordering on Y, depends on the selected level of B, and no additive representation will be possible.

The independence condition allows for the independent ordering of the factors A and B in terms of increasing values of Y. On the basis of this

Table 4.1. *The combinations (a, b) are ascending both in rows (left to right) and columns (top to bottom).*

		Factor A		
		1	2	3
Factor B	1	(a_1, b_1)	(a_2, b_1)	(a_3, b_1)
	2	(a_1, b_2)	(a_2, b_2)	(a_3, b_2)
	3	(a_1, b_3)	(a_2, b_3)	(a_3, b_3)

ordering, we can represent the structure in a table like table 4.1, which contains three levels for each factor. Factor A is represented as increasing in Y from left to right; factor B is represented as increasing from top to bottom. The entries in the table are the (monotonically transformed) values y as corresponding to each combination (a, b). Because of the independence condition, the entries are increasing both in the rows and in the columns of the table.

Now we can discuss the third axiom of conjoint measurement, which is the double cancellation axiom. It refers to relations between the diagonals of the table. Double cancellation is a consequence of additivity. Additivity requires that any entry (a, b) can be represented by the additive function $f(a) + g(b)$. Therefore, an entry, say, (a_2, b_1), must be $\succeq$ (yield a greater amount of Y) to another entry, say, (a_1, b_2), if and only if $f(a_2) + g(b_1) \geq f(a_1) + g(b_2)$. Suppose that this is the case, and that it is also the case that $(a_3, b_2) \succeq (a_2, b_3)$. Then we have the two inequalities

$$f(a_2) + g(b_1) \geq f(a_1) + g(b_2) \tag{4.1}$$

and

$$f(a_3) + g(b_2) \geq f(a_2) + g(b_3). \tag{4.2}$$

It follows that

$$f(a_2) + g(b_1) + f(a_3) + g(b_2) \geq f(a_1) + g(b_2) + f(a_2) + g(b_3), \tag{4.3}$$

which reduces to

$$f(a_3) + g(b_1) \geq f(a_1) + g(b_3). \tag{4.4}$$

Thus, additivity implies that, if $(a_2, b_1) \succeq (a_1, b_2)$ and $(a_3, b_2) \succeq (a_2, b_3)$, then it must be the case that $(a_3, b_1) \succeq (a_1, b_3)$. This hypothesis, which can be directly tested, is the condition of double cancellation ('cancellation', because of the terms cancelling out in the last step of the derivation, and 'double' because there are two antecedent inequalities). The double cancellation axiom must hold for all 3 × 3 submatrices of the larger matrix defined over all levels of A and B.

Given these conditions, we can choose an arbitrary change in A, say $a_i - a_j$. This defines the unit of measurement for B: any change in B that can 'undo' the effect of the chosen change in A is considered 'equally large'. Then we can pick one of the changes in B that has this property, say $b_k - b_l$, and define the unit of measurement on A as any change in A that can 'undo' the effect of this change in B. This allows for the construction of an infinite sequence of pairs (a_p, b_p), $p = 0, \pm 1, \pm 2, \ldots$, where each next pair goes one unit up (down) in A and one unit down (up) in B. This sequence fulfils the role of a ruler; it is a standard sequence. Because of the way the units are defined, the sequence has the property that it is always true that (a_q, b_r) is not noticeably different from (a_s, b_t) whenever $q + r = s + t$, where q, r, s, t are arbitrary integers. If one goes two units 'up' in A and two units 'up' in B, then this is equivalent to going five units 'up' in A and one unit 'down' in B, and to going three units 'up' in A and one unit 'up' in B, etc. The final axiom needed is related to this standard sequence and called the Archimedean axiom. The Archimedean axiom says that for every combination (a_i, b_l) there exists integers p and q so that $(a_p, b_p) \succeq (a_i, b_l) \succeq (a_q, b_q)$. This ensures that no combinations of A and B are so small or large that they are 'off the scale'.

Standing these axioms, one can prove that an additive representation of the empirical relations exists, and that it is unique up to linear transformations. Conjoint measurement thus constructs a mapping of an empirical relational system $\mathcal{O} = \langle A \times B, \succeq \rangle$ into $\mathcal{R} = \langle \text{Re}, \geq \rangle$ without invoking a concatenation operation, as is reflected by the omission of $\oplus$ in the notation. However, as Luce and Tukey (1964) show, within conjoint measurement there is an analogue to the concatenation operation as it figures in extensive measurement. Suppose we move from (a_i, b_l) to (a_j, b_m) and record the resulting difference $\phi(a_j, b_m) - \phi(a_i, b_l)$. Subsequently, we move from (a_j, b_m) to (a_k, b_n), and again record the difference $\phi(a_k, b_n) - \phi(a_j, b_m)$. If we now move directly from (a_i, b_l) to (a_k, b_n), the model implies that the resulting difference in scale values for these combinations will equal the sum of the preceding differences: $\phi(a_k, b_n) - \phi(a_i, b_l) = (\phi(a_j, b_m) - \phi(a_i, b_l)) + (\phi(a_k, b_n) - \phi(a_j, b_m))$. In a sense, we have laid the difference between (a_i, b_l) and (a_j, b_m) and the difference between (a_j, b_m) and (a_k, b_n) 'end to end', and this 'concatenation' of differences produces the same result as the direct shift from (a_i, b_l) to (a_k, b_n). Thus, although there is no concrete concatenation, something closely resembling it is implicitly present in the model. However, the operation cannot be said to be represented in the way this can be said of extensive measurement, because it is not a concrete, observable, operation.

The invention of conjoint measurement is, without a doubt, one of the most important theoretical contributions in the history of psychology. It shows that fundamental measurement does not require a concrete concatenation operation, and in doing so provides a justification for psychological measurement that could never have been produced within Campbell's traditional account. It provides psychology with at least the theoretical possibility of a system for measurement that is on equal footing with the ones in physics. For the way subjective loudness could be measured and quantified is exactly the same way in which density can be measured and quantified. The representationalists thus showed that the conclusion reached by the commission installed by the British Association for the Advancement of Science was false: fundamental measurement is, in principle, possible in psychology.

4.2.3 The ontological stance

Representationalism itself explicitly suggests the appropriate ontological status for its central concept, the measurement scale. The proofs in representational measurement theory are aimed at delineating the conditions that must hold in the data so that it is, in principle, possible to *construct* a representation. The theory does not presuppose more than the existence of very basic, qualitative empirical relations; representations are not assumed to exist independently of the researcher, but are rather the product of his efforts in scale construction. Representationalism does not posit hypothetical latent structures, variables, or processes, and scales are not supposed to play causal roles in the data generating process. Also, in contrast to the reasoning based on the hypothesis that a model is true, which is so common in latent variables analysis, the representationalist does not hypothesize the 'truth' of the representation – if this is a well-formed sentence at all – but derives the possibility of constructing one from the fact that empirical axioms are satisfied. There is no reason to suppose that the ontological status of measurement scales should involve realist metaphysics.

The theory thus shows how one can start by observing relations between objects with the unaided eye, and then build up theoretical terms like 'length', 'distance', or 'subjective loudness' from these relations. Thus, scales are explicitly taken to be constructions. This suggests that representationalism is an implementation of a constructivist philosophy. In particular, it is consistent with the basic tenets of logical positivism, which held that theoretical terms are related to observations by so-called correspondence rules. While the model does not preclude the possibility that there exist objective magnitudes that correspond to such scales

(Michell, 1997), it does not require one to endorse such a position; in fact, it will be argued that representationalism and realism do not sit well together. This is illustrated by the fact that representational measurement theory has problems in dealing with measurement error. Attempts to formulate what error is and how it can be dealt with require extending the model with metaphysical assumptions; doing this, however, precludes a constructivist interpretation as well as a strict reading of the central tenets of the theory and, at least in one case, leads to the latent variable model.

Logical positivism and representationalism
The logical positivists thought that a scientific theory could be divided in two languages: an observation language and a theoretical language (Carnap, 1936; Suppe, 1977). The observation language was considered to contain statements about observable objects, properties, and relations. The theoretical language, in contrast, consisted of statements that involved abstract, not directly observable objects, properties, and relations. The terms that figured in the theoretical language were considered to be anchored in the observation language. The coordination between theoretical terms and observational terms was handled by correspondence rules (Carnap, 1956). These rules specified how a sentence which involved theoretical terms could be translated into a sentence which only contained observation terms; the latter could then be verified without problems, or so the logical positivists thought, and if all the observation sentences implied by the theory were verified, then the theory was confirmed. Thus, the logical positivists imagined that there could be a kind of dictionary, which for any sentence involving theoretical concepts (say, 'neuroticism is negatively related to extraversion') gives a sentence involving only observables (say, 'In the past week, John has not attended a party, and was repeatedly observed while sitting quietly in his room with a book') by considering the appropriate correspondence rules ('more neurotic people are more often observed while reading books, and less often while attending parties'). Theoretical terms, like 'neuroticism', were not taken to refer to structures in reality, but rather to be purely theoretical terms partially defined by observation sentences through correspondence rules.

It appears that representationalism attempts to do something similar. The empirical relations, that figure in the empirical relational system, are assumed to be noticeable. It does not take a lot of imagination to see a parallel between the noticeable empirical relations mentioned in representationalism, and the observation sentences of logical positivism. Carnap (1956, p. 41) says that 'the terms of V_0 [the observational vocabulary] are predicates designating observable properties of events of things (e.g., "blue", "hot", "large", etc.) or observable relations between them (e.g., "x is warmer than y", "x is contiguous to y", etc.)'. The 'etc.' is surely meant to include such direct comparisons as 'a is longer than b' and '(a_i, b_l) is subjectively louder than (a_j, b_m)'. Thus, in a logical positivist interpretation, the empirical relational system that consists of noticeable relations of the form $(a_i, b_l) \succeq (a_j, b_m)$ could, without problems, be considered to make up (part of) the observation language in a scientific theory.

Sentences that involve measurement scales, rather than concrete observations, are of a theoretical character. As Carnap (1956, p. 44) states, 'the domain D [of theoretical entities figuring in the theoretical language] contains space–time points and regions, physical magnitudes and their values, physical systems and their states'. Mathematically specified laws that involve measurement scales, like Newton's $f = m \times a$, which says that the force an object exerts is a multiplicative function of its mass and acceleration, are the kind of sentences that, for the logical positivists, belonged to the theoretical language. Sentences of the type '$\phi(a, b) = f(a) + g(b)$', which may for example say that subjective loudness is an additive function of frequency and intensity, specify similar abstract invariance relations between measurement scales. They could, without much hesitation, be considered to make up (part of) the theoretical language in a logical positivist scheme of thinking.

Finally, the logical positivist idea of scientific theories requires a set of correspondence rules. There are several ways of constructing such rules (Suppe, 1977), but their function is always to relate theoretical statements to observation statements. Carnap (1956, p. 46): 'these rules must be such that they connect sentences of L_O [the observation language] with sentences of L_T [the theoretical language], by making a derivation in one or the other direction possible'. In our present scheme of thinking, correspondence rules ought to relate sentences of the type '$(a_i, b_l) \succeq (a_j, b_m)$' to sentences of the type '$\phi(a, b) = f(a) + g(b)$', and must moreover allow derivations of the former on the basis of the latter. It is clear that representationalism has such rules. They are, in essence, what the entire theory is about: the truth of sentences of the form '$(a_i, b_l) \succeq (a_j, b_m)$ if and only if $f(a_i) + g(b_l) \geq f(a_j) + g(b_m)$' is precisely what representation theorems are supposed to prove.

Interpreted in this way, representation theorems prove nothing less than that correspondence rules are available for the entire set of objects covered by the measurement structure. If this is the case, then it is possible to shift back and forth between the empirical and numerical relational systems; one can observe certain structures in one part of the domain, and then use the mathematics to derive what should be the case in another part of the domain. This allows for a very specific and powerful generalization of one part of a structure to another part of that structure. This is reminiscent not only of positivist thinking (Carnap, 1936), but also of instrumentalism (Toulmin, 1953), which held that this is precisely the function of laws; they license inference to as yet unobserved data.

It is clear that representationalism is fully consistent with logical positivist ideas on the relations between theory and observation. In fact, representational measurement theory does exactly what the logical positivists attempted to do. It shows how theoretical concepts, namely measurement scales, can be constructed on the basis of relations that the logical positivists, without a doubt, would have relegated to the observation language. It is also clear that, when one follows this line of reasoning, there is no need to invoke metaphysics that go beyond the observable relations. Specifically, there is no need to invoke structures in reality that directly correspond to the constructed scales. Perhaps, one *could* hold the view that 'length', as a theoretical dimension in science, exists independently of the measurement scale constructed on the qualitative relations 'not noticeably longer than', and still adhere to representationalism. But that would surely be to invoke excess metaphysics, in the sense that the existence of 'objective magnitudes' (Michell, 1997), latent dimensions, or whatever one takes to correspond to scales, is not postulated or even required by representational measurement theory. It would moreover seem that such an assumption, while perhaps not in contradiction with representationalism, is not at all in the spirit of the theory.

Logical positivism encountered great problems that eventually led to its abandonment (Suppe, 1977). One of the main difficulties was its reluctance to introduce metaphysical assumptions that go beyond the observations. As Popper (1959) observed, scientific theories posit the existence of all kinds of theoretical entities, structures, and processes; and in this sense they go beyond observations in a perfectly natural and defensible manner. Thus, at a semantic level, the introduction of metaphysics is rather common in science. In fact, a scientist cannot do without it. It can be expected that, since representationalism implements a positivist doctrine on the relation between observation and theory, it is vulnerable to criticisms of a similar nature as those that eventually proved fatal to logical positivism. It is argued in the following sections that this is indeed the case. In a strict logical positivist interpretation, representationalism cannot give a satisfactory definition of measurement; if it gave sufficient conditions, then it would include absurd cases, and if it gave necessary conditions, then many recognized cases of measurement would not be covered by the theory since it has problems in dealing with error. Both of these issues are traced to the reluctance in introducing metaphysical assumptions. Also, it is argued that the introduction of such realist metaphysics leads naturally to some form of the latent variable model.

Representation and measurement
The problem with the view that representationalism gives a definition of measurement concerns its central tenet, namely that measurement is essentially about representation. While there is a nontrivial sense in which this is true, namely, we do aim to construct a numerical system that reflects certain systematic relations in the world, there is also a nontrivial sense in which it is false. The sense in which it is false is that measurement is not exclusively representational. In particular, the fact that a representation can be constructed cannot be a sufficient condition in any sensible definition of measurement.

This is evident from the fact that we can construct situations where we have homomorphic representations which are not measurements in any meaningful sense of the word. Consider, for example, the Guttman model, which is a deterministic item response model to which the axiomatic theory applies. The Guttman model is generally seen as a deterministic model for ordinal measurement. It says that when one's position on a latent variable exceeds a certain threshold, one gives item response $X = 1$ with probability $P(X = 1) = 1$. In an intelligence context, for example, this would mean that if John's intelligence exceeds the threshold value for the item '1, 2, 3, 5, 8, ...', then he cannot give the wrong response. However, the mathematical requirements of the model by themselves do not warrant this interpretation. To see this, consider the following four items:

1. I have parents (yes: 1, no: 0)
2. I have no beard (yes: 1, no: 0)
3. I menstruate (yes: 1, no: 0)
4. I have given birth to children (yes: 1, no: 0)

Suppose that we administered these items to a group of people. Obviously, we would get a triangulated structure that looks as follows:

Item 1	Item 2	Item 3	Item 4	Sumscore
1	0	0	0	1
1	1	0	0	2
1	1	1	0	3
1	1	1	1	4

This triangulated structure is a necessary and sufficient condition for constructing a Guttman scale. The reason that we get this structure, of course, is simply that we have constructed inclusive subclasses of people. People with sumscore 1 are men with a beard; people with sumscore 2 are non-menstruating women and men without a beard, people with sumscore 3 are women without children, and people with sumscore 4 are women with children. Now, if measurement were nothing more than homomorphic representation of empirically observed relations, and the Guttman model produces an ordinal scale, then we would be forced to conclude that we have ordinally measured something here. This does not seem to be the case. However, the example surely provides a case of homomorphic representation. Therefore, representation and measurement are not the same. That a representation can be constructed is not a sufficient condition for obtaining measurements.

This argument uses a variant of underdetermination. Although a situation where a set of items depends deterministically on a latent attribute will give rise to a triangulated structure as required by the Guttman scale, there are many other ways of obtaining such a structure; the above example gives one of the more absurd cases. No doubt, the data structures required by additive conjoint measurement suffer from underdetermination too. Although a situation where two psychological factors combine additively into a third will give rise to data that satisfy the axioms of conjoint measurement, there are without a doubt many other ways of obtaining such data. The satisfaction of axioms implied by additivity at the level of data does not guarantee that the data-generation process is of an additive nature; perhaps thousands of interacting factors are responsible for the apparently additive effects, rather than two. It seems that, in order to speak of measurement, more is needed than the satisfaction of axioms and the construction of a homomorphism. What matters is not just the structure of data, but also the question how these data originated. The relations in the data must not only exist, they must exist because of the right reasons.

What are these reasons? To answer this question, it is elucidating to go back all the way to the beginning. Consider the measurement of length according to the representationalist view. Rods of are subjected to a pairwise comparison, and each time one of them is judged longer than the other, or they are judged equally long. Representationalism takes the possibility of doing this as given, and departs from the ordering so induced. But how did this ordering itself originate? How did the judge decide which stick is longer? Does that matter?

Of course it matters. Implicit in the length measurement story is an assumption every reader will grant: people are capable of performing the relevant judgments with the naked eye. They can 'see' differences in length. Differences in length are 'observable'. They are unproblematic.

However, this is exactly the reason that the story works. It is not just the ordering of sticks according to some judge that leads to the conclusion that we are measuring length. It is not merely the fact that a nice set of axioms has been satisfied that leads us to this conclusion. Crucial is the fact that the empirical relational system has the right causal antecedents: the relations recorded in the system are causally dependent on the structure of the world. In particular, they arise because there *are* differences in length between objects, and the human perceptual system is *sensitive* to these differences, so that the differences in the judgments of the observer are *causally dependent* on real differences in length. Thus, lurking behind the word 'noticeable' is a deep metaphysical assumption about the structure of the world and how that structure determines empirically observable relations. Representationalism does not articulate this assumption in its formal structure, nor does it demand its truth. This is what the theory misses, and this is the reason it cannot give sufficient conditions for measurement without being supplemented with realist metaphysics.

The problem of error

Representationalism does not give sufficient conditions for measurement that are plausible, because it does not make the appropriate requirements with respect to the the causal antecedents of the empirical relational system. However, the theory might still give necessary conditions for measurement, as is suggested, for example, by Michell (1990, 1999). It turns out that this is also difficult because the theory has a hard time dealing with the problem of error. If the ability to construct a homomorphic representation were to be a necessary condition for measurement, this entails that we should be able to gather data that fit the measurement model perfectly. This is because, strictly speaking, models like the conjoint model are refuted by a single violation of the axioms. For example, if there is a single triple of observations where transitivity is violated, or a single 3×3 submatrix that violates double cancellation, the model is falsified, because no homomorphic representation will be possible. Since we can safely assume that we will not succeed in getting error-free data – certainly not in psychology – we must choose between two conclusions: either measurement is impossible, or it is not necessary to construct a perfect homomorphic representation. If we accept the former, we may just as well stop the discussion right now. If we accept the latter, then we have to invent a way to deal with error.

The return of Mr Brown   The natural means of introducing a theory of error would be to construct a statistical formulation of representational measurement theory. In such a theory, one would have to introduce parameters to represent the true values of the objects. One way to do this would be by replacing sentences like '$a \preceq b$ if and only if $\phi(a) \leq \phi(b)$' with sentences of the form '$\tau_a \preceq \tau_b$ if and only if $\phi(a) \leq \phi(b)$'. Here, the τ variable could serve the function of denoting the true value of the objects on some instrument used to make the comparison between a and b. This instrument could be a particular metre stick, but it could also be an item in a psychological test. Scheiblechner (1999) who follows this line of reasoning, calls the indirect comparison of objects, through their true scores on an instrument, an instrumental comparison (p. 299). The model so constructed allows for error because it may be the case that a particular observer judges that $a \preceq b$ while it is actually the case that $\tau_a \succ \tau_b$.

The problem, of course, is that the introduction of error requires an account of what the true values are. The common approach to this problem in statistics is by introducing the idea that the observed values are realizations of a random variable. Conceiving of the measurement apparatus as yielding a value x for each object, we could implement this idea by interpreting x as a realization of the random variable X. We may then introduce the assumption that $\mathcal{E}(X_a) = \tau_a$, analogous to the way this is done in classical test theory. The interpretation of the so constructed sentence in terms of length would be 'the expected centimetre reading of a is not noticeably larger than the expected centimetre reading of b if and only if the number assigned to a is smaller than the number assigned to b'. Because nobody can observe the expected values, we should delete the word 'noticeably'. This implies that we should also replace the symbol $\preceq$, which stands for 'not noticeably longer than' by the symbol $\leq$ which means 'has a lower expected centimetre reading than'. That is, the instrumental comparison can only be made by examining relations between expected values, which are by necessity numerical. So, an interesting shift takes place here: while the representational measurement model aims to construct quantitative metrics from qualitative observations, the instrumental comparison introduces a kind of quantitative metric directly at the level of the comparisons made.

Expected values are not observable, and the fact that we are introducing relations between unobservables at such a fundamental level in the construction of the model has far-reaching consequences. In effect, we are now already working with a true score model. And if we aim to construct a measuring instrument that measures a single attribute with a number of observed variables, we will build a structure that strongly resembles a latent variable model. Considered in terms of a psychological test consisting of a number of items, this would work as follows. Interpreting the numerical assignment ϕ as a latent variable (now interpreted as a rescaling of the true score), which represents an item × subject Cartesian product with an ordering induced (in both items and subjects) by the τ variable, we can construct an additive conjoint representation if the item and subject effects are independent, additive, and satisfy the double cancellation axiom with respect to the values of τ (Scheiblechner, 1999). An example of a model that has these properties is the Rasch model (Rasch, 1960). Thus, this statistical decomposition of observed values, in true and error components, leads directly to the class of additive Item Response Theory models. Similar approaches to introducing probabilistic relations in models of the representationalist type are pursued in Falmagne (1989); these also lead to latent variable structures. I will have more to say about these relations between latent variable models and representationalism in chapter 5.

This approach to the problem of error is useful because it shows that the divide between representationalism and latent variable theory is formally speaking a fine line. From a philosophical viewpoint, however, crossing this line has serious consequences; in effect, the main tenets of representationalism are lost in the present approach. The first problem is that we have assumed the existence of an instrument that gives the measurements to apply the expectation operator to. The present approach merely allows for the construction of a ruler with equal intervals on the basis of comparisons made by using a ruler with unequal intervals. It can be used to show how a scale can be linearized, analogous to the way that Rasch models linearize sumscores by appropriately stretching the far ends of the scale. However, representationalism is not served by assuming, a priori, that a ruler exists. For the theory is aimed at showing how a ruler with equal intervals could be constructed on the basis of direct qualitative comparisons with respect to the variable in question – whether it is length, density, or subjective loudness – and not at showing how length can be measured given the fact that a ruler already exists. More importantly, however, the very construction of a ruler is frustrated in the present approach. The reason for this is that the construction process would have to be carried out through the evaluation of stochastic dominance relations of the above type. These relations are clearly unobservable. Moreover, expectations cannot be empirically concatenated in principle. As a result, even the possibility of extensive measurement now vanishes. The third and most troubling consequence of this move is that in most cases of measurement, but certainly in psychology, we will encounter serious problems in the interpretation of the expected values involved. In fact, we are likely to be forced to interpret the expected values in a propensity sense. So we can now hear Mr Brown knocking on the back door; and the representationalist certainly would not want to let him in. It thus seems that, in this approach, we are quickly losing the gist of the representationalist theory. For we are not building homomorphic representations of observable objects and qualitative observable relations between them; we are building isomorphic representations of unobservable true scores and equally unobservable relations between them.

Introducing the Laplacean demon A second way to introduce a concept of error would be to introduce true relations between objects, rather than to assume true scores for the objects. This could be done by replacing sentences like '$a \preceq b$ if and only if $\phi(a) \leq \phi(b)$' with sentences of the form '$a \preceq_{true} b$ if and only if $\phi(a) \leq \phi(b)$'. That this will not work is obvious from the fact that the values ϕ are, in representationalism, constructed from the data and not hypothesized a priori. Because we cannot observe the true relations, we cannot construct these values and the above formulation is nonsensical. It would be an idea, however, to take the idealization one step further and to introduce true values for the ϕ involved. These values are not to be interpreted as existing independently of the relations they figure in, as in the introduction of expected values above. Rather, they should be seen as the values that would be constructed if we could observe the true relations between objects. Their status as true values is thus derived from positing true relations, rather than the other way around. Also, the relation $\preceq$ does not have to be interpreted as a relation between propensities. It can be taken to be a completely deterministic relation between objects. So now we could get '$a \preceq_{true} b$ if and only if $\phi_{true}(a) \leq \phi_{true}(b)$'. Interpreted in terms of length, this sentence says that a is truly not noticeably longer than b if and only if the number that would be assigned to a if we could observe the true relations is smaller than or equal to the number that would be assigned to b if we could observe the true relations. We thus retain the construction of quantitative scales out of qualitative relations, and refrain from introducing relations between unobservables in the definitions. The only problem is that the relation $\preceq$ has no natural interpretation anymore. For what does 'truly not noticeably longer than' mean? Does it mean that nobody could, in principle, notice that a is longer than b if a is actually shorter than b? No, because if this were the case, we could just use representational measurement theory as it stands; for there would be no error, and consequently there would be no need for the present exercise. Does it then mean that no perfect observer could notice that a is longer than b if a is truly shorter than b? Possibly, but who is the perfect observer? A Laplacean demon?

The problem we are facing here is clearly caused by the word 'noticeably'. The use of this term suggests that somebody is actually noticing relations between objects, and the judgments of this anonymous somebody would produce transitive and ordered data when measuring attributes that sustain measurement. Upon closer inspection, the identity of this anonymous observer is mysterious. The interpretation of the word 'noticeable' is unproblematic for a constructivist reading of the theory as long as we interpret it as 'noticeable with the unaided eye', that is, noticeable in practice. Because in this interpretation the theory is unable to deal with error, we have to move beyond the practically feasible observational powers of human beings and construct the relations as noticeable for somebody with observational powers that markedly exceed our own. This is necessary because the introduction of error means that we need to be able to say that we are wrong, and being wrong is always relative to being right. That is, error is a deviation, and the natural interpretation of the concept is that it is a deviation from a standard. In a theory that works its way up from qualitative, noticeable relations, we need somebody to notice the correct relations, which could function as such a standard. And if it cannot be us, then it must be a demon with infallible observational powers. Hence the need to introduce a Laplacean demon.

Now, if we want to pursue this line of reasoning without introducing propensities, expected values, and latent variables into reality, it is obvious that we must limit the relation $\preceq$ to be a relation between objects, and not between true scores. If we do not do this, then we must again introduce expected values and relations between them for the demon to notice. This requires that such values and relations exist in reality, so that we would again be introducing the metaphysics we sought to evade; in effect, we would arrive at the same conception of measurement as in the previous attempt to deal with error. Dismissing relations between propensities, however, has a very important consequence: it excludes any model that posits relations between expected values. Thus, in this interpretation, additive models like the Rasch model (1960) and the ADISOP models (Scheiblechner, 1999) are not representational models because they posit relations between propensities.

Perhaps the representationalist would not object to the exclusion of additive IRT models. One rarely encounters a reference to these models in the representationalist literature, and I would indeed suspect that representationalists reject such models because of the fact that they introduce too much metaphysics. The advocates of additive IRT models tend to flirt with fundamental measurement theory (e.g., Wright, 1997; Bond and Fox, 2001), but the reverse is definitely not the case. However, even the pet examples of representationalism would have difficulty surviving the demands posited in the approach we are presently considering. Consider the measurement of subjective loudness. What would we have to posit in order to be able to say that, while subject i did not notice the combination (a_i, b_l) to be $\preceq$ to the combination (a_j, b_k), he erred in this response? Or to say that, while i said he preferred stimulus j to stimulus k, he was misjudging his own preferences? The problem here is, of course, that the word 'noticeable' is, in these cases, intended as 'noticeable for subject i' and not as 'noticeable for a Laplacean demon'. The very subjective nature of the comparisons on which representational measurement theory operates in these cases precludes the introduction of error. For this requires us to say that i is objectively wrong concerning his subjective state of mind. This does not seem to go in the right direction, whether we consider the situation from the representational point of view or otherwise. Thus, in this approach few of the accomplishments of representational theory are preserved: the additive IRT models are excluded from consideration, and subjective scales for loudness, preference, etc., are deprived of their intended interpretation. Thus, the measurement of psychological variables is not satisfactorily incorporated in this approach.

Reconceptualizing error A final possibility to deal with imperfect observations is not to view them as errors at all. Whatever the ontological status of error may be, in the final analysis the only epistemological criterion to detect error is as a deviation from a theoretical model. Instead of laying the blame on the observations, so to speak, one may attribute the deviations to a failure of the model. In such a view, the model is not interpreted as aspiring truth, but as an approximation. One may then choose to minimize the distance between, for instance, the conjoint representation and the data matrix. This can be done by constructing a stress measure for this distance, and then minimizing the stress of the model with respect to the data. Interpreted in this manner, representational measurement theory would be a (possibly multidimensional) scaling technique, because error is not conceptualized as inherent to the variables observed, but as the distance between the data matrix and the representation. (In multidimensional scaling it is nonsensical to ask what the 'true' representation is, in contrast to latent variable models, where the quest for the true model is often deemed very important.) Representationalism does have a structure that is similar to scaling techniques (Coombs, 1964), so that this approach would seem a natural way for representationalism to deal with error. However, in this approach the main idea of representational measurement theory is also lost, because whatever the relation between the data and the representation may be, it will not be a homomorphic mapping.

So, it seems that representational theory is stuck between a rock and a hard place: it must either say that no psychological set of data satisfies the axioms, thereby forcing the conclusion that psychological measurement is impossible after all, or it must introduce a concept of error. The three ways of doing this, as discussed above, are not satisfactory. In the first attempt, we were forced to introduce expected values for the objects. This not only requires the existence of an instrument yielding values to apply the expectation operator to, but one must also posit probabilities that can only be interpreted as propensities. In effect, the structure we end up with strongly resembles a latent variable model, and the homomorphism constructed involves unobservable relations between unobservable true scores. This can hardly be considered to maintain the spirit of representationalism. The second attempt introduced true qualitative relations between the objects, and derived true values only in virtue of these relations. However, in this interpretation we must hypothesize a supernatural being to observe the true relations. Although this conception is perhaps closest in spirit to the formulation of representational measurement, it cannot be considered a case of progress in terms of keeping a low metaphysical profile. Finally, if we choose a more pragmatic approach, and simply minimize the distance between the data and the representation, we refrain from introducing metaphysics, but at the same time lose another central idea in representationalism, which is that we are constructing a homomorphic mapping of objects into the real numbers. Thus, the inability to deal with error seems to be deeply entrenched in the structure of representationalism. Attempts to incorporate an error structure invariably seem to destroy one or another of the tenets of the theory. This does not, of course, imply that the formal structure of representational theory could not be applied to stochastic systems. It merely means that to do so requires extending the theory with latent variables, structures, and processes, which in turn means that the constructivist connotation of the theory must be given up.

Could a realist be a representationalist?
The above objections are directed at highly literal reading of the theory, which is positivist in nature. First, the theory was criticized because it does not mention the causal antecedents of the noticeable relations, but takes these relations as given – no questions asked. Second, it was shown that the theory has serious difficulties in dealing with error. To solve these problems, one needs to introduce realist assumptions. Can this be done, while maintaining the representationalist view of measurement?

Suppose that one endorses the idea, as Michell (1997) does, that measurement on interval or ratio scales involves realism about objective attributes with an inherently quantitative structure: magnitudes. This means that such magnitudes have a quantitative structure of themselves, irrespective of whether anybody is actually representing them. The relations between such magnitudes (e.g., *a* is longer than *b*) do not correspond directly to observable relations; although they might be observed, they need not be. Ratios between objective magnitudes are estimated or discovered (Michell, 1997, p. 358), not constructed. If an appropriate causal connection between these magnitudes and observed (or estimated) relations is added to the representational theory, then the objection discussed in section 4.2.3 is taken care of. It is then acknowledged that the noticeable relations in representationalism must be causally dependent on true relations between objective magnitudes or other attributes in reality. Hence, 'accidental' representations like the Guttman scale in the previous section are ruled out as candidates for measurement. Thus, the first objection can be met.

A realist position, however, immediately leads to epistemological fallibilism: if there are true ratios of magnitudes, then we might sometimes err in our estimation of them. As has been argued in chapter 3, the idea of estimation is explicitly based on such fallibilism, and therefore requires a realist semantics. Thus, we must somehow create room for error. If this is done along realist lines, then a) the existence of theoretical attributes must be assumed, and b) these attributes must bear a nondeterministic relation to the data. The most obvious way of constructing such a relation – in fact, I know of no other ways – is by hypothesizing some probabilistic function that relates the relevant attributes to the data. It may be an erratic, nonparametric function, but it must be some probabilistic function nonetheless. But once one has done this, one has formulated a latent variable model.

It thus seems to me that the question whether a realist can be a representationalist must be answered negatively, unless a representationalist could simultaneously be a latent variable theorist. This might be possible, although I would suspect such a theorist to experience some cognitive dissonance – the combination does not seem entirely consistent. I leave it to theorists of this signature, if there are any, to argue the plausibility of their views.

Representationalism as rational reconstruction
In order to be able to prove the relevant theorems, the representationalist has to idealize observable data structures to a great extent. The reason for this is that these mathematical theorems require very clean assumptions. If no assumptions that go beyond the data structure are to be made, and no probabilistic functions are introduced, then such idealization is necessary. It is, in this respect, interesting to see the difference in emphasis with latent variable theory. Where latent variable theory takes the

data to be noisy, and may be viewed as proposing an idealized latent structure, representational measurement theory refrains from introducing latent structures, and instead idealizes the observable relations. This at the same time ensures that these axioms could, at least in principle, be conclusively verified by an ideal observer, and that they will rarely if ever be satisfied when dealing with real observers, i.e., scientists.

Representationalism, then, may be viewed as giving an idealized description of the measurement process. It does not describe how real scientists construct measures in practice. For that would require them to check all of the axioms; this is impossible, especially with existential axioms like solvability and the Archimedean axiom, which involve infinities. Reichenbach (1938), who faced a similar problem in relating the logical positivist ideas on the structure of theories to the actual scientific practice of constructing theories, said that his analysis involved a *rational reconstruction* of this process. It seems to me that representationalism could be viewed in a similar way. It gives a rational reconstruction of the measurement process, by saying how a Laplacean demon with infallible observational capacities and an infinite amount of time could construct measurement instruments on the basis of pure observation. This is a significant theoretical achievement.

But not even methodologists are Laplacean demons. We do not have infallible observational capacities or an infinite amount of time. Instead, we have ideas. We have ideas on the structure of the world that underlies our observations, and these ideas are sometimes partly testable. Testing the consequences of such ideas is what we do in scientific research. We ignore deviations from our expectations if they seem small and essentially random. If we did not do that, we could not progress at all. Sometimes, ignoring such deviations works very well, especially when the disturbing effects are of an order of magnitude smaller than the effects of the attributes one measures. This, I think, is why representational measurement theory seems to capture measurement in physics so well. Even when one is constructing a ruler, one is not making an exact but only an approximate standard sequence. One is not doing exactly what the representationalists say, for no ruler is perfect, but one can safely ignore the deviations from the ideal structure without being punished for it. If the distance between the 3- and 4-centimetre marks is a micrometre smaller than the distance between 4- and 5-centimetre marks, then strictly taken we do not have a standard sequence, but we can build a bridge with it nonetheless. We can ignore the errors involved in the measurement process because they are small enough relative to our required level of precision. In effect, we can pretend that error does not exist. And this is what the representationalist, when he is honest, must admit: he pretends that error does not exist.

Obviously, the natural sciences have come a long way by ignoring error or using ad hoc solutions to the problem, rather than by using probabilistic measurement models. From a philosophical viewpoint, however, one is inclined to say that successful development of measurement procedures was accomplished *despite* the fact that observations were idealized to perfection, rather than *because of it*. From this point of view, physics is an exceptional case, blessed with a situation where ignoring error does not lead to adverse consequences. Some philosophers of science (e.g., Scriven, 1956), have indeed suggested that the enormous success in isolating and measuring variables in physics is due precisely to the fact that the physicist can ignore disturbing factors, i.e., pretend that they do not exist, but that these circumstances should be considered to be exceptional, rather than typical. I think this is a rather plausible idea.

Of course, there is no reason to assume that a similar strategy would work equally well in psychology. It actually seems plausible to assume that, even if general intelligence exists and IQ-tests measure it, there will always be a multitude of factors that also affect the scores, some in a systematic fashion, some in an unsystematic fashion. If this is correct, then the practical (rather than theoretical) contribution of representational measurement theory to psychology can be expected to be limited; it would then be unlikely that 'the revolution that never happened' (Cliff, 1992) will ever see the light of day. In any event, today the barricades are sparsely populated.

Reconstruction does not entail prescription

That representationalism has provided important theoretical insights concerning measurement stands beyond doubt. However, some theorists adhere to a stronger interpretation of the theory: they think it should not be read as an idealized description, but as a prescriptive framework. Such ideas have been expressed by those advocates of Rasch models, who think that the Rasch model is a fundamental measurement model (Wright, 1997; Bond and Fox, 2001); Kline (1998) has even adopted the view that psychology cannot be scientific without fundamental measurement. The reasoning of these scholars seems to be more or less as follows: measurement has been very successful in physics, where it obeys the structure of fundamental measurement theory, so if we construct psychological measures based on this theory, then psychology will finally become the long sought quantitative science we have all been dreaming of.

I think that this is literally science-fiction. Representationalism offers a rational reconstruction of the measurement process, and it does this well. Reconstruction, however, does not entail prescription. It is a fallacy to think that, because established forms of measurement allow for a philosophical reconstruction in terms of model x, all measurements should be constructed to obey the prescriptions of model x – regardless of whether model x is a fundamental measurement model, a latent variable model, a generalizability theory model, or some other technique. One should be wary of models that are propagated as prescriptive frameworks in such a universal sense, because whether or not a model is adequate in a given situation strongly depends on the substantive considerations that are relevant in that particular situation.

Consider the additive conjoint model, which is seen as the main candidate for elevating the status of psychology to that of physics. Additive conjoint measurement requires additivity. Now, additivity is often desirable because it is simple, but it is only desirable if substantive theory suggests that additivity should hold. Substantive theory *may* prescribe an additive model, but I do not see why it *must* do so, as Wright (1997), Kline (1998), and Bond and Fox (2001) seem to presume. To illustrate that a universal demand for additivity is inappropriate, I will consider the requirement in terms of a physical and a psychological example, both based on the Rasch model.

First, consider length measurement. Suppose that we compared the length of objects with respect to two 'items', namely rods of different lengths. Further suppose that rod a has a length of 10 centimetres, and that rod b has a length of 20 centimetres. The 'item response process' consists of comparing objects to these two items; an object gets a score of $X_a = 1$ if it is judged to be longer than rod a, and a score of 0 if it is judged less or equally long; similarly for rod b. Now, suppose θ_i represents the true length of object i, and that $P(X_{ai} = 1|\theta_i)$ is the probability of object i being judged longer than rod a, given its length θ_i. Now, imagine that additivity is violated: the item response curves are not parallel. Suppose that these curves cross at the point $\theta = 15$ cm; for objects above that length, item a is 'easier' (has a higher probability of response 1 than item b), while for objects below that length, item b is easier. This situation implies that objects which are, say, 25 centimetres long, have a higher probability of being judged to be longer than rod a (which has a length of 10 centimetres) than to be judged longer than rod b (which has a length of 20 centimetres). So far, so good. However, the crossing of item response curves implies that objects which are 5 centimetres long have a *lower* probability of being judged longer than rod a, than to be judged longer than rod b. That means that objects which are 5 centimetres long are more likely to be judged longer than the rod of 20 centimetres (rod b), than to be judged longer than the rod of 10 centimetres (rod a). This is absurd. Yet, this is what the presence of crossing interactions (as present in factor models with unequal factor loadings as well as in Birnbaum models) signifies. In the present case, what we would expect are perfectly parallel item response curves for all possible 'items'. Thus, we would expect a Rasch model to hold. Reversals of item difficulty across the theta scale do not square with what we know about the behaviour of rods with respect to the length dimension.

It might seem attractive to take this argument further by claiming that the presence of crossing interactions excludes the possibility of valid measurement in general; not only in the case of length items like the ones in the above example, but in every bona fide set of items. Wright (1997) has argued along this line. This, however, is a serious overgeneralization. The measurement of length by comparing sticks does not square with the presence of crossing interactions; but the reasons for our passing this judgment lie in our knowledge of the physical characteristics of objects, the length dimension, and the measurement process. Thus, the methodological criterion (additivity) follows naturally from substantive theory (the physics involved). This, however, is not necessarily the case in general. For example, when we move from the physical to the psychological world, there is no reason to suppose that the methodological requirement continues to hold, because substantive considerations need not support it.

As a simple illustration, suppose we asked people a number of questions to measure their height. In this case, we might certainly encounter crossing interactions. For instance, the item 'I can touch the top of a doorpost with my hands' can reasonably be considered to measure bodily height, be it indirectly. It will show a quite steep curve as a function of height, jumping from 'no' to 'yes' at about 1.75 metres. Coding the item as 'yes':1 and 'no':0, we might imagine this item to have an expected value of 0.80 for people 1.80 metres tall, and an expected value of 0.20 for people 1.70 metres tall. The item 'I am pretty tall' is less direct, but may nevertheless be considered to validly measure the trait at hand. Because it is less direct, the item characteristic curve will not jump from 0 to 1 as suddenly and steeply as the previous item. This yields the possibility that people who are 1.70 metres tall will have an expected value of 0.30, while people who are 1.80 metres tall may have an expected value of 0.70. Thus, for people who are 1.80 metres tall, the first item is 'easier' than the second, but for people who are 1.70 metres tall, the second item is easier than the first. Technically, this means that there is a crossing interaction between the subject and item factors, which implies that additivity is violated and no additive conjoint representation can be found.

Does this mean we cannot use the two items to construct a valid measure for height? No. The measurement model for these items may not be additive, but that does not imply that it is not a measurement model; only that it is not an additive one. There is no reason to draw dramatic conclusions from this observation; I certainly do not see why it would preclude measurement. Thus, the idea that measurement necessarily requires additive item response functions, as propagated by Wright (1997) and Bond and Fox (2001), is implausible. I also think it is based on a misreading of representational measurement theory. It is one of the strengths of representationalism that the structure of a model must be motivated by a strong theory of empirical relations; as Coombs, Dawes, and Tversky (1970) write, in this sense measurement is a by-product of theory. It thus seems that scholars who propagate a normative reading of additive conjoint measurement expect to obtain scientific theory by realizing its by-products.

Good science may sometimes lead to the conjoint model. But the idea that one can therefore elevate it to a *sine qua non* for measurement, without even considering whether it is motivated by substantive considerations, is to put the cart before the horse. In the absence of a rationale based on substantive, rather than philosophical, considerations that sustain various formal properties like additivity (or, for that matter, unidimensionality, measurement invariance, and the like) one should be very careful in propagating the universal demand for such properties. It amounts to pure speculation to say that constructing measures on the basis of these formal criteria will lead to better measurement.

4.3 Discussion

Representational measurement theory implements a constructivist philosophy on measurement. The theory presupposes no more than the existence of very basic, qualitative empirical relations in the world. Representationalism characterizes these relations in terms of a set of axioms. Given the empirical satisfaction of these axioms, it is shown that a representation in a number system can be devised that preserves these relations. The resulting scale is a constructed representation of empirical relations.

Representationalism provides an instantiation of the logical positivist doctrine on the relation between theoretical and observational terms (Carnap, 1956). In particular, it specifies an observational and theoretical vocabulary in precisely the way the logical positivists envisioned. The connection between these vocabularies is handled by correspondence sentences in logical positivism; in representational measurement theory, representation theorems take care of this connection. These theorems can be interpreted as proofs that correspondence rules exist for the entire domain of measurable objects.

In contrast to latent variable theory, representationalism has very few metaphysical assumptions concerning the causal antecedents of the observable relations. However, in order to be able to mathematically prove representation and uniqueness theorems, the theory strongly idealizes the level of observations. In practical situations, where data exhibit noise and measurement error, this idealization becomes a weakness of the theory. Representationalism has no natural means of incorporating error, and it seems that the theory has to abandon its central tenets when it is equipped with a method to do so. In face of this problem, a choice has to be made between two conclusions: either measurement is impossible in the presence of error, or representational measurement theory is not a theory of how measurement is, can be, or should be carried out in practice. The first conclusion is absurd, but rejecting it leads immediately to the second, and this raises the question what the status of representationalism is. It has been argued here that representationalism offers a rational reconstruction of the measurement process. That is, it elucidates measurement procedures by recasting them in idealized logical terms.

Some theorists have interpreted the theory in a stronger sense, namely as a normative or prescriptive theory. When considered in terms of probabilistic models, the prescriptive reading of additive conjoint measurement has, in the hands of theorists like Wright (1997) and Bond and Fox (2001), been transformed into an admonition to use additive item response models like the Rasch (1960) model. It has been argued that this admonition is unfounded. A rational reconstruction does not have prescriptive force, and moreover a measurement model should be motivated by substantive considerations and not by methodological dogma. This holds for latent variable models as well as for representational measurement models. Therefore, the advocates of a prescriptive reading of the theory are not justified in their position. In effect, they are trying to sell a conceptual theory of measurement as a method for test construction and analysis. A method, however, can only be used if applicable, and because the inability to deal with imperfect observations is so deeply entrenched in the structure of representational theory, its applicability in the social sciences must be considered limited.

It is interesting to see the trade-off between introducing metaphysics and idealizing observations that seems to be present in the construction of theories of measurement. Representational measurement theory does not introduce metaphysical assumptions, but instead idealizes the data; the price that is paid for this metaphysical low profile is that, in practice, the restrictions the theory imposes on the data are so heavy that real data can hardly be expected to perfectly conform to them. Latent variable theory, on the other hand, is built to deal with noisy data, and therefore has a wider range of applicability. The gain in applicability is paid for with heavier metaphysical assumptions on the existence of latent variables, structures, and processes. Representationalism presents axioms that can be directly tested, but are so strict that they virtually guarantee rejection of the model; latent variable models are not so stringent, but the key assumptions on the existence of latent variables and their causal impact are difficult to test directly. In representational measurement theory, satisfaction of the empirical requirements guarantees that a representation with the desired properties exists, while in latent variable theory the postulated model is, at best, corroborated, but cannot be conclusively confirmed. It seems that Coombs' (1964, p. 5) statement that 'we buy information with assumptions' applies here. Even in measurement theory, there is no such thing as a free lunch.

5 Relations between the models

> Three umpires are discussing their mode of operation and defending their integrity as umpires. 'I call 'em as I see 'em,' said the first. The second replied, 'I call 'em as they are.' The third said, 'What I call 'em makes 'em what they are.'
>
> R. L. Ebel, 1956

5.1 Introduction

The choice between different mathematical models for psychological measurement, of which this book has discussed three types, involves both an ontological commitment and a position concerning what one regards as measurement. The true score model is operationalist: it views any observed test score as a measure of a true score, where the true score is exhaustively defined in terms of the test score. The representationalist model is constructivist, but not operationalist. It views scales as constructed representations of the data, but it is highly restrictive in the kind of representation that counts as a measurement scale. The meaning of scales does not explicitly derive from a realist ontology regarding attributes, but neither is it defined in terms of a specific measurement procedure in the way the true score is. Latent variable models introduce an a priori hypothesis concerning the existence of theoretical entities. The latent variable model does not work its way up from the data, like representationalism, but posits an explanatory account of where the relations in the data came from. Thus, classical test theory is basically about the test scores themselves, representationalism is about the conditions that should hold among test and person characteristics in order to admit a representation in the number system, and latent variable theory is about the question where the test scores came from.

However, in spite of the fact that such philosophical differences between the approaches exist, they are also related in important ways. At one level, the relations between the models are clear. This is the level of syntax. Mathematically, it has been known for quite some time that strong relations exist between true scores and latent variables (Lord and Novick, 1968; Jöreskog, 1971; Hambleton and Swaminathan, 1985). It has also been observed that special cases of latent variable models bear a strong relation to specific versions of the representationalist model (Brogden, 1977; Fischer, 1995; Perline, Wright, and Wainer, 1979; Roskam, 1984; Scheiblechner, 1999). Such relations also exist between classical test theory and representationalism, if the classical test model is extended with the appropriate assumptions, as was suggested by Lord and Novick (1968, ch. 1) and is illustrated below.

Thus, mathematically speaking, the models are strongly related, and sometimes a special case of one model is also a special case of another model. A question that has, however, been largely neglected is what kind of interpretation has to be given to the concepts in these models in order to maintain their interrelatedness at a semantic level. And an even more interesting question that has, to the best of my knowledge, never been addressed is the question whether these relations could also be conceptualized to hold at the ontological level. That is, does there exist an ontological viewpoint upon which the models are not in contradiction, but supplement each other? It will be argued in this chapter that such a viewpoint exists under one condition. The condition is that the probability semantics in the true score and latent variable models are interpreted at the level of the individual, that is, if the probabilities in the models are interpreted as propensities. If this is the case, then the models are syntactically, semantically, and ontologically related, and merely address different levels of the measurement process. However, as soon as the existence of propensities is denied, the models are decoupled in all these senses. In that case, the true score model is necessarily false, the latent variable model is exclusively about relations between characteristics of subpopulations, and the representationalist model is solely about deterministic relations.

5.2 Levels of connection

We can address the individual theoretical terms in the measurement models at different levels, and therefore we can also discuss the relations between these terms at different levels. I will concentrate here on the levels of syntax, semantics, and ontology. It will be shown that, while the syntactical connections are easily established and straightforward, the semantical and ontological connections leave much freedom of interpretation. An integrated theoretical framework for discussing the models will be presented, but it will also be shown that this framework collapses as soon as the propensity interpretation of the probabilities in the models is denied.

5.2.1 Syntax

Latent variables and true scores Syntactically, the true score model and the latent variable model are closely connected. In fact, they are so closely connected that the distinction between true scores and latent variables may get blurred in certain situations. It is suggested by Schmidt and Hunter (1999, p. 185), for example, that the relation between true scores and latent variables is 'usually close enough to linear' so that the latent variables approach has no conceptual or practical advantage. This is not the case, because whether there is any relation in the first place depends on the dimensionality of the latent variable model, which is not tested in the classical test model. The mistake made by Schmidt and Hunter (1999) is understandable, however, because *if* a unidimensional model holds *then* it will often be possible to construct a simple sumscore that can reasonably be used as a proxy for the latent variable in question.

Consider the Item Response Theory model for dichotomous items. It is well known (e.g., Lord and Novick, 1968; Hambleton and Swaminathan, 1985) that in this case the expectation of the sumscore is a function of the latent variable. Suppose subject i's sumscore X is defined as the sum of his item responses on N items, $1, \cdots, j, \cdots, N$. Let U_{ij} denote i's response to the jth item. Thus, $X_i = \Sigma_{j=1}^{N} U_{ij}$ and i's true test score is $t_i = \mathcal{E}(X_i)$. For a fixed test consisting of dichotomous items, there exists a monotonic relation between t and the latent variable θ. The true score is the sum of the individual item response probabilities under the IRT model:

$$t_i = \mathcal{E}(X_i \mid \theta_i) = \sum_{j=1}^{N} P(U_{ij} = 1 \mid \theta_i). \tag{5.1}$$

If the IRT model is parametric, then the function relating t to θ is also parametric and can be used to linearize the sumscore so that equal distances in the latent variable match equal distances in the transformed sumscore. For some models, like the Rasch model, the function that does this is so simple (the natural logarithm of $(X_i/N)/[1 - (X_i/N)]$) that it can be implemented on a pocket calculator. For nonparametric IRT models, no parametric function for the relation exists, but under relatively mild assumptions the latent variable still is stochastically ordered by the sumscore (Hemker, Sijtsma, Molenaar, and Junker, 1997). Thus, conditional on the assumption that a unidimensional model holds, the true score will often be strongly related to the latent variable. This can also be seen from the fact that Jöreskog (1971) actually derived the congeneric model for continuous responses by introducing the requirement that the true scores be perfectly correlated. In this case, each true score is a linear function of every other true score, which means that all true scores can be conceptualized to be a linear function of a single factor score. Although the true score model is usually seen as weaker than the latent variable model, Jöreskog in fact introduced the congeneric model by replacing the classical test theory assumption of essential tau-equivalence with the weaker assumption that the tests are congeneric. The true score model for continuous test scores that satisfy essential tau-equivalence is thus nested under the common factor model; it can be derived by introducing the restriction that the factor loadings are equal.

These results are easily misinterpreted and overgeneralized to the conclusion that there is basically no difference between the latent variable and true score models. This conclusion is erroneous because the relation does not hold in general. For instance, in the case of polytomous IRT models, the latent variable is generally not even stochastically ordered by the sumscore. In latent variable models with correlated errors, which are not uncommon in SEM, the relations will also be more complicated, and in case of multidimensional latent variable models the relations break down quickly. Finally, if no latent variable model holds at all, we may still conceptualize a true score, because the only assumption that is necessary for the definition of a true score is that the propensity distribution on which it is defined is nondegenerate and has finite variance (Novick, 1966). However, it is obvious that, under the proper conditions, the true score bears a functional rather than stochastic relation to the sumscore. Thus, the relation between the true score model and the latent variable model is mathematically explicit in some cases, and indeed is a strong one.

Latent variables and scales There are also strong connections between the latent variable model and the additive conjoint measurement model. Specifically, special cases of latent variable models, in particular additive versions of such models, can be considered to be mathematically covered by the additive conjoint model. The class of models for which this connection can be set up is quite general (Scheiblechner, 1999), but for clarity of exposition attention is limited here to the Rasch (1960) model. The Rasch model hypothesizes the expected item responses (true item scores) to be a logistic function of the latent variable. Thus, subject i's response to item j is assumed to follow the function

$$P(U_{ij}) = \frac{e^{\theta_i + \beta_j}}{1 + e^{\theta_i + \beta_j}}, \tag{5.2}$$

where $P(U_{ij})$ is the probability of a correct or affirmative answer and β_j is the location of item j, conceptualized as the point on the θ scale where $P(U_{ij}) = 0.5$. Now, a monotonic transformation of the item response probabilities will yield a simple additive representation. Specifically, the model can be rewritten as

$$\ln\left[\frac{P(U_{ij})}{1-P(U_{ij})}\right] = \theta_i + \beta_j, \tag{5.3}$$

where ln denotes the natural logarithm. The axioms of additive conjoint measurement hold for the model in stochastic form.

First, the $P(U_{ij})$ form a weak order by definition: transitivity (if $P(U_{ij}) \succeq P(U_{kl})$, and $P(U_{kl}) \succeq P(U_{mn})$, then $P(U_{ij}) \succeq P(U_{mn})$) and connectedness (either $P(U_{ij}) \succeq P(U_{kl})$, or $P(U_{kl}) \succeq P(U_{ij})$, or both) must hold because probabilities are numerical, and numbers are ordered. This interesting fact seems to result from the imposition of the Kolmogorov axioms on the probabilities, which, as a result, are ordered by assumption.

The independence condition also holds. That is, item difficulty and person ability are seen as the two independent variables, and items and subjects are independently ordered on ability and difficulty, respectively, by the dependent variable $P(U_{ij})$. Rasch (1960) actually derived the model from the requirement of parameter separation, i.e., it should be possible to estimate the ordering of items and subjects independently, which basically comes down to the same type of requirement as posed by the independence axiom in the additive conjoint model. Rasch called this property specific objectivity. Statistically, this implies that the item and person parameters can be estimated independently, because the sumscore is a minimally sufficient statistic for the person parameter, which enables parameter estimation by Conditional Maximum Likelihood (Andersen, 1973).

Further, if the Rasch model is true, then the double cancellation condition is satisfied. If, for any three levels of ability and any three levels of item difficulty, if it is true that

$$\theta_2 + \beta_1 \geq \theta_1 + \beta_2 \tag{5.4}$$

and it is also true that

$$\theta_3 + \beta_2 \geq \theta_2 + \beta_3 \tag{5.5}$$

then

$$\theta_2 + \beta_1 + \theta_3 + \beta_2 \geq \theta_1 + \beta_2 + \theta_2 + \beta_3, \tag{5.6}$$

so that

$$\theta_3 + \beta_1 \geq \theta_1 + \beta_3 \tag{5.7}$$

and double cancellation holds.

Finally, the solvability and Archimedean axioms hold by assumption; the solvability axiom because the person ability and item difficulty scales are continuous, the Archimedean axiom because they are unbounded. As is the case in additive conjoint measurement, the Rasch model represents a trade-off; here, the trade-off is between person ability and item difficulty. Thus, the model gives a representation of person ability and item difficulty on interval scales with a common unit.

The structure of the Rasch model sustains representational measurement theory. As soon as the model is extended with a discrimination parameter, as in Birnbaum's (1968) model, this resemblance vanishes because the independence condition will no longer hold.

Scales and true scores The fact that the latent variable model can be constructed from the imposition of restrictions on the relations between true scores, and the fact that additive latent variable models are special cases of representational measurement theory, suggests that appropriately constructed versions of the classical model can be written in representational form too. For instance, the true score model for essentially tau-equivalent tests assumes that for any two true scores of person i on tests j and k, denoted t_{ij} and t_{ik}, it is true that $t_{ij} = c + t_{ik}$, where c is constant over persons. The structure of the model can be written in terms of a common factor model (Jöreskog, 1971):

$$\mathcal{E}(X_{ij}) = \nu_j + \lambda\theta_i \tag{5.8}$$

where the ν_j parameter is a test-specific intercept term that absorbs the effect of the constant c in the definition of essential tau-equivalence, λ is the factor loading, and θ_i is subject i's position on the latent variable. Because, by the definition of essential tau-equivalence, λ is constant over tests, it has no test subscript as in the congeneric model. We may set it to unity without loss of generality. This gives the additive representation

$$\mathcal{E}(X_{ij}) = \nu_j + \theta_i \tag{5.9}$$

The axioms of conjoint measurement then hold for the so constructed model. The instrumental comparison is made through the true scores on the tests, as it is made through the item response probabilities in the Rasch model. The true scores induce an ordering because, like probabilities, true scores are numbers and numbers are ordered. The condition of independence holds because the item and person effects do not interact (this would occur if the factor loadings differed across items): persons can be stochastically ordered by true scores, regardless of which test is used for this purpose, and tests can be stochastically ordered by true scores, regardless of which person is used for this purpose. That the double cancellation axiom holds is obvious, because the additive decomposition of the observed scores into a test and person specific part guarantees this to be the case; one may follow the line of reasoning as discussed above for the Rasch model and substitute v_j for β_j.

Because the fundamental measurement model works its way up from relations between objects, and the presently formulated relations are indistinguishable from the relations assumed to hold in the true score model with essential tau-equivalence, the classical test theory model allows for an additive conjoint representation under the restriction of essential tau-equivalence. It is interesting to note that such a representation cannot be constructed under the stronger conditions of tau-equivalence and parallelism. Both tau-equivalence and parallelism assume equal true scores across tests, which means that the intercept terms v_j are equal across tests. This implies that the true scores cannot induce an ordering in these tests, so that the additive conjoint model cannot be formulated.

So, the true score, latent variable, and additive conjoint models are strongly related syntactically. Imposing appropriate restrictions on the models allows one to juggle the terms around so as to move back and forth between the mathematical structures. The true score model with the essential tau-equivalence restriction seems to serve as a bridge between the latent variable model and the additive conjoint model: it is a special case of the latent variable model, and the restrictions it poses on the true scores guarantee that an additive representation is possible. On the other hand, there are syntactical differences between the models that should not be forgotten; one can formulate latent variable models that are nonadditive and therefore do not generate the possibility of constructing an additive conjoint representation; the true score model can be formulated without invoking a latent variable, and latent variable models can be constructed where the true score bears no direct functional relation to the latent variable (i.e., multidimensional models, models with correlated errors, or models for polytomous items); and the additive conjoint model can generate deterministic structures that render the true score undefined (i.e., the propensity distribution is non-existent or degenerate, depending on one's point of view) and the latent variable model obsolete (i.e., trivial or unnecessary, depending on one's point of view). Nevertheless, under the right conditions, there is a strong correspondence between the models. The question now becomes: what kind of semantics do we need to relate the models not only in terms of mathematics, but to keep a consistent interpretation of these relations, and what kind of overall conceptualization of the measurement process would this give?

5.2.2 Semantics and ontology

The semantics of true score theory, latent variable models, and representational measurement are markedly different, as should be clear from the preceding chapters. The reason that the models can nevertheless be related syntactically is that, in the above discussion, the models were uncritically defined on probabilities and relations among them. However, we have seen in the preceding chapters that the interpretation of the probability calculus is not straightforward in the case of psychological testing. In the true score model, probabilities must be interpreted as propensities which are defined at the level of the individual; in the latent variable model, they may either be interpreted as such propensities, or as characteristics of subpopulations; in the additive conjoint measurement model, the observations are assumed to be free of measurement error, so that no interpretation of probability is necessary at all. In order to set up the above connections, we have required the representational model to take a step back from its constructivist foundation, and to grant the existence of probabilities of some kind, but we have not yet interpreted these probabilities. Neither have we made a choice with regard to the conceptualization of the item response probabilities in latent variable models. If we are going to interpret the connections between the models, we will have to make such a choice.

Admitting propensities As is so often the case, the most elegant situation occurs if we introduce the strongest metaphysics. This, of course, comes down to a propensity interpretation of the probabilities in the model. In this case, we conceptualize the probabilities as propensities that are uniquely defined for a particular person at a particular time point. Interpretation of these probabilities will in general require a thought experiment like Mr Brown's infamous brainwash.

In this interpretation, the true score, latent variable, and representationalist models are strongly related. Semantically, true score theory discusses the relation between propensities and observables; latent variable theory posits a hypothesis to explain the relations between propensities; and representationalism shows the conditions necessary to construct a representation that preserves the relations between subjects, where these relations are defined indirectly via the propensities. Thus, true score theory describes, latent variable theory explains, and fundamental measurement represents. Moreover, under appropriate conditions the models are not at odds with each other; they simply focus on different levels of the measurement process. This is graphically represented in figure 5.1.

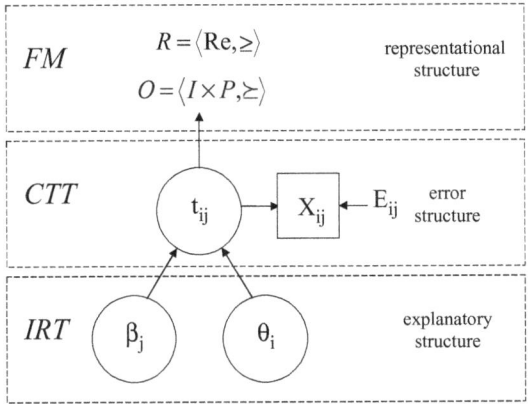

Figure 5.1. The relation between Item Response Theory, Classical Test Theory, and Fundamental Measurement Theory.

As the figure illustrates, we have a division of labour between the different theories. Classical test theory provides a theory of the error structure. It does so by defining the true score as the expected value of the propensity distribution for subject i on item or test j. Latent variable models, such as the item response theory model, provide a hypothesis concerning the data generating process. The hypothesis is that there exists variation on an attribute (the latent variable) which produces variation in the true scores. The item difficulty (which could be the intercept term in a continuous model) also produces such variation. In the figure, these person and item effects are represented as independent.

The true scores can be used for the instrumental comparison $\succeq$ of the Cartesian product terms (i, j), which are defined on the Items × Persons matrix, denoted $I \times P$ in figure 5.1. The true scores will form a weak order because they are already numerical. Because the effects of item difficulty and latent variable are independent, the instrumental comparison will allow for the independent ordering of items and subjects. This gives the empirical relational system $\mathcal{O} = \langle I \times P, \succeq \rangle$. Perhaps, it should be called a quasi-empirical relational system, because it is defined on unobservable propensities. The fact that the effects of person ability and item difficulty are independent guarantees that, if the model is true, a transformation of the true scores can be found that yields an additive representation, as is the case in the Rasch model. The representation so constructed is the numerical relational system $\mathcal{R} = \langle \text{Re}, \geq \rangle$. Together $\mathcal{O}$ and $\mathcal{R}$ form an additive conjoint measurement structure. What is represented is the trade-off between item and person effects in producing true scores. The representation of this trade-off is invariant up to a linear transformation, so it is measured on an interval scale.

The division of labour highlights the different functions of the theories. For instance, in the present conceptualization one would not say that the Rasch model is a fundamental measurement model, but one would say that the Rasch model describes (one of the) hypothetical data generating mechanisms that would produce data that allow for an additive representation in the fundamental measurement theory sense. This is a large conceptual difference, that lies primarily in the different ontological status of the numerical representation, which is a construction even if based on relations between propensities, and the latent variable, which is a hypothetical attribute that underlies relations between propensities. A related difference is that the latent variable model is a hypothesis on the data generating process, and therefore claims more than the relations it implies in the data. The representation does not have this property, because it is not a posited explanation of the relations in the data, but a representation of these relations. That is, one can say that the latent variable model is true or false, but one cannot say that a homomorphic representation is true or false; one can only say that it can or cannot be constructed.

Note also that the representation is purely hypothetical: because unsystematic variance is introduced in the error structure, there is no representation of observed relations as in typical fundamental measurement theory models. So, strictly taken, it is impossible to actually construct the desired representation on the basis of observed data. It is, however, the case that, if the model were true, then a representation could be constructed if the true scores were observed. True scores cannot be observed, so that the representational account must then be viewed as inherently based on a counterfactual line of reasoning. So, even if the latent variable model were true, the representation would stay counterfactual as long as we cannot observe true scores. It think that this is why, in latent variable models, it is more usual to say that one estimates a person's position on the latent variable than to say that one measures that position. This difference in terminology also seems to reflect the ontological difference between a latent variable and a measurement scale. Thus, in the present scheme, the models are about as closely connected as possible, but the difference in ontological tenets remains: latent variables are entities that figure in an explanation of how relations in the data arise, while measurement scales are constructed representations of the relations in the data.

The truth of a latent variable model must be considered conceptually independent of the possibility of constructing a fundamental measurement theory representation. In principle, the latent variable model may be true, while it is impossible to construct a homomorphic representation, and it may be possible to construct such a representation, while the latent variable model is not true. An example of the former situation would occur in case a common factor model with unequal factor loadings, or a Birnbaum model, were true. An example of the latter situation would occur when the relations in the data would admit a fundamental measurement representation, although no latent variable were responsible for these relations, as in the case of spurious Guttman scaling discussed in section 4.2.3., and in the coin-tossing example discussed by Wood (1978). This does not mean that either theory is in some sense inadequate, but that latent variable and fundamental measurement theory are concerned with distinct problems.

Dismissing propensities Assuming the existence of propensities allows for connecting the latent variable, true score, and fundamental measurement models. However, if one dismisses the existence of propensities, the unified picture discussed above falls like a house of cards.

First, if propensities do not exist, then the true score model in the Lord and Novick (1968) formulation is necessarily false. This is because in this interpretation, the observed score can no longer be viewed as a realization of a random variable at the level of the individual, which means that the true score model cannot be constructed. If no randomness is associated with the item response process, then the probability distribution on which the true score should be defined is degenerate, and the core assumption of the true score model (Novick, 1966) is therefore violated. Sentences like 'the reliability of this test is 0.88 in population X' cannot, in principle, be true in this interpretation. At most, one could rephrase such sentences in the counterfactual form, and state that 'if the observed scores had been generated by a random process, etc., then the reliability of the test scores would have been 0.88 in population X'. Such counterfactuals may be useful and informative, but the place and conceptual status of counterfactual information about test scores would require some serious rethinking of the use of classical test theory in test analysis.

The latent variable model could be true without a propensity interpretation if a repeated sampling perspective is adopted. The validity of latent variable models would then be relevant only at the level of aggregate statistics; because there is no randomness associated with an individual's item responses, the models would be necessarily false at the individual level. In this interpretation, the connection between true score theory and latent variable models breaks down. Since there is no randomness at the individual level, there is no true score, and a statement to the effect that the true score is monotonically related to the latent variable cannot be made.

In a repeated sampling interpretation, the latent variable model states that differences between subpopulations at the latent level lead to differences between subpopulations at the observed level, and nothing more. The model uses probability semantics and the expectation operator, but only to deal with sampling variation; the expectation is conceptualized as a population mean, as it is in standard population-sampling schemes in statistics, and not as a true score. To interpret such models as process models that apply at the level of the individual amounts to a logical fallacy. Nevertheless, the basic idea of latent variable models, which is that variation in the latent variable produces variation in the observed scores, may be maintained, elaborated upon, and endowed with a substantive theoretical interpretation.

For fundamental measurement theory, denying the validity of probability assignments at the individual level has no theoretical consequences. Since the model is most naturally stated in deterministic terms in the first place, the theory does not have to be modified or reinterpreted when responses are stripped of randomness at the level of the individual. Such a view does lead to the conclusion that the axioms of fundamental measurement are usually not satisfied by empirical data, either in psychology or elsewhere. This observation, of course, is hardly surprising, given the strict demands of the theory. What is interesting, however, is that the connection between probabilistic latent variable models and fundamental measurement breaks down if the propensity interpretation is denied. For instance, the stochastic dominance relations as discussed by Scheiblechner (1999) no longer apply, because they are defined on true scores, which are no longer admitted in the present interpretation. Thus, the only item response model that is properly admitted as a case of fundamental measurement in this interpretation, is the deterministic Guttman model. It is thus clear that the popular view, which holds that the Rasch model 'is' a fundamental measurement model (Perline, Wright, and Wainer, 1979; Scheiblechner, 1999; Bond and Fox, 2001), is parasitic on the stochastic subject interpretation of the item response model. Once that interpretation is denied, the Rasch model has little to do with fundamental measurement. In fact, the only thing that conjoint measurement and Rasch models have in common, in this interpretation, is additivity.

Thus, there are at least two ways of looking at the relations between the different theories of measurement discussed in this book. The similarities and dissimilarities between these models depend on a rather high level philosophical assumption, namely on whether one wants to admit propensities into psychological measurement or not. Admitting propensities gives a consistent and unified picture, in which the different approaches focus on different parts of the measurement process, but are

Relations between the models

not necessarily at odds. Denying the existence of propensities immediately destroys the classical test model, and leaves one with two models that have relatively little to do with each other.

5.3   Discussion

This chapter has aimed to clarify the relations between the models discussed in this book. It has been shown that the models are syntactically related in quite a strong sense. However, when viewed from a semantic perspective, whether these connections continue to hold depends on the interpretation of probability: probability must be interpreted in a propensity sense, otherwise the models are unrelated. In spite of this, the difference in ontological tenets with respect to the central concepts in the models (i.e., true scores, latent variables, and scales) remains, regardless of the interpretation of probability. These conclusions will be examined in somewhat greater detail in the next sections. First, the general problem concerning the theoretical status of measurement concepts will be discussed. Second, I will shortly review arguments for and against the propensity and repeated sampling interpretations of probability. Third, the models will be evaluated in terms of the semantics they yield for validity; in this section, it will become apparent that, when the models are required to specify a relation between the observed scores and a theoretical attribute, both the classical test theory model and the representationalist model converge to a latent variable formulation; classical test theory because it has to be strengthened, and representationalism because it has to be weakened. The conceptualization of measurement so reached has important consequences for psychometrics in general and validity theory in particular; these will be discussed in the next chapter.

5.3.1   *Theoretical status*

It is instructive to review the conclusions reached in this book with respect to the theoretical status of the central concepts in the measurement models discussed. We have seen that classical test theory defines the true score in terms of the expectation of a series of replications of the same item or test. It has been argued in chapter 2 that it does not make sense to say that two tests x and y 'measure' the same true score, as is suggested in the definitions of parallelism and tau-equivalence. It does make sense to say that the true scores on test x and test y have the same numerical value, but this is a statement of an entirely different character. The fact that the true score is explicitly defined in terms of a particular test implies that the meaning of the true score is exhausted by reference to the operations that lead to it. That the operations require brainwashing and cannot be carried out is peculiar, but does not refute this conclusion. Thus, the psychologist who defines intelligence as a true score takes an operationalist position with respect to the construct. He cannot do otherwise.

Latent variable theory supplements classical test theory precisely by broadening the meaning of the theoretical terms in the model. Latent variables are not exhaustively defined by a series of operations, otherwise two distinct tests could not measure the same latent variable. That latent variable theory allows for the statement that different tests can measure the same latent variable is obvious; if this were not possible, common applications like test equating and adaptive testing would lack a theoretical basis. That they do not lack such a basis means that the latent variable has surplus meaning over the observation statements and the operations that lead to them. It is not an operationalist concept. Upon this conclusion, the question occurs whether the theoretical term 'latent variable' must be taken to refer to reality or not. It seems to me that it should be taken to do so. Several arguments for this conclusion have been adduced in chapter 3. I would like to discuss one other argument because it brings out clearly the difference with representationalism.

It has been observed several times that the syntactical equivalence between probabilistic versions of additive conjoint measurement and latent variable theory breaks down if we allow the slope of item response functions to differ across items, as is the case in the congeneric model and in the Birnbaum model. Mathematically speaking, the reason for this is very simple, because it means that no additive representation is possible if additivity is violated, which comes down to the trivial observation that additivity is violated if additivity is violated. Conceptually, however, there are more interesting things going on.

What the existence of nonadditive latent variable models illustrates is that latent variable theory not only allows for the possibility that different items measure the same latent variable, but that it also allows for the even stronger claim that a given set of items can measure the same latent variable differently in different subpopulations. This is clear from the fact that nonadditive latent variable models imply that items have different difficulty orderings in subpopulations high and low on the trait.

Similar considerations play a role in the definition of bias with respect to group membership. The concept of bias means that the expected value of an item response differs across groups, conditional on the latent variable, for at least one position on that latent variable. Such a situation occurs, for instance, when females have a lower expected item response on an IQ-item than males, where the comparison is between subpopulations of males and females that have the same level of intelligence. This method of conditioning on the latent variable is very common in latent variable models. It is highly interesting.

The reason for this is the following. What do we assert when we say that an item has different expected values across groups, conditional on the latent variable? It seems to me that we are in effect asserting that the item has different expected values across groups, conditional on the *same* latent variable. What we have to assume, then, is that the item *does* measure the same latent variable across groups. Otherwise it would be meaningless to condition on this latent variable. The problem formulated in item bias is not, therefore, that the item in question measures a different latent variable in each group, but that it measures the same latent variable differently in each group. Thus, not only is it the case that latent variables are not exhaustively defined by the items that measure them; they are not even exhaustively defined by the item response functions. For if the latter were the case, this would preclude the formulation of item bias. And nothing precludes the formulation of item bias.

The common practice of conditioning on the latent variable across groups with different response functions presupposes a kind of meaning invariance of the latent variable concept. Now, this invariance cannot be reduced to the fact that a particular set of items is used, as in operationalism, for this would preclude the possibility of unidimensionality and adaptive testing. It cannot be reduced to the ordering of the items, for in a nonadditive model this ordering is not invariant across trait levels. It cannot be reduced to the invariance of item response functions, for these may be different across groups. And it cannot be reduced to the invariance of theoretical relations in which the latent variable enters, for these will also be different across groups (for instance, a latent variable may be correlated to some other variable in one group but not in another, while we are still talking about the same latent variable). Where, then, does this meaning invariance come from? What would allow us to say that we are measuring the same latent variable in all these cases? It seems that this meaning invariance can only be upheld if the latent variable is granted an existential status that is essentially independent of the measurement procedure or the theory in which it figures. Thus, the psychologist who views a theoretical concept like intelligence as a latent variable must subscribe to a realist position.

It has been argued in chapter 4 that representationalism is based on an constructivist philosophy of science. In particular, it implements logical positivism. Its central concept, the measurement scale, is a constructed representation of relations between the objects measured. Can a representationalist formulate a concept such as item bias? It seems to me that this will be fairly difficult. Suppose that we have two populations, A and B, and that in each population the responses on a three item scale, consisting of items j, k, and l, conform to a Rasch model. Further suppose that item l is, in latent variable terms, biased, and that it is biased to such a degree that it is more diffcult than item k in population A, but less difficult than item k in population B. So, in each population an additive conjoint representation is possible, but in the union of these populations it is not. Now, the latent variable theorist could, in principle, allow for the different item orderings in each population and still estimate the position on the latent variable. He could even compare the populations with respect to the latent variable distributions. This may, in many cases, be objectionable from a substantive point of view, but it is logically and technically possible (see Borsboom, Mellenbergh and Van Heerden, 2002b, for some examples where this procedure may also be plausible from a substantive point of view). However, the important point is not whether this would be generally appropriate, but that nothing in the formulation of the latent variable model precludes it. The representationalist does not seem to be in a position to take such a course of action. The qualitative relations mapped into the numerical domain in population A are different from those in population B. Because measurement is representation, it seems to me that the representationalist must say that something different is being measured in each population, not that the same attribute is being measured differently. The representationalist cannot therefore assume the kind of meaning invariance that the latent variable theorist can.

The reason for this lies in the different ontological tenets of the models. If the representationalist cannot construct a representation, nothing is measured; he cannot reify a measurement scale without contradicting himself. The latent variable theorist can imagine the wildest situations because he takes the ontological freedom to postulate a latent variable, and take it from there; the representationalist cannot imagine any measurement situation where he could not construct a homomorphic representation on the basis of empirical relations, for such a situation would not allow for use of the term measurement. Thus, the representationalist model does not have the metaphysical richness to allow one to posit the existence, in reality, of more than the relations in the data to be represented. Where the latent variable theorist cannot keep a consistent position *without* a realist interpretation of latent variables, the representationalist cannot keep a consistent position *with* a realist interpretation of measurement scales.

The researcher who views intelligence as a measurement scale thus takes a constructivist position with respect to the attribute in question. Because the existence of a measurement scale depends on the fact that it is possible to construct it, such a researcher must moreover conclude that general intelligence does not exist at the present time, because nobody has constructed a general intelligence test that allows for a homomorphic representation. However, all is not lost, because it also follows from the identification of intelligence with a measurement scale, that general intelligence may come to exist tomorrow at 2.14 p.m. if someone were to construct a homomorphic mapping of general intelligence test items at that particular time. This kind of relativism with respect to theoretical entities is strongly reminiscent of positivism.

These observations are relevant with respect to the theoretical status of psychological constructs in general. Of course, positions of all kinds can be defended for a construct like intelligence. The reason for this is that the theory of intelligence is not formulated in sufficient detail to imply a realist, constructivist, or operationalist position. So, one may hold the view that intelligence is a causally effcient entity, or that it is just a heuristic concept, useful to organize our observations, or that it is a dispositional characteristic, or that it is a social construction, and so forth. But when a construct like intelligence is related to the observations, some kind of measurement model must come into play. And it is at this point that the researcher must commit to an ontology for the construct. If he is an operationalist or constructivist, he should not let himself be drawn into latent variable models; for then he will have to posit an ontological position that is too strong. If he is a realist, then research conducted within the framework of classical test theory cannot be considered to put the proposed ontology to the test. If he does not want to commit to realism, but neither to operationalism, he may opt for representational measurement theory.

If I am correct in my analysis, psychology suffers from a substantial conceptual confusion in the interpretation of its theoretical terms. For instance, some researchers in personality give the impression that executing a principal components analysis tests the hypothesis that the Five Factors of personality are real and causally efficient entities. A principal component analysis, however, is a special case of the formative model discussed in chapter 3, so as far as I am concerned this specific ontological tenet (which is the subject of heated discussions; Pervin, 1994) has not been tested in such research. Similarly, many people working in latent variable theory seem to regard latent variables as nothing more than economic representations of the data. However, commonly used latent variable model are usually not representations of the data in a rigorous fundamental measurement theory sense, and it is unclear why one would need latent variables analysis for economic representations in a less rigorous sense; principal components seem good enough, and are much easier to obtain. Others think that a factor in a factor analysis is the 'common content' of the items; but this is also inconsistent, for common content is a characteristic of items, while a latent variable is a characteristic of subjects. Finally, I suspect that the majority of researchers in psychology, who hold a realist position with respect to their constructs, will not hesitate to equate these constructs with true scores; a position that is, in general, inconsistent.

Is this important? That depends on the situation. I personally feel that the most serious mistake consists in asserting realism about constructs on the basis of the wrong model. Somebody who thinks that he has proven the existence of general intelligence because one principal component had an Eigenvalue larger than one, or because Cronbach's α was over 0.80, has never tested the ontological claim involved. Such cases abound in psychology. Of course, someone who has successfully fitted a unidimensional latent variable model has not proven the existence of a latent variable either, but at least that hypothesis has been tested, however indirectly. Mistaken reification seems to me the most serious fallacy that can be made with respect to the problems discussed here. The other mistake, i.e., claiming that no theoretical concept in the models discussed could ever exist, does not seem so grave. I see no particular problem with an intelligence researcher who neither believes that intelligence exists, nor that such a hypothesis is tested in a model of any kind. One could say such a person is perhaps being overly sceptical, but the sceptic has a philosophical problem, not necessarily a scientific one. Moreover, sceptics usually play a healthy role in the scientific discussion, while communities of believers seem to be able to propagate mistaken conclusions indefinitely. This is especially true of psychology, where ontological realists about attitudes, personality traits, and general intelligence, are hardly ever pressed to use the right model for testing their claims.

5.3.2 The interpretation of probability

The interpretation of the theoretical status of the discussed models, the theoretical terms figuring therein, and the relations between these models, were seen to depend crucially on the interpretation of probability. Obviously, neither the stochastic subject nor the repeated sampling interpretation of probability is logically imposed upon us. Can we nevertheless force a choice between these interpretations? For example, could such a choice be defended on more general metatheoretical principles?

From this point of view one may, for instance, argue that the stochastic subject interpretation is flawed, because Mr Brown's brainwash is simply a ridiculous and inadmissible thought experiment. However, the interpretation of probability in models like the ones discussed here always requires a thought experiment of one variety or another. Mr Brown's brainwash is the variant that goes with the stochastic subject interpretation. The repeated sampling interpretation, however, no less requires a thought experiment. Usually, we are not sampling at random from well defined populations, as the statistician would like us to do. In fact, generally nothing that resembles the statistician's idea of sampling has occurred in the first place; in psychology, 'sampling' often merely means that not all six billion people on this earth have been tested. Thus, the random sampling view must also take recourse to a thought experiment – this time in terms of hypothetical repeated sampling from a subpopulation of people with the same position on the latent variable – if an interpretation of its terms is asked for. Moreover, the population in question will often be idealized. For instance, the population may be assumed to be normally distributed over a continuous latent variable, which is unrealistic if only because there are not enough people to realize that assumption. Thus, the introduction of a thought experiment seems unavoidable in both interpretations, and it may well be unavoidable in applied statistics in general (Borsboom, Mellenbergh, and Van Heerden, 2002a). One cannot argue that the propensity interpretation must be discarded because it invokes a thought experiment, for the repeated sampling interpretation does so too. At best, one could argue that one of the interpretations should be favoured because it introduces a 'better' thought experiment, but I do not see what the grounds for such an argument could be.

One could also claim that propensities should be cut away by Occam's razor, because they are superfluous: the model can be formulated without mentioning propensities. Ellis (1994, p. 5) quotes a personal communication with Paul Holland, in which the latter is reported to have said that '··· the stochastic subject hypothesis is a bad hypothesis. Like God, it is not needed'. Such an argument may seem attractive, but I think it oversimplifies the problem. First, it is most certainly not the case that propensities do no theoretical work at all: we have seen in this chapter that, at the very least, they yield a unified and consistent picture of psychometric theory. And unification could be seen as a metatheoretical principle with force about equal to the parsimony principle. Moreover, the psychologist who maintains that his theory is about propensities is justified in using these propensities to derive predictions with respect to between-subjects data. That his predictions could also be derived from a theory which does not mention individual level propensities means that the theory is underdetermined by empirical data; but this cannot be taken to be a decisive argument against his use of propensities, because every theory is underdetermined by empirical data. And that there is usually an alternative explanation of the between-subjects data, which does not use propensities, does not imply that such an alternative explanation is plausible; in fact, it may well be that no substantive interpretation is available for that explanation, so that it remains a purely statistical oddity. Thus, although the introduction of propensity undoubtedly introduces a metaphysical element in a psychological theory, one cannot say that it should therefore be considered inadmissible, unless one holds an unduly narrow view of what is admissible in scientific research.

Many more philosophical arguments for one or another interpretation could perhaps be given. However, I think that none will be decisive. Methodological principles or philosophical arguments do not have enough force to clinch this problem. This may have to do with the fact that the interpretation of probability is an intricate problem in general, and not just in psychometric models (e.g., Nagel, 1939; Fine, 1973; De Finetti, 1974; Popper, 1963; Hacking, 1965). No decisive argument has, to my knowledge, ever been presented for or against a specific interpretation of probability, and there seems no reason to expect that such an argument would be available in the present situation. If this is correct, i.e., if the choice between these interpretations cannot be motivated on general principles, then it must be motivated on other grounds. It would seem that the problem should then be passed on to substantive psychological theory. And this brings us back to a problem that was already discussed in chapter 3: namely, what is the range of application of theoretical constructs? That is, do they apply to individuals, or solely to interindividual comparisons, or to both? I am aware of the fact that I am passing on a difficult problem to psychologists. On the other hand, it would be strange if the interpretation of a term so crucial as probability would be given by methodological considerations. If psychology constructs probabilistic laws, as has often been said in the philosophy of science (Hempel, 1962; Nagel, 1961), then it is up to psychology to decide in which sense they are probabilistic.

5.3.3 *Validity and the relation of measurement*

Because the theories discussed in this book entertain a radically different conception of what it means to measure something, one may expect them to give different accounts of what it means for a measurement procedure to be valid. In this respect, it is remarkable that influential treatises on validity, a concept deemed central to measurement, only superficially address theories of measurement, if at all. It seems to be tacitly assumed that it does not really matter whether one conceives of measurement from a true score perspective, a latent variables perspective, or a fundamental measurement theory perspective. As these theories conceive of the measurement process differently, however, it is likely that the semantics of validity that they give will differ. To investigate this matter, consider a simple sentence like 'IQ-tests measure intelligence'. Let us enquire what would make this sentence true in each of the theories discussed.

First, consider the measurement process from a classical test theory perspective. We have seen in chapter 2 that classical test theory conceives of measurement in a statistical fashion. As Lord and Novick (1968, p. 20) put it, a test score is a measure of a theoretical construct if its expected value increases monotonically with that construct. At first sight, the theoretical construct could be taken to be the true score. Oddly enough, however, the true score is itself defined as the expected test score. Because true scores are identical to expected scores, and because any variable increases monotonically with itself, every test must measure its own true score perfectly. Therefore, if the true score on an IQ-test is considered to be identical to intelligence, the proposition 'IQ scores measure intelligence' is true by definition. This is because the proposition 'IQ-scores measure intelligence' is transformed to 'the expected IQ-scores are monotonically related to the true scores on the IQ-test' which is vacuously true since the true scores are identical to the expected scores. Because the line of reasoning succeeds for every conceivable test, in this interpretation every psychological test is valid. However, it is only valid for its own true score. This is the price of operationalism: if the construct is equated with the true score, each distinct test defines a distinct construct, because it defines a distinct true score.

An alternative interpretation of classical test theory is that the observed scores do not measure the true scores (after all, it is rather odd to say that an expected value measures itself), but that the true scores measure something else, in the sense that they are themselves monotonically related to the theoretical construct in question. Viewing the issue in this way, the sentence 'IQ-scores measure intelligence' is true if the true scores on the test are monotonically related to intelligence. From a classical test theory perspective, this means that the theoretical construct cannot be conceived of as represented in the measurement model for the test in question, but must be viewed as an external variable. This prompts the conceptualization of validity as correlation with a criterion variable, which yields the concept of criterion validity.

Criterion validity has been extremely important to the theoretical development of the validity concept, for the following reason. Originally, the criterion was considered to be an observed variable, such as grades in college. Because the validity question refers to measurement and not to prediction, and because IQ-scores do not attempt to measure college grades (which are, after all, observable) but intelligence, the criterion validity view was never an adequate conceptualization of test validity. One possible response to this is to sweep the criterion variable under the carpet of unobservability, and to grant it the status of a hypothetical entity. In such a view, the definition of validity in terms of a statistical relation (i.e., the true score increases monotonically with the theoretical construct) is typically retained. The measurability of the intended construct (intelligence) is thereby hypothesized a priori, and the validity of the measurements (IQ-scores) is conceptualized as a monotone relation of the true scores on the IQ-test with this hypothetically measurable attribute.

In this view, validity is external to the measurement model, because in classical test theory a theoretical construct such as intelligence cannot be non-vacuously represented inside the measurement model. The proposition 'IQ-scores measure intelligence' thus becomes 'the true IQ-scores increase monotonically with a hypothetical criterion variable called intelligence'. Attempts to find 'perfect' measurements of intelligence that could function as a standard, analogous to the standard metre in Paris, have, of course, proven fruitless. The type of thinking introduced by looking at intelligence as a criterion variable outside the measurement model is, however, still a very common way of thinking about test validity. That is, there is 'something out there', and the question of validity is how high the correlation between our test scores and that something is. This renders the semantics of validity dependent on two assumptions: (1) there really is something out there (intelligence), and (2) the test scores have a monotonically increasing relation with that something. If this is the case, then the proposition 'IQ-scores measure intelligence' is true. An interesting aspect of this view is that, because expected test scores will have monotonic relations with many attributes, any given test measures an indeterminate number of attributes. Thus, measures are not uniquely tied to a construct. If measurement is further reduced to correlation, everything measures everything else to a certain extent, and all tests must be valid. However, the requirement that true scores be monotonically related to the attribute to be measured is highly similar to the latent variable model; in fact, latent variable theory can be viewed as an elaboration of this idea.

The reason that classical test theory must consider theoretical constructs as external to the measurement model is that the syntactical machinery of the theory is not rich enough to represent constructs inside the model. As we have seen, the true score cannot perform this function without rendering a completely trivial account of measurement. Latent variable models do possess the required terminology. As has been discussed in chapter 3, such models can be viewed as relating the true scores on a number of items or tests to a latent variable, or as relating subpopulation parameters to a latent variable. In either case, the latent variable must be considered to function as a representative for the theoretical construct (to be distinguished from the function of fundamental measurement scales, which are representations of observed relations). The relation of measurement in latent variable models is rather similar to the statistical formulation of classical test theory; namely, it is conceived of in terms of a stochastic relation that the observed scores have with the latent variable. However, these models do have the power to dispose of the problem that tests are valid for any attribute they are monotonically related to, because the dimensionality of the latent space can be specified in the model.

For example, in the unidimensional case, a latent variable model specifies that the true scores on each of a number of indicators are monotonically related to the same latent variable. Moreover, within such unidimensional models it is assumed that the indicators measure only this latent variable and nothing else. This implies that the indicators are independent, conditional on the latent variable. If, conditional on the latent variable, the indicators are still related to another variable (for example, group membership), the indicators are considered biased. Thus, if unidimensionality is posited, measurement can be seen as a monotonic relation of the expected scores with a latent variable, and only with this latent variable (in the sense that they do not systematically relate to another variable, given the latent variable). The proposition 'IQ-scores measure intelligence' then becomes 'the expected IQ-scores increase monotonically with the latent variable intelligence, and, given the latent variable, with nothing else'. It follows that the semantics of unidimensional latent variable models do not allow indicators to be valid for more than one latent variable, in contrast to the classical test model.

In representationalism, measurement is a process of representing observed relations between subjects and items in a number system, which results in a measurement scale. This scale is a product of human activity: it is therefore not necessary to assume, a priori, that scales exist independently of the act of measurement, and that they are somehow responsible for the observed relations. This is in sharp contrast to latent variable models. Scales represent relations, they do not cause relations. Now, if observed relations can be represented in the number system (that is, if a homomorphism can be constructed), the resulting scale is an adequate representation by definition, and therefore measurement has succeeded. If the procedure fails, measurement has not taken place.

Let us consider our paradigm example, and interpret the proposition 'IQ-scores measure intelligence' from this perspective. In order for such a conclusion to hold, a strict set of empirical relations between people and items must hold. Michell (1986) has observed that, in particular, a set of dichotomous IQ-items should form a Guttman scale. This is not the case. Therefore, from a representationalist viewpoint, IQ-tests cannot be considered valid for measuring intelligence; for the required relations between people and items have not been shown to hold. IQ-tests cannot possibly measure intelligence, for they cannot be said to measure anything at all. The proposition 'IQ-scores measure intelligence' is thus false. Moreover, from a fundamental measurement perspective, measurement is extremely rare in psychology (if it occurs at all), because very few psychological tests produce the type of consistencies required for representational theory to operate. Thus, according to this definition of measurement, most or all psychological tests are invalid. Still, this does not answer the question where representationalism would put validity; it merely says that psychological tests are invalid. Suppose for a moment that IQ-tests did conform to the empirical requirements of representational measurement theory. Wherein would the property of validity then consist?

I think that, if representationalists took the theoretical presuppositions of psychologists seriously, they would end up with a relation that is highly similar to, or in fact even the same as, the one posited in latent variable theory. The representationalist would first need to accommodate for the problem of error, that is, he would need to incorporate probabilistic relations. It has been argued in chapter 4, and in the present chapter, that this will almost unavoidably lead to a latent variable model formulation. Second, he would have to introduce exactly the kind of realism that latent variable theory presupposes, in order to prevent every single case of representation to count as an instance of measurement. The empirical relations should not just exist; they should exist because they are causally dependent on the measured attribute. This requires the representationalist to abandon the constructivist position completely; for now he will have to hold that the attribute exists and has causal relevance for the observed variables. It thus seems that, if the representationalist gave up the constructivist foundation of the theory, and incorporated a probabilistic relation between the attribute and the observed variables, he could occupy the same philosophical position with respect to the validity concept, as the latent variable theorist.

So, with respect to the relation of validity, we must conclude the following. Classical test theory does not formulate a serious account of measurement, and therefore is inadequate to deal with the question of validity. In fact, if it begins to formulate such an account, it invokes a kind of embryonic latent variable model. Latent variable theory is able, by its very conceptualization, to hold that measurement is a causal relation between the latent variable and its indicators. In fact, this is a natural interpretation of the theory, because it is virtually equivalent to a common cause model (Glymour, 2001). Representationalism works on observable relations between objects, and therefore has no place for the relation of validity: the very fact that we are supposed to be able to judge relations like 'not noticeably longer than' with the unaided eye, means that validity is presupposed in the model. However, if the representationalist drops the condition that relations between objects be 'noticeable', which is unrealistic in the first place, he turns out to have been hiding a latent variable model under the cloak of noticeability all this time. Thus, when considered in terms of validity, the representational measurement model and the latent variable model converge to a surprising extent.

5.3.4 Theoretical consequences

So far, I have discussed the different mathematical models one might choose to conceptualize psychological measurement, and have discussed the relations between them. In this process, it has been shown how these models implement different positions in the philosophy of of science, and what the strengths and weaknesses of these positions are. I will now present my own view on these matters.

The classical test theory model presents exactly one good idea. That idea is the introduction of a stochastic structure in the measurement model. The way in which this is done, however, is devoid of a serious motivation. The mathematical formulation is not based on a theory of test scores, but on the statistical theory of composite random variables; accordingly, the interpretation of the model in terms of measurement is entirely post-hoc. In fact, it is surprisingly difficult to come up with a reasonable interpretation of the central terms in the model, like true and error scores, or even to make sense of what is actually being meant by a term so central as reliability. At a philosophical level, the consequences of fully endorsing the model are those of operationalism: it is impossible to even consistently state the hypothesis that two tests measure the same true score. If one stays within the conceptual framework that classical test theory offers, that means that it is impossible for different measurement procedures to measure the same attribute, magnitude, or dimension. This is a well-known consequence of the operationalist position (Suppe, 1977). However, this strikes me as absurd; it seems to me that the possibility of measuring the same attribute with different measurement procedures is not a matter of philosophical deliberation, but a fact of life.

Representationalism shows how far one can go with an absolute minimum of metaphysics. The theory is elegant and deep; and the ideas presented in additive conjoint measurement may be among the best ever to have been introduced in psychological measurement. However, in order to make its mathematically rigorous treatment work, representational measurement theory idealizes data to perfection. This precludes the possibility of dealing with measurement error in a satisfactory way. Also, the theory mentions empirical relations and scales that represent them, but it is silent on the way the empirical relations are supposed to originate. Representationalism says what one can do, once one has an empirical relational structure that has a weak order, but not why this order should exist or where it came from. In my opinion, a theory of measurement that does not treat this issue is not really a theory of measurement, but rather a theory of representation alone. Equating measurement with representation, however, is not an option because it would include absurd cases as instances of measurement. It seems that the only satisfactory way of solving this problem is by introducing realism about the measured attributes. This directly implies the specification of a latent variable model.

The latent variable model, then, seems to take the best of both worlds. It includes a stochastic structure, which makes it applicable to real measurement situations, where data are noisy. It can also be interpreted as instantiating exactly the realist position that representationalism fails to explicate, because it says that observed relations must be a function of the attributes one measures. These attributes are specified inside the measurement model, namely as latent variables. The characterization of such attributes may be given in terms of the empirical relational systems that are provided by representational measurement theory; if this is done, these are hypothesized to hold at the latent level. In such an interpretation, one would use the formal apparatus of representationalism (i.e., set theory) but not the associated philosophical framework (i.e., logical positivism).

I think that latent variable theory gives a plausible picture of measurement, and I will take it as my starting point in what follows. However, I add to the statistical formulation of the model the requirement that the indicators must not merely be statistically associated with the latent variable, but must be causally dependent on it. This is not usually explicitly stated in the assumptions of latent variable theory, but latent variable models are almost always consistent with a common cause relation since they require local independence. The philosophical way of saying this is that the latent variable 'screens off' the correlations between the observables.

Measurement should then be conceptualized as follows. First, it requires an attribute to exist and to have a determinate structure (e.g., a qualitative or quantitative structure of certain dimensionality). Second, it requires a measurement instrument that is set up in such a way as to be sensitive to that structure. The word 'sensitive' means that the instrument works in such a way that it transmits variation in the measured attribute; this means nothing more (or less) than that variation in the observable measurement outcomes depends causally on variation in the attribute. Thus, this requires a causal chain that runs from variation in the attribute to variation in the measurement outcomes. It need not do so in a deterministic manner; the causal chain may be disturbed by various factors other than the measured attribute, and this means that we may expect some noise in the observations.

One example of making the required causal chain is by constructing a ruler to measure length, for instance. The ruler transmits differences in length into differences in recorded measurement outcomes. Because length has a quantitative structure, and we are smart enough to see that it has such a structure, we can make measurement instruments that transmit the causal effect in a quantitative way. This is what we do when we measure length with a ruler. Another attempt to construct such a chain is by making an IQ-test to measure general intelligence. If general intelligence exists, and the IQ-test items have the property of transmitting variation in general intelligence, then we can use somebody's responses on these items to assess his position on general intelligence. In this case, the causal process supposedly at work is somewhat mysterious and has never been clearly articulated; hence we must doubt the validity of such tests, for we do not know how they work. But causality in measurement need not be complicated, even if it depends in part on psychological processes. An example of a simple causal chain that depends on psychological concepts like memory and knowledge is put to work when we measure sex by asking a person to which sex he or she belongs: the person ticks the box 'male' because he knows he is male, and he knows that he is male because he *is* male. Because the same process holds for females, we may conclude that the variation in sex is directly transmitted into variation in the item responses. In statistics, it is common to say of such variables that they are 'observed'. However, that is a curious mode of speech; one does not 'observe' the variable 'sex' walking down the street. What 'observed' means here is that the causal process that links the variable sex to the item response (e.g., to a person's striking the box for 'male' when asked for his sex) is so transparent and simple that we may consider it to be deterministic.

Thus, in the present scheme of thinking, there is always a conceptual distinction between the attribute measured and the measurement outcomes: they are never identical. When we say that a variable was 'observed', this must be considered a metaphorical mode of speech, and not a statement that could possibly be factually correct. For what we observe are men and women, not the variable 'sex'. Thus, variables are theoretical terms by definition. However, there is no ontological distinction between 'latent' and 'observed' variables. This distinction is a function of the measurement process. 'Observed' variables are attributes that bear a deterministic causal relation to the item response (e.g., to a person's striking the box for 'male' when asked for his sex). 'Latent' variables are attributes for which this is not the case. Clearly, this is an epistemological distinction that depends on the characteristics of the measurement process, not an ontological distinction between different 'kinds' of variables.

In conclusion, if a causal chain is present and links variation in the attribute to variation in the observed measurement outcomes, then these outcomes can be used to infer an object's or person's place in the attribute structure. This can only happen if the attribute exists and has a determinate structure; otherwise it cannot enter in a causal relation. It is important to realize that variables need not be 'inside' a person in order to fulfil this role. Thus, the between-subjects structure and within-subject structure need not be identical in form or dimensionality in order for measurement to be possible. Sex is an example of an attribute that is, for instance, not present within a person. All we can say is that a person occupies one of its levels: it is a between-subjects attribute, for it does not vary within a person. Mood is an example of an attribute that is, in a sense, present within a person; the sense in which this is true is that a person varies in mood over time: it is a within-subject attribute. Note, however, that even in this case, at any given time point t, it is strictly speaking only true that the person occupies a position on the variable mood; that variable itself is not present 'inside' the person at time t. Like sex 'stretches out' in the between-subjects space, mood does so in the within-subject space. Mood is, of course, also a between-subjects attribute, but it is a complicated one: it cannot unproblematically be assumed that mood has the same structure or dimensionality within each person. In contrast, for the variable 'age' we can make this assumption: it has a unidimensional structure both within and between persons. The between-subjects and within-subjects dimensions are, in this case, of the same form. Much research in psychology silently assumes this to be true for psychological attributes in general, but I think that, if psychologists ever reach the point where they start to put this assumption to serious tests, they will find that it is the exception rather than the rule. For the present discussion, however, this is immaterial. What is important is that locally homogeneous, locally heterogeneous, and locally irrelevant attributes are all potential candidates for measurement: no assumptions regarding the equivalence of between- and within-subject structures are required.

This picture of measurement is, in my view, simple and plausible. The consequences of this scheme of thinking for the conceptualization of psychological measurement, however, are surprisingly serious. In the next chapter, this will be illustrated through the examination of the concept of test validity. It turns out that the past seventy years of validity theory either stand in flagrant contradiction to the ideas at which we have now arrived, or fail to articulate them.

6 The concept of validity

6.1 Introduction

That the conceptual problems inherent in measurement in general, and psychological measurement in particular, are poorly understood is obvious from the lack of agreement on the meaning of the term 'measurement', the multitude of conceptually different models for implementing it, and the fact that no psychologist can point to a field where psychological measurement has succeeded without eliciting an immediate claim to the contrary from another psychologist. Given that virtually all aspects of the measurement problem are the subject of ongoing debates, many of which have been discussed in previous chapters, one would expect these debates to culminate in fierce discussions on the most central question one can ask about psychological measurement, which is the question of validity. It is therefore an extraordinary experience to find that, after proceeding up through the turmoil at every fundamental level of the measurement problem, one reaches this conceptually highest and presumably most difficult level only to find a tranquil surface of relatively widespread consensus (Kane, 2001; Shepard, 1993).

A remarkable aspect of this consensus in validity theory is that the concept with which validity theorists are concerned seems strangely divorced from the concept that working researchers have in mind when posing the question of validity. That is, many researchers are under the impression that the problem of validity simply concerns the question whether a test measures what it should measure, but most validity theorists have come to see the validity concept as embracing a much wider variety of test-related problems (Cronbach, 1988; Messick, 1989; Shepard, 1993). This is because, in the past century, the question of validity has evolved from the question whether one measures what one intends to measure (Cattell, 1946; Kelley, 1927), to the question whether the empirical relations between test scores match theoretical relations in a nomological network (Cronbach and Meehl, 1955), to the question whether interpretations and actions based on test scores are justified – not only in the light of scientific evidence, but with respect to social and ethical consequences of test use (Messick, 1989). Thus, validity theory has gradually come to treat every important test-related issue as relevant to the validity concept, and aims to integrate all these issues under a single header. In doing so, however, the theory fails to serve either the theoretically oriented psychologist or the practically inclined tester: the theoretically oriented are likely to get lost in the intricate subtleties of validity theory, while the practically oriented are unlikely to derive a workable conceptual scheme with practical implications from it. A theory of validity that leaves one with the feeling that every single concern about psychological testing is relevant, important, and should be addressed in psychological testing, cannot offer a sense of direction to the working researcher.

The objective of the present chapter is to show that validity theory can do better. I aim to analyse the considerations that have led to the present state of affairs, to show that many of these are irrelevant, and to offer a simple, clear, and workable alternative. It is my intent to convince the reader that most of the validity literature either fails to articulate the validity problem clearly, or misses the point entirely. Validity is not complex, faceted, or dependent on nomological networks and social consequences of testing. It is a very basic concept and was correctly formulated, for instance, by Kelley (1927, p. 14), when he stated that a test is valid if it measures what it purports to measure.

The argument to be presented is exceedingly simple; so simple, in fact, that it articulates an account of validity that may seem almost trivial. It is this: if something does not exist, then one cannot measure it. If it exists, but does not causally produce variations in the outcomes of the measurement procedure, then one is either measuring nothing at all or something different altogether. Thus, a test is valid for measuring an attribute if and only if a) the attribute exists, and b) variations in the attribute causally produce variations in the outcomes of the measurement procedure. The general idea is based on the causal theory of measurement (e.g., Trout, 1999). When considered within a latent variable framework, the position is similar to that taken by Bollen (1989). Also, several theorists in the previous century have hinted at similar conceptions (e.g., Cattell, 1946; Loevinger, 1957). Finally, it is likely that most researchers think of construct validity in causal terms, so that one could consider the proposed conception to be a kind of 'underground' interpretation of construct validity.

Nevertheless, in the consensus on validity that has emerged in the past two decades, it is difficult to find an explicit formulation resembling the above. In the writings of leading theorists (i.e., Cronbach, 1988; Kane, 2001; Messick, 1981, 1989, 1998; Shepard, 1993), one will not find much that sustains it; rather, one is likely to find this type of idea in a discussion of historical conceptions of validity (Kane, 2001, pp. 319–23). More importantly, even though many working researchers may be inclined to agree with the proposed conception if pressed for a definition of validity, its consequences are not followed through in mainstream validation research. These consequences are not trivial. The fact that the crucial ingredient of validity involves the causal effect of an attribute on the test scores implies that the locus of evidence for validity lies in the processes that convey this effect. This means that tables of correlations between test scores and other measures cannot provide more than circumstantial evidence for validity. What needs to be tested is not a theory about the relation between the attribute measured and other attributes, but a theory of response behaviour. Somewhere in the chain of events that occur between item administration and item response, the measured attribute must play a causal role in determining what value the measurements outcomes will take; otherwise, the test cannot be valid for measuring the attribute. Importantly, this implies that the problem of validity cannot be solved by psychometric techniques or models alone. On the contrary, it must be addressed by substantive theory. Validity is the one problem in testing that psychology cannot contract out to methodology.

In the course of developing the conception of validity as put forward above, I aim to do two things. First, to offer a simple, yet adequate, semantics for the validity concept. This is done through a juxtaposition of the proposed validity concept with existing theory in three domains: ontology versus epistemology, reference versus meaning, and causality versus correlation. Second, to indicate future directions in research that may demystify, pinpoint, and solve the widespread validity problem in psychology. Here, the benefits of a trimmed-down validity concept will be illustrated through a discussion of some clear theoretical and practical implications that may improve both the theory and practice of psychological measurement.

6.2 Ontology versus epistemology

If the crucial issue in validity concerns the existence of an attribute that causally influences the outcome of the measurement procedure, then the central claim is ontological, and not epistemological. This is to say that one is claiming something about which things inhabit reality, and how they relate to each other. Thus, the realm of ontology includes both the existence of phenomena and their causal influences. These constituents are fleshed out in the following sections, which address reference and causality in turn.

The truth of ontological claims is distinct from the ability to find out about reality, which is the central issue in epistemology. Measurement, of course, is the prototypical epistemological activity in science, and it is therefore easy to make the mistake that we are primarily claiming something on this front. This is because *if* the ontological claim holds, *then* the measurement procedure can be used to find out about the attributes to which it refers. Put more simply: if differences in intelligence cause differences in IQ-scores, then the IQ-score differences can be used to find out about the intelligence differences. Thus, in this very special case, the truth of the ontological claim guarantees the epistemological access. Note that the truth of the ontological claim is logically prior to the process of measurement itself, because it is a necessary condition for measurement to be possible. Nevertheless, the ontological claim that underlies the measurement procedure is itself conceptually distinct from the measurement process. One can see this by considering the following analogy. It may be a necessary condition for entering a room that the door leading to that room is not locked. Still, the fact that the door is not locked is conceptually distinct from walking through it to enter the room.

It would seem, however, that to talk about the ontology is to talk about the epistemology, and there surely is a sense in which this is correct. Now, it is a small step to conclude that, instead of laying down the ontological claims involved in measurement, which make so abundantly clear the strong assumptions we are making about psychological attributes (Kagan, 1988; Michell, 1999), the discussion could just as well be limited to the epistemological side of the endeavour, which is respectable and familiar, without addressing the ontological issues. It is another small step to conclude that the essential question of validity is about particular aspects of this epistemological process called measurement. The final step, leading to some very dark philosophical dungeons from which escape is impossible, is to start talking about some presumed universal characteristics of this epistemological process (usually derived from a few paradigm cases like length or temperature measurement) that, if present, would allow one to somehow be rationally justified in concluding that the ontological claims are true.

This, of course, will not work. The family of procedures, that scientists – as opposed to philosophers – regard as instances of measurement, is diverse and incoherent and has few universal characteristics. Length and temperature, blood pressure and brain size, pathology, and intelligence all could be said to involve measurement, but the associated measurement practices are based on vastly different lines of reasoning and employ vastly different methodologies. So now one gets into trouble. What could it be that successful measurement procedures have in common? Is it the way

The concept of validity 153

the test looks? Representative sampling from a universe of behaviours? The line of reasoning on which it is constructed? The correlation between a test and some external variable called the 'criterion'? The (presumed) fact that the test figures in a 'nomological network' of 'constructs'? Or is it just that one can do something 'useful' with regard to some 'purpose' which is presumably *different* from measuring the hypothesized attribute? Or are we on the wrong track here, because what is important is not a characteristic of tests or test scores, but of test score interpretations – which are, again, presumably *different* from the obvious ones like 'IQ-scores measure intelligence'?

This line of reasoning quickly gets us nowhere. The reason is that there *are* no universal characteristics of measurement, *except* the ontological claim involved. The only thing that all measurement procedures have in common is the either implicit or explicit assumption that there is an attribute out there that, somewhere in the long and complicated chain of events leading up to the measurement outcome, is playing a causal role in determining what values the measurements will take. This is not some complicated and obscure conception but a very simple idea. If one, however, fails to take it into account, one ends up with an exceedingly complex construction of superficial epistemological characteristics that are irrelevant to the validity issue. And because the measurement processes and models are diverse and complicated, one is likely to buy into the mistaken idea that the concept of validity must also be complicated. So now one gets a multiplication of terms. For the human condition is such that someone will inevitably distinguish between 'kinds of validity' and 'degrees of validity' and so we are bound to come up with a hundred or so 'validities', which all come in 'degrees', until someone stands up because this is clearly ridiculous, and claims that 'all validation is one' (Cronbach, 1980, p. 99) so that all kinds of validity can be integrated and subsumed under one giant umbrella (Messick, 1989). And since we are now thoroughly convinced that we are concerned with characteristics of an epistemological process rather than with an ontological claim, we are going to reach the conclusion that all this time we were really just talking about the one grand epistemological process – scientific research (Cronbach and Meehl, 1955; Loevinger, 1957; Messick, 1989). However, given that every attempt at drawing a line between 'scientific' and 'unscientific' research either fails or duplicates the distinction between good and bad research, the exciting fact discovered here is that validation research is research. In other words, nothing has been discovered at all. And the reason for this is that there was nothing to be discovered in the first place.

When claiming that a test is valid, one is taking the ontological position that the attribute being measured exists and affects the outcome of the measurement procedure. This is probably one of the more serious scientific claims one can make, and it is difficult to prove or refute it. This, however, does not mean that the validity concept itself is complicated. Every test constructor in every scientific discipline has the stated line of reasoning in mind when she is constructing, administering, or interpreting a test. It is the only aspect that measurement procedures have in common. If one is going to search for homogeneity in the superficial characteristics of these procedures one is not going to find any, and one is likely to build ever more complicated systems covering different 'aspects' of validity. These systems, however, do not cover different aspects of validity but describe different research procedures for validation. So 'asking people what they think about the test' becomes 'face validity'; 'checking whether we can predict some interesting things with it' becomes 'predictive validity'; 'investigating whether the data fit our theory about the attribute' becomes 'construct validity'; and so on.

The union of all possible test related activities of this kind is not validity, but validation. These terms are sometimes used interchangeably in the literature, but they are not the same. This is clear from the fact that validity is a property, while validation is an activity. In particular, validation is the kind of activity we undertake to find out whether a test has the property of validity. Validity is a concept like truth; it represents an ideal or desirable situation. Validation is more like theory testing; the muddling around in the data to find out which way to go. Validity is about ontology; validation is about epistemology. The two should not be confused. Now, most of the validity literature has not dealt with the problem of validity, but with the problem of validation. While there is nothing wrong with describing, classifying, and evaluating validation strategies, such activities are not likely to elucidate the concept of validity itself. In fact, if one concentrates on the epistemological problems long enough, one will move away from the validity concept rather than towards it. Consider, for example, Messick's (1989) widely cited definition of validity: 'validity is an integrated evaluative judgment of the degree to which empirical evidence and theoretical rationales support the *adequacy* and *appropriateness* of *inferences* and *actions* based on test scores or other modes of assessment' (p. 13; italics in the original). No view could be farther apart from the one advanced here. Validity is not a judgment at all. It is the property being judged.

6.3 Reference versus meaning

That the position taken here is so at variance with the existing conception in the literature is largely due to the fact that, in defining validity, I have reversed the order of reasoning. Instead of focusing on accepted epistemological processes and trying to fit in existing test practices, I start with the ontological claim, and derive the adequacy of epistemological practices only in virtue of its truth. This means that the central point in validity is one of *reference:* the attribute to which the psychologist refers must exist in reality, otherwise the test cannot possibly be valid for measuring that attribute. This does not imply that the attribute cannot change over time, or that that psychological attributes are 'unchanging essences' (cf. Kagan, 1988). It does imply that to construe theoretical terms as referential requires a realist position about the phenomena to which such terms refer. Thus, measurement is considered to involve realism about the measured attribute. This is because I cannot see how the sentences 'Test X measures the attitude towards nuclear energy' and 'Attitudes do not exist' can both be true. If you agree on this point, then you are in disagreement with some very powerful philosophical movements which have shaped validity theory to a large extent.

Of course, the strongest of these movements was logical positivism. Philosophers and scientists endorsing this theory saw it as their mission to exorcise all reference of theoretical terms (like 'attitude'), because such reference introduces metaphysics, which the logical positivists thought was bad. They therefore constructed theoretical terms as non-referential. This led them to focus on the *meaning* of theoretical terms. Meaning and reference are easily confused, but are very different concepts. To give a classic example (Frege, 1892), 'the morning star' and 'the evening star' have different meanings (namely 'the last star still to be seen at morning' and 'the first star to be seen at evening'), but refer to the same thing (namely the planet Venus). Because the positivists had a slightly phobic attitude towards metaphysics, they wanted to explain the use of theoretical terms like 'attitude' without letting these terms refer to reality.

This was an interesting endeavour but it failed (see Suppe, 1977, for a good overview). However, one of the relics of the approach has plagued validity theory to this day. This is the nomological network. A nomological network is a kind of system of laws relating the theoretical terms to each other and to the observations. For the positivists, this network served to create meaning without reference for the theoretical terms. The idea is that the meaning of a theoretical term is solely determined by the place of that term in the nomological network: the meaning of the term 'energy' is fixed by the network and by nothing else – certainly not by a reference to actual energy. Thus, in this view one can have meaning without reference, and can invoke theoretical terms without automatically engaging in ontological claims, which always introduce a lot of metaphysics.

This idea was used by Cronbach and Meehl in 1955 to put forward their idea of 'construct validity'. Many people think that construct validity is the same as the kind of validity proposed in this chapter, but this is not the case. The construct validity position does not invoke reference (it does not say that the attribute to be measured should exist), and it does not talk about causality (it is not necessary for the attribute to have a causal role in determining the measurement outcomes). The classic position, as articulated by Cronbach and Meehl (1955), holds that a test can be considered valid for a construct if the empirical relations in which the test stands to other tests, match the theoretical relations, in which the construct stands to other constructs. One can imagine this as two path models, one hovering over the other. One model stands for theoretical relations, the other for empirical relations. If the models match, then there is 'construct validity' for test score interpretations in terms of the nomological network. For instance, suppose the nomological network says that the construct 'intelligence' is positively related to the construct 'general knowledge' and negatively to the construct 'criminal behaviour'. Further suppose that one observes a correlation of 0.5 between an IQ-test and a test for general knowledge, and a correlation of -0.4 between the IQ-test and the number of months spent in prison. There is thus a match between empirical and theoretical relations. In construct validity theory, it is this match that constitutes and defines the validity concept.

To define construct validity, no reference to the existence of theoretical entities is necessary, and their causal impact on the measurement outcomes is not even a topic of discussion. Read Cronbach and Meehl (1955) to see how carefully they avoid this issue. As an illustration of the ambiguity of Cronbach and Meehl's (1955) paper, one may compare Bechtold (1959) and Loevinger (1957), who both discuss construct validity, but are talking about two completely different interpretations of the concept – one positivist, the other realist. In principle, however, within the construct validity perspective there is no friction between 'Test X measures the attitude towards nuclear energy' and 'Attitudes do not exist.' As long as the empirically observed relations, between test X and other tests, match the theoretical relations in the nomological network, all is fine.

The problem, of course, is that there are few, if any, nomological networks in psychology that are sufficiently detailed to do the job of fixing the meaning of theoretical terms. To fix this meaning requires a very restrictive nomological network. The reason is that, if one wants to evade realist metaphysics, one cannot say 'intelligence is a real attribute with causal impact on our measurements', but only that 'intelligence is a theoretical term that is defined in terms of the relations it has to other constructs in

The concept of validity 157

the nomological network'. Now, it is crucial for the ideas formulated in Cronbach and Meehl (1955) that the latter type of descriptive, nonreferential account is possible, because otherwise one is forced to invoke a referent for a theoretical term like intelligence, which brings in the very metaphysics to be avoided through the back door - and introducing such metaphysics changes the rules of the game considerably.

In some highly developed theories, like the ones in physics, one could at least begin to consider this account, because they are restrictive enough to single out one particular theoretical term, which is the only one that has all the right relations. In psychology, such an account does not work because one does not have the required theories. We do have loosely specified ideas on how largely undefined attributes relate to each other under limited sets of circumstances, but this is not enough. That this is not just an academic point, but a decisive argument against using a descriptive, nonreferential account can immediately be seen by considering the intelligence example discussed above. One does not get anywhere by saying that 'intelligence is whatever is positively related to general knowledge and negatively to criminal behaviour', because there are too many theoretical terms that will satisfy this description, and many of them will evidently not be the same as intelligence. No theoretical term in psychology can be unambiguously identified in this way. Thus, this theory will not be able to single out theoretical terms merely by describing where they stand in a nomological network. Cronbach and Meehl (1955) do discuss the problem that nomological networks are incomplete and vague in psychology, but they do not mention the most important implication of that problem: it is fatal to any positivist reading of their account, because it shows that reference, and the accompanying realist metaphysics of measurement, cannot be avoided.

In this context, it has been noted by validity theorists (Shepard, 1997; Kane, 2001), that requiring the existence of a nomological network is unrealistic in psychology, which is correct. However, if one removes the nomological network from construct validity theory, one is left with very little indeed. In fact, dropping the nomological network leaves one without the heavily needed theory of meaning, and one is likely to be forced to introduce reference again, that is, to interpret the theoretical terms as referring to things out there in the world. I think that this is a plausible move, as will be evident, but the consequence is that the main idea of construct validity, as put forward by Cronbach and Meehl (1955), loses its bite. That is, if one reintroduces reference, then it is difficult to maintain that what constitutes validity is a match between empirical relations and theoretical relations. For this match is now rendered a helpful epistemological criterion, which may be given a signalling function, but not much more. Thus, if there is a grave discrepancy between the theoretical and empirical relations, one knows that something is wrong somewhere; but this can hardly be considered news. If the theoretical and empirical relations match, this match does nothing more than corroborate the theory, to use a Popperian term. The match is no longer constitutive of validity, however, because the reintroduction of the realist metaphysics forces one to shift back to reference as the primary defining feature of validity.

The emphasis that is placed on the importance of ruling out alternative rival hypotheses for corroborating data (Cronbach and Meehl, 1955; Messick, 1989) partly acknowledges this. One can readily see this by introducing the question to what hypothesis the alternative one should be considered a rival. Obviously, to the hypothesis that there is an attribute in reality that produces variation in the measurement outcomes. What, then, is to be seen as the defining feature of validity if not exactly the truth of that hypothesis? And if this is correct, then where does this leave the instrumentalist, positivist, and empiricist? Consider, for example, instrumentalism. This view does not invoke truth, but usefulness as the primary criterion for the adequacy of scientific theories and measurements. However, we are surely not seriously considering the idea that we have to rule out rivals to the hypothesis that intelligence tests are useful. The Wechsler Adult Intelligence Scale comes in a big heavy box, which is very useful to hit people on the head with, but the hypothesis that the WAIS is valid for inflicting physical injury is certainly not the kind of hypothesis we are interested in. Clearly, from the viewpoint of ruling out alternative hypotheses, the hypothesis that the test is useful is neither intended nor relevant, except for the very special hypothesis that it can be used to measure intelligence *because variation in intelligence produces variation in IQ-scores*.

However, the flip side of this coin should not be overlooked: if no attribute answers the referential call, the test is not valid for measuring that attribute, no matter how useful the test may be for prediction, selection, or how well it may fulfil other functions. As Kagan (1988, p. 619) has said, this 'urges care in the use of descriptive terms', because if such a term is treated as referential but has no referent, then one is reifying terms that have no other function than that of providing a descriptive summary of a set of distinct attributes and processes. For instance, one then comes to treat a name for a group of test items as if it were the common cause of the item responses. That, of course, is a mistake. Kagan (1988) has further noted some difficult problems in constructing referential connections for theoretical terms. Most important is the observation that this connection may not work in the same way, or even refer to the same attribute or process, in different contexts, situations, or persons, a problem that has been discussed in chapter 3: the latent space underlying a set of item responses may not have the same dimensionality or structure across persons. This is a complicated issue, but that does not mean that we may therefore neglect it. To state that one measures an attribute, but that that attribute does not exist, is not to put forward some sophisticated philosophical position, but to make an empty gesture to evade the difficulties involved.

In conclusion, a positivist or instrumentalist reading of construct validity requires a descriptive theory of meaning which must invoke nomological networks. Cronbach and Meehl (1955) tried to construct an account of validity on this basis. However, the nomological network interpretation of construct validity is inadequate, as has been recognized in the literature. Dropping the nomological network from consideration simply means that one has to go back to a realist interpretation of psychological attributes. In a realist interpretation, however, the crucial issue is reference and not meaning. Therefore, a question like 'are IQ-tests valid for intelligence?' can only be posed under the prior assumption that there does exist, in reality, an attribute that one designates when using the term 'intelligence'; and the question of validity concerns the question whether one has succeeded in constructing a test that is sensitive to variations in that attribute.

6.4 Causality versus correlation

Although construct validity theory is, in its original form, inadequate, it does represent a serious attempt to forge a validity concept that has an account of meaning, a function for theory, and that stresses the fact that there is no essential difference between validation research and research in general. Moreover, if one removes the nomological network from consideration, replaces meaning with reference, and reintroduces the realist perspective, much of what is said in construct validity theory remains consistent and plausible. Also, the idea of construct validity was introduced to get rid of the atheoretical, empiricist idea of criterion validity, which is a respectable undertaking because criterion validity was truly one of the most serious mistakes ever made in the theory of psychological measurement. The idea, that validity consists in the correlation between a test and a criterion, has obstructed a great deal of understanding and continues to do so. The concept continues to exert such a pervasive influence on the thinking of psychologists, because many are under the impression that construct validity is really criterion validity with the criterion replaced by the construct (this fallacy cannot be attributed to construct validity theorists, as is evident from the writings of Cronbach and Meehl, 1955;

Kane, 2001; and Messick, 1981, 1989). However, the inadequacy of this view does not depend on whether one views the criterion as a variable to be predicted from test scores, or as an 'infallible' measure of the theoretical construct to be measured, or as the theoretical construct itself. The crucial mistake is the view that validity is about correlation. Validity concerns measurement, and measurement has a clear direction. The direction goes from the world to our instruments. It is very difficult not to construct this relation as causal. Criterion validity employs correlation and similarity, where it should employ direction and causality.

Of course, causality is a loaded term, and many researchers seem afraid to use it. The platitude 'correlation is not causation' is deeply inscribed in the conscience of every researcher in psychology, and in the literature the word 'causes' is often replaced by euphemisms like 'determines', or 'affects', or 'influences'; in measurement, we see traits 'manifesting' or 'expressing' themselves. What is meant is that traits cause observed scores. It is perfectly all right to say this because hypothesizing a causal account does not mean that one interprets every correlation as a causal relation. This, again, is the epistemological side of the issue which remains as problematic as ever – although progress has been made in this respect, as is evidenced in the work of writers like Pearl (2000) as well as in the development of latent variable models. The primary power of causality lies in the theoretical opportunity to think directionally rather than in terms of similarity or correlation (see, for some good examples, Pearl, 2000; Glymour, 2001). These causal relations can either be constructed to apply to intra-individual variation over time, to inter-individual variation in a population, or to both, and in each of these cases the concept of validity can be applied. Now, measurement is a causal concept, not a correlational one, and validity is so too. To clarify this, some absurdities to which any theory based on a correlational account of validity leads are pointed out. The criticisms must be explicitly understood as applying not just to the criterion validity view, but to any view that does not invoke a causal arrow pointing from the attribute to the measurement outcomes.

First, it has been observed by Guilford (1946) that the idea of criterion validity leads to the conclusion that a test is valid for measuring many things, as epitomized in his famous statement that a test is valid for anything with which it correlates. However, it can be shown that the set of zero correlations is a null set, which means that the likelihood of encountering a zero correlation in real life is exceedingly small (Meehl, 1978), and it has also been observed that in the social sciences everything tends to correlate with everything. Therefore, the upshot of any line of thinking that sees correlation as a defining feature of validity is that everything is, to some degree, valid for everything else. This absurdity does not arise in a causal theory because it is not the case that everything causes everything else.

Second, the idea has the unfortunate consequence of equating degrees of validity with the value of the correlation coefficient: the higher the correlation, the higher the validity. The limiting case is the case where two variables correlate perfectly, which would imply perfect validity. That is, if one views validity as correlational, one is bound to say that if two constructs have a perfect correlation, then 'they are really the same construct under two different labels' (Schmidt and Hunter, 1999, p. 190). This is very problematic. For instance, suppose one is measuring the presence of thunder. The readings will probably show a perfect correlation with the presence of lightning. The reason, of course, is that both are the result of an electrical discharge in the clouds. However, the presence of thunder and the presence of lightning are not the same thing under a different label. They are strongly related, one can be used to find out about the other, and there is a good basis for prediction, but they are not the same thing. When one is validly measuring the presence of thunder, one is not validly measuring the presence of lightning for the simple reason that one is not measuring the presence of lightning at all. The limiting case of the correlational view implies that perfect correlation is perfect validity, and this leads to the idea that deterministically related attributes are the same thing. This absurdity does not arise in a causal theory because variations in the presence of lightning do not play a causal role in producing variations in the presence of thunder.

Third, the correlation is a population dependent statistic, that is, it is sensitive to the amount of variability in the attribute to be measured across populations. A well known instance is the attenuating effect of restriction of range in the presence of imperfect relationships between variables. Any correlational view must therefore hold that validity itself is by necessity variable over populations. Corrections for unreliability and restriction of range (Lord and Novick, 1968) are going to solve some of the trouble here but not all of it. In particular, there is one important, well-established case of valid measurement where the population dependence of correlations raises serious problems. This is the case of extensive measurement (Campbell, 1920; Krantz, Luce, Suppes, and Tversky, 1971). This is very troubling because extensive measurement is more or less the paradigm example of measurement in general (Narens and Luce, 1986). To take a familiar example of extensive measurement, suppose that one is measuring the length of rods, and that the measurement apparatus used is a ruler. Further suppose that one is measuring without error. The correlation between the measurement outcome and the real length will be unity in most populations, as it should be, but there is an important class of populations where it will be zero. This is the class of populations of rods of equal length. Therefore, one must conclude that, in such a population, the ruler is not valid for measuring length. This is a strange result. In extensive measurement, it is quite meaningful to say that all objects in such a subpopulation are, say, 4.2 feet long, and that this measurement is valid. In the causal account, this absurdity does not arise. This is because causality is directional and conditional: the causal account says that, *if* there are differences in the attribute, then these will produce differences in the measurement outcome. However, if there are no differences in the attribute, no differences in the measurement outcomes are expected. This in no way precludes the validity of the measurement outcomes themselves, which is exactly as it should be.

Correlations are epistemologically relevant because they are sometimes indicative of causality, but they are not, and cannot be, constitutive of validity. Perhaps, I have refuted this view in somewhat greater detail than is strictly necessary, as criterion validity has been considered inadequate at least since Cronbach and Meehl's (1955) introduction of construct validity (Messick, 1989; Kane, 2001). I considered a thorough refutation important, however, because it is my impression that many people who do not subscribe to the criterion validity perspective still entertain a correlational conception of validity – the only difference is that they have replaced the criterion with the construct itself. However, it is clear that if attribute differences do not play a causal role in producing differences in measurement outcomes, then the measurement procedure is invalid for the attribute in question. Correlations are not enough, no matter what their size. Height and weight correlate about .80 in the general population, but this does not mean that the process of letting people stand on a scale and reading off their weight gives one valid measurements of their height. To state otherwise is to abuse both the concepts of measurement and of validity. The very fact that a correlational view of measurement allows for this kind of language abuse must be considered to be a fundamental weakness; and any theory of validity that sustains such absurdities should immediately be dropped from consideration. Therefore, not just criterion validity, but any correlational conception of validity is hopeless. The double-headed arrows of correlation should be replaced by the single-headed arrows of causation; and these arrows must run from the attribute to the measurements.

6.5 Where to look for validity

The proposed theory of validity now stands. Validity is a property of tests: a valid test can convey the effect of variation in the attribute we intend to measure. This means that the relation between test scores and attributes is not correlational but causal. A test is valid for measuring an attribute if variation in the attribute causes variation in the test scores. In this case we say that it is true that the test measures the attribute in question. The concept of validity thus expresses nothing less, but also nothing more, than that an attribute, designated by a theoretical term like 'intelligence', exists and that measurement of this attribute can be performed with a given test, because the test scores are causally affected by variation in the attribute. This conception does the job we want validity to do, and it does it in a simple and effective way.

The analysis has direct relevance for the practice of test construction and analysis. In particular, it seems that the emphasis on the role of constructs in theories, and their place in nomological networks, has prompted validation research to adopt what has been called a top-down strategy (Cervone, 1997). This basically comes down to the fact that much validation research is concerned with creating tables of correlation coefficients, and then checking whether these go in the right direction. Although such macro-level relations are important, it would seem that the primary objective of validation research is not to establish that the correlations go in the right directions, but to offer a theoretical explanation of the processes that lead up to the measurement outcomes. That is, there should be at least a hypothesis concerning the causal processes that lie between the attribute variations and the differences in test scores. To use Embretson's (1983) terminology, validation should be concerned primarily with construct representation and only secondarily with nomothetic span.

The upshot of this line of reasoning for test construction is clear. Purely empirical methods, based on the optimization of external correlations, are very unlikely to generate tests that can be considered valid measurements. This is because focusing on predictive properties will destroy, rather than enhance, measurement properties such as validity. The reason for this is simply that items that measure the same attribute will be correlated. Correlated items, however, are relatively useless in prediction, because they generate multicollinearity (they do not explain unique variance in the criterion; Lord and Novick, 1968, p. 332; Smits, Mellenbergh, and Vorst, 2002). What one selects when optimizing predictive utility are items that are mutually uncorrelated, but highly correlated with the criterion. This is not what one expects or desires in measurement. Note that this does not preclude that tests constructed in this manner may be highly useful for prediction. It does imply that optimizing measurement properties and optimizing predictive properties are not convergent lines of test construction.

What is missing in such empirically oriented methods is a theory on what happens between the attribute and the test scores. Maximizing correlations will not remedy this problem, but aggravate it. One has to start with an idea of how differences in attribute will lead to differences in test scores; otherwise the project of test construction is unlikely to generate tests that are valid for more than prediction. This may be one of the few instances where psychology may actually benefit from looking at the natural sciences. In the more exact quarters, nobody starts constructing measurement instruments without the faintest idea of the processes that lead to the measurement outcomes. And, interestingly, the problem of validity appears never to have played the major and general role it has played in psychology. These two observations may well be related: the concept of validity may never have been necessary because the instruments were generally set up based on an idea of how they would work. In that case, the question what it is, precisely, that is measured, can simply be resolved by pointing to the processes that lead to the measurement outcomes.

In contrast, the question what do psychological instruments measure is generally not answered by pointing to the way the instruments work, but by pointing to the relation they have with other instruments. This way of working makes the question 'what is measured?' a question to be answered after the test has been constructed. Thus, the contrast here is between a conception that sees validity as something that one puts into an instrument, and a conception that views validity as something to be discovered afterwards. Psychologists have tended to construe validity as an empirical matter, that is, the question what is measured is to be answered by data. However, a century of experience with test construction and analysis clearly shows that it is very hard to find out where the scores are coming from, if tests are not constructed on the basis of a theory of item response processes in the first place. Therefore, I would like to push my validity conception one step further, and to suggest not only that epistemological issues are irrelevant to validity, but that their importance may well be overrated in validation research too. A large part of test validity must be put into the test at the stage of test construction, a stage of the testing process that has received little attention compared with the enormous emphasis that has been placed on test analysis. Thus, it is suggested here that the issue may not be first to measure, and then to find out what it is you are measuring, but rather that the process must run the other way. It does seem that, if one knows exactly what one intends to measure, then one will probably know how to measure it, and little if any validation research will be necessary. If this is correct, then the problem of validation research is not that it is difficult to find out what is measured; the problem is that it is difficult to find out what we intend to measure.

In this view, validation is not, and cannot be, a purely or even mainly methodological enterprise. This does not mean that methodological and psychometric techniques are irrelevant to validation research, but that the primary source for understanding how the test works must be substantive and not methodological. Thus, I consider it impossible to argue for test validity solely on the basis of a multi-trait multi-method matrix. Such a matrix is helpful, but a favourable matrix configuration is not constitutive of validity. What is constitutive of validity is the existence of an attribute and its causal impact on our scores. Therefore, if one does not have an idea of how the attribute variations produce variations in measurement outcomes, one cannot have a clue as to whether the test measures what it should measure. No table of correlations, no matter how big, can be a substitute for knowledge of the processes that lead to item responses. The knowledge of such processes must be given by substantive psychological theory and cannot be based on methodological principles.

There are certainly tests for which a considerable body of knowledge has accumulated in this respect. Examples of research in this direction are, for instance, the cognitive modelling approach in spatial reasoning tests (Embretson, 1994) and the latent class approach in the detection of developmental stages (Dolan, Jansen, and Van der Maas, 2004; Jansen and Van der Maas, 1997). Such approaches are distinct from mainstream validation research because they look for evidence of validity in different places. The balance scale task (Inhelder and Piaget, 1958; Siegler, 1981) is a good example. In this task, which is intended to measure the level of cognitive development, children are confronted with a balance scale. The balance scale has weights on both sides, and children have to indicate whether the scale will tip, and, if so, to which side. The weights vary in number, and are placed at varying distances from the centre of the balance scale. The point of departure, in this work, is the formulation of a theory that characterizes the attribute. In this particular case, the theory says that children go through four discrete stages in cognitive development (Inhelder and Piaget, 1958). This theory is translated in a formal model, in this case a latent class model, which conceptualizes developmental stages as latent classes, and development as an ordered series of discrete transitions between these classes (Jansen and Van der Maas, 1997).

Second, class membership is related to response behaviour. Specifically, the theory formulates how children in different stages will approach the items in the task. For instance, children in the first stage will simply count the number of weights on both sides of the centre to reach a decision; children in the second stage will take distances between the weights into account, but only if the number of weights on each side of the balance scale are equal; children in the third stage will incorporate both the number of weights and the distance of weights from the centre, but will start guessing if these cues conflict; and children in the fourth stage will compare products of weights and distances on both sides of the scale.

Third, these response strategies are linked to item response patterns. This is possible because children in different stages make different kinds of mistakes. Therefore, one can construct items for which the response strategies give conflicting responses, so that on some items, children in an earlier stage outperform children in a later stage. Through this chain of theory, the classes can be characterized with sufficient precision to allow for testing the adequacy of the model against observed response patterns (Jansen and Van der Maas, 1997, 2002). Here, the use of latent variable modelling can provide an excellent method for testing the theory against empirical data. The example shows how much can be achieved through a coordinated pattern of theory, test construction, and data analysis. It also shows how little remains of the validity problem, which is virtually reduced to the question whether this theory of response behaviour is true.

Of course, the evidence for the validity of the balance scale test is not conclusive, as evidence hardly ever is; and both the theory of discrete stage transitions, as well as the number and character of the response strategies, are not settled issues. In the present context, however, the main point is not primarily that there is a *correct* theory of response behaviour, but that there is *a* theory of response behaviour. And when such a theory is present, the problem of validity loses much of its mysterious quality and elusive character, because it is clear what must be the case in reality for this test to be valid for the developmental stages in question. The clarity is achieved because the entire chain of events that leads from the attribute to the test scores is characterized. We know what has to happen between item administration and item response for the test to be valid. In other words, we know how the test is supposed to work.

Contrast this with mainstream validation research, e.g., with research on personality tests. Of course, we do now have the methodology to test the hypothesis that the covariation between item scores is due to a number of common causes, namely confirmatory factor analysis (Jöreskog, 1971). However, as is often the case in psychology, we have beautiful models but too little theory to go with them. We can formulate the hypothesis that extraversion is the common cause of the scores for a number of different items of subtests, but there is no good theory available to specify how different levels of extraversion lead to different item responses. Thus, there is, at present, no detailed hypothesis of how the causal effect of extraversion on the test scores is being conveyed. The causal model may be set up, but the arrows in it are devoid of interpretation. Of course, this does not show that personality tests are invalid, or that no such thing as extraversion exists. However, it does preclude any firm treatment of the problem of validity. The reason for this is that we expect to get an answer to the question what the test measures, without having a hypothesis on how the test works. If one attempts to sidestep the most important part of test behaviour, which is what happens between item administration and item response, then one will find no clarity in tables of correlation coefficients. No amount of empirical data can fill a theoretical gap.

It is disconcerting to find that a large proportion of test research is characterized by an almost complete absence of theories of response behaviour, and that so few researchers recognize that the problem of psychological measurement is not a matter of following the 'right' methodological rules, but of tackling one of the most challenging problems in psychology: how do psychological characteristics relate to empirical observations? Fortunately, there are various recent developments in theoretically inspired modelling (e.g., Embretson, 1994, 1998; Jansen and Van der Maas, 1997; Mislevy and Verhelst, 1990; Süss, Oberauer, Wittmann, Wilhelm, and Schulze, 2002; Wilhelm and Schulze, 2002) that show how much is gained when one starts to consider the processes involved in item response behaviour, and to utilize advanced test theory models that have been developed in the past century. However, studies that proceed in this manner are still scarce throughout psychology, and it is therefore no surprise that the problem of validity is so widespread. What I hope to have shown is that it need not be that way.

6.6   Discussion

I have proposed a simple conception of validity that concerns the question whether the attribute to be measured produces variations in the measurement outcomes. This theory of validity is based on ontology, reference and causation, rather than on epistemology, meaning and correlation. Although epistemological issues are central to validation, and consequential issues are central to test use, both are considered irrelevant to the concept and definition of validity itself. The conjunction of these theses produces a viewpoint that is almost diametrically opposed to the currently endorsed conceptions of validity, which state that the concept applies to evaluative judgments of test score interpretations, that it depends on nomological networks, that it is complex and faceted, and that social, ethical, and political consequences are relevant to validity. I do not see the need for a 'unified' validity concept (Messick, 1989; Moss, 1992; Shepard, 1993; Ellis and Blustein, 1991), because I think there is nothing to unify. The consequences of the proposed conception are far-reaching, but the overall picture that emerges is consistent and fits the intuitive notions most researchers have about validity quite well. I therefore think that a realist, causation based concept of validity is a viable alternative to the current consensus in validity theory.

The philosophical assumptions involved in the present conception are strong; stronger, perhaps, than in any previous discussion of validity. Therefore, it may be argued that, by invoking realism about psychological attributes and causal relations, I am engaging in metaphysical speculation. I concede this point, but it does not bother me. I think that the very idea that metaphysics and science are necessarily opposed is a relic that stems from logical positivism; in fact, I think that science is the best way of doing metaphysics we know. To the hard-boiled empiricist, I reply that it is naive to think that *any* scientific theory can get off the ground without introducing an ontological picture of how the world works, which will always contain metaphysical ingredients. Given that this is the case, the metaphysics better be good.

Other objections may come from the postmodern or social constructivist camp. An obvious one is the objection that psychological attributes are social constructions, and that I am engaging in an unjustified reification of such constructions. However, that a realist ontology is necessary in order to apply the concept of validity says nothing about the kind of attributes that can and cannot be invoked. Now, if the supposition that psychological attributes are social constructions is meant in an eliminative way, and thus is taken to mean that such attributes do not exist, then they cannot have any causal effects whatsoever, and it is impossible to measure them. However, this is not an argument against the semantics of validity as discussed in this chapter; it rather expresses the opinion that psychological tests are invalid, and it does so in terms of the very same semantics I have proposed in this chapter. Another position could be taken by researchers who are prepared to defend the thesis that psychological attributes do exist, although they exist as social constructions. Such researchers may hypothesize that these social constructions in fact do have causal effects, for instance on measurement outcomes. In that case, the concept of validity applies as usual, and it invites constructivists to work out the causal chains involved in the process of social construction. In my view, neither eliminative nor 'liberal realist' conceptions of social constructivism provide an argument against the proposed semantics.

There are various other questions about validity that stand in need of further theoretical investigation. For instance, while the present validity concept can be applied directly to reflective latent variable models used in psychological measurement, it seems that formative models (Edwards and Bagozzi, 2000; Bollen and Lennox, 1991) do not allow for such application. In such models, the observed indicators are not considered to be causally affected by the latent variable, but to cause such a latent

The concept of validity 169

variable. In this case, it is difficult to see how these observed indicators could be conceptualized as measures of the attribute in question, because the arrows between the attribute and the observations run in the opposite direction. Consider, as an example of a construct typically addressed with formative models, Socio-Economic Status (SES). A formative model conceptualizes SES as a latent variable that is regressed on indicators such as annual income, educational level, etc. Now, it would be odd to ask whether the question 'what is your annual income?' is a valid measure of SES, because, according to the theory proposed here, this question does not measure SES; rather, it measures one of the determinants of SES, namely annual income. And at this level, one can consistently ask the question of validity, namely when one asks whether variation in annual income has a causal effect on variation in the responses to the question.

One may also imagine that there could be procedures to measure constructs like SES reflectively – for example, through a series of questions like 'how high are you up the social ladder?'. Thus, the fact that attributes like SES are typically addressed with formative models does not mean that they could not be assessed reflectively, in which case the concept of validity, as defined here, can be applied. However, validity does not apply to the relation between formative indicators and the corresponding constructs. Because validity explicitly concerns the relation of measurement, one wonders whether it is appropriate to view formative models as measurement models in the first place. They might be better conceptualized as models for indexing or summarizing the indicators, or as causal models that do not involve a measurement structure for which one can ask the question of validity as defined in this chapter. It would be interesting to further enquire how such models relate to the logic of measurement.

A second issue concerns the distinction between intraindividual and interindividual measurement structures, as made in chapter 3. In my view, the proposed validity concept can be applied to both of these levels, although it is important not to confuse them. If the measurement outcomes are obtained in a group of people at a single time point, then the variation in scores ranges over people, and the only thing that can cause variation over people is something that also varies over people. Conversely, if the variation in scores ranges over time within a person, then the cause of this variation must also vary over time within that person. Your developmental trajectory on a Raven item does not cause differences between people on responses to that item, and that there exists a given source of differences between people does not cause your response to the Raven item. The reason that such suppositions do not make sense is not that the Raven is invalid either for measuring developmental processes, or for measuring differences between people; it could be valid for both. The problem is rather that there is a mismatch between the domain of variation in the cause, and the domain of variation in the effect. It may be countered that, assuming complete homogeneity of processes across persons, it is possible to make inferences about the structure of intraindividual processes based on the measurement of interindividual differences or the other way around. This is true. However, that one can generalize to another domain does not mean that one has measured something in that domain. It is simply impossible to measure intraindividual variation in attributes with interindividual variation in scores, or to measure interindividual variation in attributes with intraindividual variation in scores. This is not an empirical hypothesis that could be refuted by research, but a matter of logic. Nevertheless, the validity concept applies with equal force to measurement at the interindividual and the intraindividual level – although not necessarily at the same time or with respect to the same attributes.

A third theoretical consequence of the present chapter is that it raises the question whether validity should be conceptualized as a matter of degree. This has become more or less a dogma of construct validity. Cronbach and Meehl (1955, p. 290) state that 'the problem is not to conclude that the test "is valid" for measuring the construct variable', but that 'the task is to state as definitely as possible the degree of validity'. Similarly, Messick (1989, p. 13) writes that 'it is important to note that validity is a matter of degree, not all or none'. However, the question whether an attribute exists and has causal impact on the observations can be answered by a simple 'yes' or 'no'. Thus, the present theory is naturally compatible with the possibility of conceptualizing validity as a qualitative, rather than quantitative, concept, as is commonly done with the similar concept of truth. It would be worthwhile to investigate this possibility further.

These ideas point to another issue that would deserve further study. Namely, how does validity line up with other test theoretic concepts like reliability, unidimensionality, measurement invariance, and bias? For instance, if validity is conceptualized as a qualitative concept, it would hardly make sense to say that reliability provides an upper bound for validity (Lord and Novick, 1968). One would rather say that validity is a necessary condition for reliability estimates to make sense. This is not implausible, because reliability is an index of measurement precision (Mellenbergh, 1996), and it does seem strange to say that test x measures intelligence with a certain precision, but that the test does not measure intelligence. Similarly, the concept of validity as defined here does not imply absence of bias in tests, which is a commonly held idea (but see Borsboom, Mellenbergh, and Van Heerden, 2002b). More generally, my definition suggests a decoupling of the terms 'valid measurement' and 'optimal measurement', which are often seen as identical. Upon the present definition, a valid test need not be the best available test, and not all valid tests are on equal footing. Two tests may both be valid, but one may be more reliable. One may consider the possibility that psychometric characteristics like reliability, unidimensionality, and measurement invariance, do not provide necessary conditions for valid measurement, as is often thought, but rather presuppose validity as defined in this paper. This would mean that validity is not in the same league as other test theoretic concepts. As has been suggested above, the reason may be that validity is not so much a methodological as a substantive problem.

The validity concept proposed here has been stripped of all excess baggage. The benefit is that this lends substantial clarity and force to the concept, but the price is that it covers less ground. For instance, when one claims validity, one is not thereby claiming reliability, predictive adequacy, or absence of bias. However, these are important properties, and one may still want to introduce a kind of umbrella term to express one's opinion on the overall quality of a testing procedure. I suggest that, to express this judgment, 'overall quality' is not such a bad choice. The accompanying plain English terms 'better' and 'worse' further allow one to express one's opinion that some tests are better than others in a given situation, without having the connotation of precision and objectivity that the jargon of 'degrees of validity' suggests. Which testing procedure is 'best' for you depends on your situation, your goals, a very diverse set of test properties that are sometimes desirable and sometimes not, and on the amount of time and money at your disposal. But if you want to measure something, then your test must be valid for that something, however suboptimal it may be with respect to properties like reliability. This distinction should not be blurred. Also, the usage of 'better' and 'worse' does not interfere with the concept of validity as defined here, and, perhaps most importantly, such usage emphasizes that in saying 'the WAIS is a good test' one is expressing one's enthusiasm about the WAIS, rather than proposing a refutable hypothesis. In conclusion, the present conception of validity is more powerful, simple, and effective, than the consensus position in the validity literature. However, it does seem that it puts conventional thinking on test theory on its head, which necessitates further investigation of the way validity relates to psychometrics, philosophy of science, and substantive psychological theory. Also, the integration of psychological theory, test construction, and data analysis, advocated here as the best way to tackle the problem of validity, needs to be worked out in greater detail. It would be worthwhile to develop theories of response behaviour in different domains, which could lead to a greater degree of integration between psychometrics and psychology than exists at present. Psychometric techniques and models have great potential for improving measurement practice in psychology, but only if they are driven by a substantive theory of response processes. I think that, with such theory in hand, the problem of validity will turn out to be less difficult than is commonly thought.

References

Andersen, E. B. (1973). A goodness of fit test for the Rasch model. *Psychometrika*, 38, 123–40.
Bartholomew, D. J. (1987). *Latent variable models and factor analysis*. London: Griffin.
Bechtold, H. P. (1959). Construct validity: a critique. *American Psychologist*, 14, 619–29.
Bentler, P. M. (1982). Linear systems with multiple levels and types of latent variables. In K. G. Jöreskog and H. Wold (eds.), *Systems under indirect observation* (pp. 101–30). Amsterdam: North Holland.
Birnbaum, A. (1968). Some latent trait models and their use in inferring an examinee's ability. In F. M. Lord and M. R. Novick (eds.), *Statistical theories of mental test scores*. Reading, MA: Addison-Wesley.
Bock, R. D. (1972). Estimating item parameters and latent ability when responses are scored in two or more nominal categories. *Psychometrika*, 37, 29–51.
Bollen, K. A. (1989). *Structural equations with latent variables*. New York: Wiley.
  (2002). Latent variables in psychology and the social sciences. *Annual Review of Psychology*, 53, 605–34.
Bollen, K. A. and Lennox, R. (1991). Conventional wisdom on measurement: a structural equation perspective. *Psychological Bulletin*, 110, 305–14.
Bollen, K. A. and Ting, K. (2000). A tetrad test for causal indicators. *Psychological Methods*, 5, 3–22.
Bond, T. G. and Fox, C. M. (2001). *Applying the Rasch model: fundamental measurement in the social sciences*. Mahwah, NJ: Lawrence Erlbaum Associates.
Borkenau, P. and Ostendorf, F. (1998). The big five as states: how useful is the five factor model to describe intraindividual variations over time? *Journal of Research in Personality*, 32, 202–21.
Borsboom, D. and Mellenbergh, G. J. (2002). True scores, latent variables, and constructs: a comment on Schmidt and Hunter. *Intelligence*, 30, 505–14.
Borsboom, D., Mellenbergh, G. J., and Van Heerden, J. (2002a). Functional thought experiments. *Synthese*, 130, 379–87.
  (2002b). Different kinds of DIF: a distinction between absolute and relative forms of measurement invariance and bias. *Applied Psychological Measurement*, 26, 433–50.
  (2003). The theoretical status of latent variables. *Psychological Review*, 110, 203–19.
  (2004). The concept of validity. *Psychological Review*, 111, 1061–71.

Brennan, R. L. (2001). An essay on the history and future of reliability. *Journal of Educational Measurement, 38*, 295–317.
Bridgman, P. W. (1927). *The logic of modern physics*. New York: Macmillan.
Brogden, H. E. (1977). The Rasch model, the law of comparative judgment, and additive conjoint measurement. *Psychometrika, 42*, 631–4.
Brown, J. R. (1991). *The laboratory of the mind: thought experiments in the natural sciences*. London: Routledge.
Browne, M. W. and Cudeck, R. (1992). Alternative ways of assessing model fit. *Sociological Methods and Research, 21*, 230–58.
Cacioppo, J. T. and Berntson, G. G. (1999). The affect system: architecture and operating characteristics. *Current Directions in Psychological Science, 8*, 133–7.
Campbell, N. R. (1920). *Physics, the elements*. Cambridge: Cambridge University Press.
Carnap, R. (1936). Testability and meaning (I). *Philosophy of Science, 3*, 419–71.
  (1956). The methodological character of theoretical concepts. In Feigl, H. and Scriven, M. (eds.), *Minnesota studies in the philosophy of science, Vol. I* (pp. 38–77). Minneapolis: University of Minnesota Press.
Cartwright, N. (1983). *How the laws of physics lie*. Oxford: Clarendon Press.
Cattell, R. B. (1946). *Description and measurement of personality*. New York: World Book Company.
Cattell, R. B. and Cross, K. (1952). Comparisons of the ergic and self-sentiment structures found in dynamic traits by R- and P-techniques. *Journal of Personality, 21*, 250–71.
Cervone, D. (1997). Social–cognitive mechanisms and personality coherence: self-knowledge, situational beliefs, and cross-situational coherence in perceived self-efficacy. *Psychological Science, 8*, 43–50.
  (2004). The architecture of personality. *Psychological Review, 111*, 183–204.
Cliff, N. (1992). Abstract measurement theory and the revolution that never happened. *Psychological Science, 3*, 186–90.
Coombs, C. H. (1964). *A theory of data*. New York: Wiley.
Coombs, C. H., Dawes, R. M., and Tversky, A. (1970). *Mathematical psychology: an elementary introduction*. Englewood Cliffs, NJ: Prentice-Hall.
Cronbach, L. J. (1957). The two disciplines of scientific psychology. *American Psychologist, 12*, 671–84.
  (1980). *Validity on parole: how can we go straight? New directions for testing and measurement: measuring achievement over a decade*. Paper presented at the Proceedings of the 1979 ETS Invitational Conference, San Francisco.
  (1988). Five perspectives on validation argument. In H. Wainer and H. Braun (eds.), *Test validity* (pp. 3–17). Hillsdale, New Jersey: Erlbaum.
Cronbach, L. J. and Meehl, P. E. (1955). Construct validity in psychological tests. *Psychological Bulletin, 52*, 281–302.
Cudeck, R. and Browne, M. W. (1983). Cross validation of covariance structures. *Multivariate Behavioral Research, 18*, 147–67.
De Finetti, B. (1974). *Theory of probability (Vol. 1)*. New York: Wiley.
Devitt, M. (1991). *Realism and truth* (2nd edn). Cambridge: Blackwell.
Dolan, C. V., Jansen, B., and Van der Maas, H. (2004). Constrained and unconstrained normal finite mixture modeling of multivariate conservation data. *Multivariate Behavioral Research* (in press).

References

Ebel, R. L. (1956). Must all tests be valid? *American Psychologist, 16*, 640–7.
Edgeworth, F. Y. (1888). The statistics of examinations. *Journal of the Royal Statistical Society, 51*, 598–635.
Edwards, J. R. and Bagozzi, R. P. (2000). On the nature and direction of relationships between constructs and measures. *Psychological Methods, 5*, 155–74.
Ellis, J. L. (1994). Foundations of monotone latent variable models. Unpublished doctoral dissertation.
Ellis, J. L. and Van den Wollenberg, A. L. (1993). Local homogeneity in latent trait models: a characterization of the homogeneous monotone IRT model. *Psychometrika, 58*, 417–29.
Ellis, M. V. and Blustein, D. L. (1991). The unificationist view: a context for validity. *Journal of Counseling and Development, 69*, 561–3.
Embretson, S. (1983). Construct validity: construct representation versus nomothetic span. *Psychological Bulletin, 93*, 179–97.
  (1994). Applications of cognitive design systems to test development. In C. R. Reynolds (ed.), *Cognitive assessment: a multidisciplinary perspective* (pp. 107–35). New York: Plenum Press.
  (1998). A cognitive design system approach for generating valid tests: approaches to abstract reasoning. *Psychological Methods, 3*, 300–96.
Epstein, S. (1994). Trait theory as personality theory: can a part be as great as the whole? *Psychological Inquiry, 5*, 120–2.
Falmagne, J. C. (1989). A latent trait theory via stochastic learning theory for a knowledge space. *Psychometrika, 54*, 283–303.
Feldman, L. A. (1995). Valence focus and arousal focus: individual differences in the structure of affective experience. *Journal of Personality and Social Psychology, 69*, 153–66.
Fine, T. L. (1973). *Theories of probability*. New York: Academic Press.
Fischer, G. H. (1995). Derivations of the Rasch model. In G. H. Fischer and I. W. Molenaar (eds.), *Rasch models: foundations, recent developments, and applications* (pp. 15–38). New York: Springer.
Fischer, G. H. and Parzer, P. (1991). An extension of the rating scale model with an application to the measurement of change. *Psychometrika, 56*, 637–51.
Fisher, R. A. (1925). *Statistical methods for research workers*. London: Oliver and Boyd.
Frege, G. (1952/1892). On sense and reference. In P. Geach and M. Black (eds.), *Translations of the philosophical writings of Gottlob Frege*. Oxford: Blackwell.
Gaito, J. (1980). Measurement scales and statistics: resurgence of an old misconception. *Psychological Bulletin, 87*, 564–7.
Gergen, K. (1985). The social constructionist movement in modern psychology. *American Psychologist, 40*, 266–75.
Glymour, C. (2001). *The mind's arrows*. Cambridge, MA: MIT Press.
Goldstein, H. and Wood, R. (1989). Five decades of item response modelling. *British Journal of Mathematical and Statistical Psychology, 42*, 139–67.
Goodman, L. (1974). Exploratory latent structure analysis using both identifiable and unidentifiable models. *Biometrika, 61*, 215–31.
Guilford, J. P. (1946). New standards for test evaluation. *Educational and Psychological Measurement, 6*, 427–39.

Gulliksen, H. (1950). *Theory of mental tests*. New York: Wiley.
Guttman, L. (1945). A basis for analyzing test–retest reliability. *Psychometrika, 10*, 255–82.
  (1950). The basis for scalogram analysis. In S. A. Stoufer, L. Guttman, E. A. Suchman, P. L. Lazarsfeld, S. A. Star, and J. A. Clausen (eds.), *Studies in social psychology in World War II: vol. IV. Measurement and prediction* (pp. 60–90). Princeton, NJ: Princeton University Press.
Hacking, I. (1965). *Logic of statistical inference*. Cambridge, MA: Cambridge Univeristy Press.
  (1983). *Representing and intervening*. Cambridge: Cambridge University Press.
  (1990). *The taming of chance*. Cambridge: Cambridge University Press.
  (1999). *The social construction of what?* Cambridge: Harvard University Press.
Hamaker, E. L., Dolan, C. V., and Molenaar, P. C. M., (in press). Statistical modeling of the individual: rationale and application of multivariate time series analysis. *Multivariate Behavioral Research*.
Hambleton, R. K. and Swaminathan, H. (1985). *Item Response Theory: principles and applications*. Boston: Kluwer-Nijhoff.
Hemker, B. T., Sijtsma, K., Molenaar, I. W., and Junker, B. W. (1997). Stochastic ordering using the latent trait and the sum score in polytomous IRT models. *Psychometrika, 62*, 331–47.
Hempel, C. G. (1962). Deductive–nomological vs. statistical explanation. In H. Feigl and G. Maxwell (eds.), *Minnesota Studies in the Philosophy of Science, vol. 3: Scientific explanation, space, and time* (pp. 98–169). Minneapolis: University of Minnesota Press.
Hershberger, S. L. (1994). The specification of equivalent models before the collection of data. In A. von Eye and C. C. Clogg (eds.), *Latent variables analysis*. Thousand Oaks: Sage.
Holland, P. W. (1986). Statistics and causal inference. *Journal of the American Statistical Association, 81*, 945–59.
  (1990). On the sampling theory foundations of item response theory models. *Psychometrika, 55*, 577–601.
Inhelder, B. and Piaget, J. (1958). *The growth of logical thinking from childhood to adolescence*. New York: Basic Books.
Jackson, P. H. and Agunwamba, C. C. (1977). Lower bounds for the reliability of the total score on a test composed of non-homogeneous items: I. Algebraic lower bounds. *Psychometrika, 42*, 567–78.
Jansen, B. R. J. and Van der Maas, H. (1997). Statistical tests of the rule assessment methodology by latent class analysis. *Developmental Review, 17*, 321–57.
  (2002). The development of children's rule use on the balance scale task. *Journal of Experimental Child Psychology, 81*, 383–416.
Jensen, A. R. (1998). *The g factor: the science of mental abilities*. Westport, CT: Praeger.
Jöreskog, K. G. (1971). Statistical analysis of sets of congeneric tests. *Psychometrika, 36*, 109–33.
Jöreskog, K. G. and Sörbom, D. (1993). *LISREL 8 User's reference guide*. Chicago: Scientific Software International, Inc.

References

Judd, C. M., Smith, E. R., and Kidder, L. H. (1991). *Research methods in social relations*. Fort Worth: Harcourt Brace Jovanovich College Publishers.
Kagan, J. (1988). The meanings of personality predicates. *American Psychologist*, 43, 614–20.
Kane, M. T. (2001). Current concerns in validity theory. *Journal of Educational Measurement*, 38, 319–42.
Kelley, T. L. (1927). *Interpretation of educational measurements*. New York: Macmillan.
Kelly, K. T. (1996). *The logic of reliable inquiry*. New York: Oxford University Press.
Klein, D. F. and Cleary, T. A. (1967). Platonic true scores and error in psychiatric rating scales. *Psychological Bulletin*, 68, 77–80.
Kline, P. (1998). *The new psychometrics: science, psychology, and measurement*. London: Routledge.
Kolmogorov, A. (1933). *Grundbegriffe der Warscheinlichkeitsrechnung*. Berlin: Springer.
Krantz, D. H., Luce, R. D., Suppes, P., and Tversky, A. (1971). *Foundations of measurement, vol. I*. New York: Academic Press.
Lamiell, J. T. (1987). *The psychology of personality: an epistemological inquiry*. New York: Columbia University Press.
Lawley, D. N. (1943). On problems connected with item selection and test construction. *Proceedings of the Royal Society of Edinburgh*, 62, 74–82.
Lawley, D. N. and Maxwell, A. E. (1963). *Factor analysis as a statistical method*. London: Butterworth.
Lazarsfeld, P. F. (1950). The logical and mathematical foundation of latent structure analysis. In S. A. Stoufer, L. Guttman, E. A. Suchman, P. L. Lazarsfeld, S. A. Star, and J. A. Clausen (eds.), *Studies in social psychology in World War II: vol. IV. Measurement and prediction* (pp. 362–412). Princeton, NJ: Princeton University Press.
  (1959). Latent structure analysis. In S. Koch (ed.), *Psychology: a study of a science*. New York: McGraw-Hill.
Lazarsfeld, P. F. and Henry, N. W. (1968). *Latent structure analysis*. Boston: Houghton Mifflin.
Lee, P. M. (1997). *Bayesian statistics: an introduction*. New York: Wiley.
Levy, P. (1969). Platonic true scores and rating scales: a case of uncorrelated definitions. *Psychological Bulletin*, 71, 276–7.
Lewis, D. (1973). *Counterfactuals*. Oxford: Blackwell.
Loevinger, J. (1957). Objective tests as instruments of psychological theory. *Psychological Reports*, 3, 635–94.
Lord, F. M. (1952). *A theory of test scores*. New York: Psychometric Society.
  (1953). On the statistical treatment of football numbers. *American Psychologist*, 8, 260–1.
Lord, F. M. and Novick, M. R. (1968). *Statistical theories of mental test scores*. Reading, MA: Addison-Wesley.
Luce, R. D. (1996). The ongoing dialog between empirical science and measurement theory. *Journal of Mathematical Psychology*, 40, 78–95.
  (1997). Several unresolved conceptual problems of mathematical psychology. *Journal of Mathematical Psychology*, 41, 79–87.

Luce, R. D. and Tukey, J. W. (1964). Simultaneous conjoint measurement: a new type of fundamental measurement. *Journal of Mathematical Psychology*, *1*, 1–27.

Lumsden, J. (1976). Test theory. *Annual Review of Psychology*, *27*, 251–80.

Maxwell, G. (1962). The ontological status of theoretical entities. In H. Feigl and G. Maxwell (eds.), *Minnesota Studies in the Philosophy of Science, Vol 3: Scientific explanation, space, and time* (pp. 3–28). Minneapolis: University of Minnesota Press.

McArdle, J. J. (1987). Latent growth curve models within developmental structural equation models. *Child Development*, *58*, 110–33.

McCrae, R. R. and Costa, P. T. (1997). Personality trait structure as a human universal. *American Psychologist*, *52*, 509–16.

McCrae, R. R. and John, O. P. (1992). An introduction to the five factor model and its applications. *Journal of Personality*, *60*, 175–215.

McCullagh, P. and Nelder, J. (1989). *Generalized linear models*. London: Chapman and Hall.

McDonald, R. P. (1982). Linear versus nonlinear models in item response theory. *Applied Psychological Measurement*, *6*, 379–96.

(1999). *Test theory: a unified treatment*. Mahwah, NJ: Lawrence Erlbaum Associates.

McDonald, R. P. and Marsh, H. W. (1990). Choosing a multivariate model: noncentrality and goodness of fit. *Psychological Bulletin*, *107*, 247–55.

McGuinness, B. (ed.) (1976). *Ludwig Boltzmann. Theoretical physics and philosophical problems*. Dordrecht: Reidel.

Meehl, P. E. (1978). Theoretical risks and tabular asterisks: Sir Karl, Sir Ronald, and the slow progress of soft psychology. *Journal of Consulting and Clinical Psychology*, *46*, 806–34.

Mellenbergh, G. J. (1989). Item bias and item response theory. *International Journal of Educational Research*, *13*, 127–43.

(1994a). Generalized linear item response theory. *Psychological Bulletin*, *115*, 300–7.

(1994b). A unidimensional latent trait model for continuous item responses. *Multivariate Behavioral Research*, *19*, 223–36.

(1996). Measurement precision in test score and item response models. *Psychological Methods*, *1*, 293–9.

(1999). Measurement models. In H. J. Adèr and G. J. Mellenbergh (eds.), *Research methodology in the social, life, and behavioural sciences*. London: Sage.

Mellenbergh, G. J. and Van den Brink, W. P. (1998). The measurement of individual change. *Psychological Methods*, *3*, 470–85.

Meredith, W. (1993). Measurement invariance, factor analysis, and factorial invariance. *Psychometrika*, *58*, 525–43.

Messick, S. (1981). Constructs and their vicissitudes in educational and psychological measurement. *Psychological Bulletin*, *89*, 575–88.

(1989). Validity. In R. L. Linn (ed.), *Educational Measurement* (pp. 13–103). Washington, DC: American Council on Education and National Council on Measurement in Education.

(1998). Test validity: a matter of consequence. *Social Indicators Research, 45,* 35–44.
Michell, J. (1986). Measurement scales and statistics: a clash of paradigms. *Psychological Bulletin, 100,* 398–407.
  (1990). *An introduction to the logic of psychological measurement.* Hillsdale, NJ: Erlbaum.
  (1997). Quantitative science and the definition of measurement in psychology. *British Journal of Psychology, 88,* 355–83.
  (1999). *Measurement in psychology: a critical history of a methodological concept.* New York: Cambridge University Press.
  (2000). Normal science, pathological science, and psychometrics. *Theory and Psychology, 10,* 639–67.
  (2001). Measurement theory: history and philosophy. In N. J. Smelser and P. B. Baltes (eds.), *International encyclopedia of the social and behavioral sciences*: Elsevier Science.
Mill, J. S. (1843). *A system of logic.* London: Oxford University Press.
Mischel, W. (1968). *Personality and assessment.* New York: Wiley.
  (1973). Toward a social cognitive learning reconceptualization of personality. *Psychological Review, 80,* 252–83.
Mischel, W. and Shoda, Y. (1998). Reconciling processing dynamics and personality dispositions. *Annual Review of Psychology, 49,* 229–58.
Mislevy, R. J. and Verhelst, N. (1990). Modeling item responses when different subjects employ different solution strategies. *Psychometrika, 55,* 195–215.
Mokken, R. J. (1970). *A theory and procedure of scale analysis.* The Hague: Mouton.
Molenaar, P. C. M. (1985). A dynamic factor model for the analysis of multivariate time series. *Psychometrika, 50,* 181–202.
  (1999). Longitudinal analysis. In H. J. Adèr and G. J. Mellenbergh (eds.), *Research methodology in the social, life, and behavioural sciences.* Thousand Oaks: Sage.
Molenaar, P. C. M. and Von Eye, A. (1994). On the arbitrary nature of latent variables. In A. von Eye and C. C. Clogg (eds.), *Latent variables analysis.* Thousand Oaks: Sage.
Molenaar, P. C. M., Huizenga, H. M., and Nesselroade, J. R. (2003). The relationship between the structure of inter-individual and intra-individual variability: a theoretical and empirical vindication of developmental systems theory. In U. M. Staudinger and U. Lindenberger (eds.), *Understanding human development* (pp. 339–60). Dordrecht: Kluwer.
Moss, P. A. (1992). Shifting conceptions of validity in educational measurement: implications for performance assessment. *Review of Educational Research, 62,* 229–58.
Moustaki, I. and Knott, M. (2000). Generalized latent trait models. *Psychometrika, 65,* 391–411.
Muthén, L. K. and Muthén, B. O. (1998). *Mplus User's Guide.* Los Angeles, CA.
Nagel, E. (1939). *Principles of the theory of probability.* Chicago: University of Chicago Press.
  (1961). *The structure of science.* London: Routledge and Kegan Paul.
Narens, L. and Luce, R. D. (1986). Measurement: the theory of numerical assignments. *Psychological Bulletin, 99,* 166–80.

References

Neale, M. C., Boker, S. M., Xie, G., and Maes, H. H. (1999). *Mx: statistical modeling* (5th edn). Richmond, VA: Department of Psychiatry.

Neyman, J. and Pearson, E. S. (1967). *Joint statistical papers*. Cambridge: Cambridge University Press.

Novick, M. R. (1966). The axioms and principal results of classical test theory. *Journal of Mathematical Psychology*, 3, 1–18.

Novick, M. R. and Jackson, P. H. (1974). *Statistical methods for educational and psychological research*. New York: McGraw-Hill.

Nunally, J. (1978). *Psychometric theory*. New York: McGraw-Hill.

O'Connor, D. J. (1975). *The correspondence theory of truth*. London: Hutchinson University Library.

Pearl, J. (1999). Graphs, causality, and structural equation models. In H. J. Adèr and G. J. Mellenbergh (eds.), *Research methodology in the social, behavioural, and life sciences*. Thousand Oaks: Sage.

(2000). *Causality: Models, reasoning, and inference*. Cambridge: Cambridge University Press.

Perline, R., Wright, B. D., and Wainer, H. (1979). The Rasch model as additive conjoint measurement. *Applied Psychological Measurement*, 3, 237–55.

Pervin, L. A. (1994). A critical analysis of current trait theory (with commentaries). *Psychological Inquiry*, 5, 103–78.

Popham, W. J. (1997). Consequential validity: right concern – wrong concept. *Educational Measurement: Issues and Practice*, 16, 9–13.

Popper, K. R. (1959). *The logic of scientific discovery*. London: Hutchinson Education.

(1963). *Conjectures and refutations*. London: Routledge and Kegan Paul.

Rasch, G. (1960). *Probabilistic models for some intelligence and attainment tests*. Copenhagen: Paedagogiske Institut.

Reese, T. W. (1943). The application of the theory of physical measurement to the measurement of psychological magnitudes, with three experimental examples. *Psychological Monographs*, 55, 6–20.

Reichenbach, H. J. (1938). *Experience and prediction*. Chicago: University of Chicago Press.

(1956). *The direction of time*. Berkeley: University of California Press.

Rorer, L. G. (1990). Personality assessment: a conceptual survey. In L. A. Pervin (ed.), *Handbook of personality: theory and research* (pp. 693–720). New York: Guilford.

Roskam, E. E. and Jansen, P. G.W. (1984). A new derivation of the Rasch model. In E. Degreef and J. van Bruggenhaut (eds.), *Trends in mathematical psychology*. Amsterdam: North-Holland.

Rozeboom, W. W. (1966a). *Foundations of the theory of prediction*. Homewood, IL: The Dorsey Press.

(1966b). Scaling theory and the nature of measurement. *Synthese*, 16, 170–233.

(1973). Dispositions revisited. *Philosophy of Science*, 40, 59–74.

Russell, J. A. and Carroll, J. M. (1999). On the bipolarity of positive and negative affect. *Psychological Bulletin*, 125, 3–30.

Ryle, G. (1949). *The concept of mind*. London: Penguin.

Samejima, F. (1969). Estimation of latent ability using a response pattern of graded scores. *Psychometrika Monograph*, 17.

Scheiblechner, H. (1999). Additive conjoint isotonic probabilistic models. *Psychometrika*, *64*, 295–316.
Schmidt, F. L. and Hunter, J. E. (1999). Theory testing and measurement error. *Intelligence*, *27*, 183–98.
Scott, D. and Suppes, P. (1958). Foundational aspects of theories of measurement. *Journal of Symbolic Logic*, *23*, 113–28.
Scriven, M. (1956). A possible distinction between traditional scientific disciplines and the study of human behavior. In H. Feigl and Scriven, M. (eds.), *Minnesota studies in the philosophy of science, Vol. I* (pp. 330–40). Minneapolis: University of Minnesota Press.
Shepard, L. A. (1993). Evaluating test validity. *Review of research in education*, *19*, 405–50.
  (1997). The centrality of test use and consequences for test validity. *Educational Measurement: Issues and Practice*, *16*, 5–8.
Siegler, R. S. (1981). Developmental sequences within and between concepts. *Monographs for the Society of Research in Child Development*, *46*, 1–74.
Skinner, B. F. (1987). Whatever happened to psychology as the science of behavior? *American Psychologist*, *42*, 780–6.
Smits, N., Mellenbergh, G. J., and Vorst, H. C. M. (2002). The measurement versus prediction paradox in the application of planned missingness to psychological and educational tests. Unpublished manuscript.
Sobel, M. E. (1994). Causal inference in latent variable models. In A. von Eye and C. C. Clogg (eds.), *Latent variables analysis*. Thousand Oakes: Sage.
Sörbom, D. (1974). A general method for studying differences in factor means and factor structures between groups. *Psychometrika*, *55*, 229–39.
Sorensen, R. (1992). *Thought experiments*. Oxford: Oxford University Press.
Spearman, C. (1904). General intelligence, objectively determined and measured. *American Journal of Psychology*, *15*, 201–93.
Sternberg, R. J. (1985). *Beyond IQ: a triarchic theory of human intelligence*. Cambridge: Cambridge University Press.
Stevens, S. S. (1946). On the theory of scales of measurement. *Science*, *103*, 667–80.
  (1968). Measurement, statistics, and the schemapiric view. *Science*, *30*, 849–56.
Stigler, S. M. (1986). *The history of statistics*. Cambridge, MA: Harvard University Press.
Suppe, F. (1977). *The structure of scientific theories*. Urbana: University of Illinois Press.
Suppes, P. and Zanotti, M. (1981). When are probabilistic explanations possible? *Synthese*, *48*, 191–9.
Suppes, P. and Zinnes, J. L. (1963). Basic measurement theory. In R. D. Luce, R. Bush, and E. Galanter (eds.), *Handbook of mathematical psychology* (pp. 3–76). New York: Wiley.
Süss, H., Oberauer, K., Wittmann, W. W., Wilhelm, O., and Schulze, R. (2002). Working-memory capacity explains reasoning ability – and a little bit more. *Intelligence*, *30*, 261–88.
Sutcliffe, J. P. (1965). A probability model for errors of classification I: General considerations. *Psychometrika*, *30*, 73–96.

Takane, Y. and De Leeuw, J. D. (1987). On the relationship between item response theory and factor analysis of discretized variables. *Psychometrika, 52,* 393–408.

Thissen, D. and Steinberg, L. (1984). A response model for multiple choice items. *Psychometrika, 49,* 501–19.

(1986). A taxonomy of item response models. *Psychometrika, 51,* 567–77.

Thurstone, L. L. (1947). *Multiple factor analysis.* Chicago: University of Chicago Press.

Toulmin, S. (1953). *The philosophy of science.* London: Hutchinson.

Townshend, J. T. and Ashby, F. G. (1984). Measurement scales and statistics: the misconception misconceived. *Psychological Bulletin, 96,* 394–401.

Trout, J. D. (1999). Measurement. In W. H. Newton-Smith (ed.), *A companion to the philosophy of science.* Oxford: Blackwell.

Van Fraassen, B. C. (1980). *The scientific image.* Oxford: Clarendon Press.

Van Heerden, J. and Smolenaars, A. (1989). On traits as dispositions: an alleged truism. *Journal of the Theory of Social Behaviour, 19,* 297–309.

Van Lambalgen, M. (1990). The axiomatization of randomness. *Journal of Symbolic Logic, 55,* 1143–67.

Velleman, P. F. (1993). Nominal, ordinal, interval, and ratio typologies are misleading. *American Statistician, 47,* 65–72.

Wiley, D. E., Schmidt, W. H., and Bramble, W. J. (1973). Studies of a class of covariance structure models. *Journal of the American Statistical Association, 86,* 317–21.

Wilhelm, O. and Schulze, R. (2002). The relation of speeded and unspeeded reasoning with mental speed. *Intelligence, 30,* 537–54.

Wilson, M. (1989). Saltus: a psychometric model of discontinuity in cognitive development. *Psychological Bulletin, 105,* 276–89.

Wittgenstein, L. (1953). *Philosophical investigations.* New York: Macmillan.

Wood, R. (1978). Fitting the Rasch model: a heady tale. *British Journal of Mathematical and Statistical Psychology, 31,* 27–32.

Wright, B. D. (1997). A history of social science measurement. *Educational Measurement: Issues and Practice, 16,* 33–45.

Index

additive conjoint measurement, *see* measurement
additivity 97–8, 105, 116–18, 132, 134
  violation of 116–18
admissible transformations 186–7
Alzheimer's disease 33–4
anti-realism 7–8
Archimedean axiom 99, 114, 126
attitudes 1, 46, 79–80, 138, 155–6

balance scale 76, 165–6
Bayesian statistics 64–5
Big Five 1, 51, 56, 61, 73–4, 79, 137

causality 6, 68–81, 137, 159–62
  and covariation 69–70
  and representationalism 106, 112–13, 118, 144
  and validity 150, 151, 153, 156, 159–62, 163, 165, 166, 168, 169, 170
  between subjects 68–9, 77–8, 82–3
  counterfactual account of 69, 70–1
  in latent variable models 68–81, 82, 83, 146–7
  within subjects 69–77, 78, 82–3
central limit theorem 15
classical test theory 3, 4, 9, 141–3, 145
  and latent variable model 49, 50, 51, 54, 56, 59, 81, 84, 121, 123–6
  and representationalism 107, 121, 144–5
concatenation 71, 89–94, 99–100
congeneric model 39, 53, 123–4, 126, 134
constructivism 7–9, 40, 45, 58, 60–8, 88, 100–1, 110, 112, 118, 121, 135–7, 144, 168
correction for attenuation 47
correspondence rules 7, 100–2, 118
counterfactuals 13, 70–1, 131
Cronbach's α 23, 30, 47, 138

developmental stages 165–6
dispositions 19, 31, 42–4, 46–7
double cancellation 97–9, 106, 108, 125, 127

empirical adequacy 63, 65–7
empirical relational system 89, 91, 93, 99, 101–2, 106, 129, 146
empiricism 7, 58
error score 12, 13, 20, 21, 145
  definition of 14
  independence of 14
  interpretation of 36–8
  normal distribution of 17
  zero expectation of 14, 21
essential tau-equivalence 22, 27, 30, 124, 126–7

fallibilism
  and parameter estimation 64
  and representationalism 113
  and truth 65–7
falsificationism 6, 88

general intelligence 5, 6, 8, 9, 53, 61, 64, 71, 74, 76, 81, 82, 115, 137, 138, 147
God 139
goodness of fit 49

homomorphism 90, 92–4, 104–6, 109, 111, 112, 130–1, 136, 137, 143

independence
  in conjoint measurement 97–8, 125–6
  local 53, 61, 146
  of true and error scores 14
instrumentalism 7–8, 59, 63, 103, 158, 159
item bias 135

latent variable
  and sumscore 57
  constructivist interpretation of 60–8

latent variable *(cont.)*
  emergence of 80–1
  formal 54, 57–9
  operational 57–9, 64, 68, 82
  operationalist interpretation of 58–60
  realist interpretation of 60–8
  semantics of 54–6
latent variable model
  and classical test theory 123–4
  and representationalism 124–6
  Birnbaum model 53, 116, 126, 131, 134
  dynamic factor model 72, 78
  factor model 5, 22, 52, 53, 56, 73, 74, 82, 87, 116
  formative 61–3, 137, 168–9
  generalized linear item response model 50–2
  Guttman model 104–5, 113, 131, 143
  Item Response Theory 32, 39, 50, 52, 55, 61, 110–11, 123, 124, 129
  latent class model 34, 50, 53, 76, 165
  latent profile model 50, 53, 56
  latent structure model 50
  Rasch model 50, 53, 57, 87, 97, 108, 110, 115–19, 123–7, 129, 130, 132, 136
  reflective 61–3, 80, 168–9
levels of measurement 86, 90
local
  heterogeneity 78–9, 83, 84, 148
  homogeneity 77–8, 148
  independence 53, 61, 146
  irrelevance 79–80, 83, 84, 148
logical positivism 6–9, 155, 168
  and representationalism 88, 100–4, 118, 135, 146

magnitude 89, 100, 102, 103, 112–14
meaningfulness 87
measurement
  additive conjoint 93–5, 97, 105, 108, 116–19, 124–8, 134, 136, 145
  and representation 89–90, 104–6
  extensive 89, 90–3, 96, 99, 108, 161–2
  fundamental 4, 9, 11, 85–7, 89, 91–2, 96, 100, 107, 110, 115
  in classical test theory 32–5, 44, 46, 141–3
  in latent variable theory 52–6, 59, 142–3
  in representationalism 88–95, 143–4
  structure 90, 102, 129
measurement error
  in classical test theory, *see* error score
  in latent variable theory 61–5

  in representationalism 106–12
misspecification 66
multi-trait multi-method matrix 165
multidimensional scaling 111–12

nomological network 149, 150, 153, 155–9, 163, 167

observational vocabulary 7, 101
observed variables 17, 25, 50, 56, 57, 61, 67, 79, 82, 107, 141, 144
Occam's razor 36, 139
operationalism 9, 41–2, 45, 58–9, 93–4, 135, 137, 141, 145

P-technique 72
parallel tests 13, 20, 42
  correlation between 24, 26
  definition of 22
  interpretation of 28–9
parameter separability 97
probability
  frequentist interpretation of 16, 18, 64
  propensity interpretation of 18–19, 108–10, 112, 128–33
  subjectivist interpretation of 16
process homogeneity 75–6

rational reconstruction 88, 113–15, 119
realism 6, 40, 42, 45, 46, 58, 60–8, 82, 89, 101, 112, 137, 138, 144, 146, 155, 168
  entity realism 58, 60, 61–3
  theory realism 60, 63–8, 81
reliability 11, 13, 22, 23–32, 44–7, 131, 145, 170, 171
  and validity 17, 30, 33
  definition of 23
  internal consistency 26, 28–30, 47
  lower bounds for 26, 30, 47
  parallel test method 28–9
  population dependence of 23, 47
  split-halves method 29
  stability coefficients 26
  test-retest method 26–7, 30, 31
repeated sampling 52, 54–6, 68, 71, 131–3, 138–9
representation theorem 90, 95, 102, 118
representational measurement
  model 3, 4, 9, 107, 119, 145
  and classical test theory 107, 121, 144–5
  and latent variable model 124–6
  prescriptive reading of 115–18

Index

scale
　constructivist interpretation of 100, 101–4, 110, 112, 118
　interval 90, 95
　nominal 90
　ordinal 90, 105
　ratio 86, 90, 92, 112
　realist interpretation of 89, 112–13
　semantics of 90–5
social constructivism 7, 8, 168
socio-economic status 2, 61, 169
solvability 96, 114, 126
Spearman–Brown correction 29
standard sequence 91, 99, 114
statistical equivalence 56, 66–8
stochastic subject 20, 52, 54–6, 69, 73, 132, 138, 139

tau-equivalence 22, 30, 124, 126–7, 133
theoretical terms 6–8, 100–1, 122, 137, 138, 147
　meaning of 134, 154–9
　multiplication of 36, 38–40, 41, 45, 153
theoretical vocabulary 7, 118
theory of errors 11, 14–21, 35, 44, 46
thought experiments
　brainwashing 17, 19, 20, 23, 25, 27–9, 36, 38, 43–5, 54, 56, 73, 106–8, 128, 134, 138
　functional 20
　Laplacean demon 109–11
　repeated sampling 54–6, 131–3, 138–9
　replication of subjects 20
　semantic bridge function of 20

true score
　constructivist interpretation of 40–1
　definition of 14
　dispositional interpretation of 19, 42–6
　multiplication of 38, 40
　realist interpretation of 12, 36, 38–41, 43, 45
　semantics of 14–21
true gain score 25
truth
　and empirical adequacy 63, 66–8
　and fallibilism 64, 113
　and underdetermination 56–7
　coherence theory of 63
　correspondence theory of 63–6, 68
　true model 65–6, 111

underdetermination 56, 66, 82, 105, 139
uniqueness theorem 90, 119

validity
　and causality 147–8, 159–62
　and correlation 33, 141–2, 159–62
　and reliability 17, 30–3
　and validation 154
　construct validity 150, 154, 156–9, 162
　in classical test theory 17, 32, 141–2
　in latent variable theory 142–3
　in representationalism 117, 143–4
verificationism 7, 88
Vienna Circle 6, 88

weak order 96, 125, 129, 146

Lightning Source UK Ltd.
Milton Keynes UK
UKHW042134290919
350707UK00001B/32/P